The Great Reporters

The Great Reporters

David Randall

Pluto Press

LONDON • ANN ARBOR, MI

First published 2005 by Pluto Press
345 Archway Road, London N6 5AA
and 839 Greene Street, Ann Arbor, MI 48106

www.plutobooks.com

British Library Cataloguing in Publication Data
A catalogue record for this book is available from the British Library

ISBN   0 7453 2297 2 hardback
ISBN   0 7453 2296 4 paperback

Library of Congress Cataloging-in-Publication Data

Randall, David, 1951–
    The great reporters / David Randall.
       p. cm.
    ISBN 0–7453–2297–2 (hardback) — ISBN 0–7453–2296–4 (pbk.)
  1. Journalists—United States—Biography. 2. Reporters and reporting—United
States—History—19th century. 3. Reporters and reporting—United States—
History—20th century. I. Title.
    PN4871.R38 2005
    070.92'273—dc22
                                                                2005006707

10 9 8 7 6 5 4 3 2 1

Designed and produced for Pluto Press by
Chase Publishing Services Ltd, Fortescue, Sidmouth, EX10 9QG, England
Typeset from disk by Stanford DTP Services, Northampton, England
Printed and bound in the European Union by Gutenberg Press, Malta

Contents

*To all the fixers, drivers and translators who,
invariably unsung and often at some peril,
helped reporters get the story out*

Introduction

HOW THE GREAT REPORTERS WERE CHOSEN

So how do you go about selecting the best reporters who ever lived? Well not, if my experience is anything to go by, with all that much difficulty. The key, I suspect, was going for such a small number. It set the bar very high. The top 40 would have been a different matter: all kinds of very good reporters would have been in with a shout. But a dozen or so? Relatively easy. And why 13? Because that's the number of them who I reckon occupy that tallest of journalistic plinths.

The first thing I did was decide to confine myself to press reporters. Radio and television reporting depends on a team effort; relies on sound and pictures – more, sometimes, than the reporter's words – and it often needs, for its sense and completeness, an introduction from an anchor or newscaster. The rule on teamwork ruled out Watergate's Woodward and Bernstein (and their almost equally crucial editors, Ben Bradlee and Howard Simons). Also out were those whose reporting was done for books, on the grounds that they have length, deadlines expandable by weeks, if not months, and besides, how do you compare work written in two years with that turned out in 45 minutes? Out, too, were those who were essentially columnists or roving commentators. That meant no H.L. Mencken, an exclusion I felt would look eccentric until I scanned his greatest pieces for what you might – at a stretch – call reporting, and found surprisingly little.

Having set these boundaries, I then chose the reporters the only way that, as someone who had news edited three

British national newspapers, I could: I imagined I was running a celestial newsroom and could pick my staff from all the reporters who had ever lived. Most of the people profiled here went down on my rota within half an hour, and the only reporter hitherto unknown to me that I 'discovered' during my research was Meyer 'Mike' Berger of the *New York Times*.

Those who came close, but didn't quite make it onto the roster, were: I.F. Stone (I preferred George Seldes as a member of the awkward squad); Lincoln Steffens; Marguerite Higgins (great story-getter, shame about the writing); Ida Wells-Barnett (her exposé of lynchings was historic, but she spent too little of her life reporting); Gloria Emerson of the *New York Times*; Winifred Bonfils; Marvel Cooke; Gay Talese; John Pilger of the *Daily Mirror*; and Robert Fisk of the *Independent*. Maybe next time...

Finally, some will point out that there are no representatives of minorities here. The explanation is simple: no one in this book is representative of anything other than their own talent and work. Their sexuality, physical appearance, gender and cultural antecedents played no part in their selection. While I can defend this utterly, I was much troubled by the fact that the faces in this book are all white ones. So I searched and searched the journalistic record for an exception who could be included. It was when I was on the verge of putting in Marvel Cooke at the expense of someone whose researching and writing was, to my mind, far better, that I realised this was patronising and wrong. So I stopped. If anyone can suggest a non-Caucasian reporter whose life's work is the equal of those here, I'll be delighted to hear about it and will include them in any future edition.

Having selected my greats, I then had to put them into some sort of order. What should it be – alphabetical? Too boring. Chronological? Ditto. So I decided to put them in my own rank of merit, partly out of a sense of mischief, but also in the hope that my selections, and ordering of them, would provoke some debate, not only about names, but also about the criteria for greatness in reporting. What I was looking for in reporters who could be included was: the driven curiosity to research – on paper, screen and in person – to the maximum depth and detail possibly in the time available; the determination to accept no barriers to the pursuit of the story (or the wit and slipperiness to evade them); a considerable intelligence brought to bear on the material (not thinking about what the story really adds up to is still the greatest failing of the average reporter); a sense of perspective, of context, and of how what has been uncovered may not be the whole story; and a fresh, imaginative way with words (cliché-wielders need not apply). The combination of these talents is rare in journalism (although not as rare as some critics think); and the possession of them all, in high degree, is what sorted the wholegrain wheat of my selection from the general chaff.

Which leads me, finally, to why this book was written. First, because for many years I had wanted to salute in print the best of a breed – reporters – whom I think represent the most useful part of journalism. Without reporters, newspapers (and society) would merely be conjecturing and commenting and rumour-mongering. Reporters are our hunter-gatherers, out looking for fresh information while the rest of us merely sit round the campfire chewing last week's fat until they return. Second, I hoped that a book attempting to identify the greats might give reporters a set of role models; or, at least, some sense that such paragons might exist somewhere beyond their own offices, or even beyond their own times. And, third, I'd like to think that the people included here are, for new generations of reporters, not just benchmarks to be admired and learnt from, but, as they would be in sport, previous record-holders to be equalled and maybe even surpassed. After all, no age needs outstanding reporters more than the present. For the benefit of the future, reporters may, as the truism goes, compile the first rough draft of history; but to the here and now they provide something even more valuable than that: the raw material with which we judge our world and those who seek authority within it. And our best defence against demagogues, charlatans, rabble-rousers, smooth operators and all the lies and half-truths they peddle is reporters, especially the great ones.

The World of the Reporter

Each generation of journalists, at least until its muscles start to sag, assumes it is unique in having to face challenges unknown to previous generations. History, for people geared to thinking of the day before yesterday as dead meat and next week as long-term planning, is not generally thought to offer much in the way of instruction. The reporters of the past, especially those of more than 50 years ago, are seen as generally verbose characters who had it easy – not, like our contemporary selves, having to contend with competition from many other media, the sophisticated wiles of spin-doctoring sources, ever more complex technologies, and the uncertainties of modern life.

How very silly; and, as I discover in scores of conversations every year, how very common. Hence this brief effort to set out how the world of the reporter has changed in the period covered by this book. If nothing else, it might provide a few chronological bearings and make the less historically literate realise why, for instance, reporters covering the American Civil War did not simply pick up the phone, call their offices collect and file. (For why not, see the date of the invention of the telephone, below.)

The first person in this book, historically speaking, is William Russell of *The Times*, whose fame is based on his reporting of the Crimean War in 1854 and 1855. He inhabited a world where Pitman's shorthand and the typewriter ribbon already existed, as did the cable (a message via telegraph was first used as the basis for a newspaper story in 1844, by *The Times* of London). The telegraph was, however, too costly, and its wiring insufficiently extensive, to be used for foreign reporting in the 1850s. Russell's stories, therefore, were hand-written (in pencil – so much more practical in the field than a pen, which required ink), and posted to the newspaper in the form of a letter. Hence the word 'correspondent'. Other features of Russell's professional landscape were: the lack of rivals (which meant his only regular competition were terse, official communiqués); the absence of press agencies (the Associated Press, founded in 1848, did not do foreign reporting in those days, and Reuters, founded in 1851, was a mere fledgling); very little inhibition on the length of his stories (he basically wrote all he could and the paper printed it, not necessarily all at once, nor always in the order in which he wrote it); no way of knowing whether his copy had arrived; the absence of any means for papers to publish photographs (which accounts for the purple prose of some Victorian reporters); and the lack of any management of him by the military (good, in the sense that there were no restrictions on where he could go; bad in that he got virtually no official guidance or information).

By the time the American Civil War ended, ten years later, newspapers had proliferated to such an extent that more than 150 correspondents covered that conflict, and AP was well established (in 1861, for instance, the government stopped distributing its statements merely to a few favoured papers, and begin issuing them through AP to all who subscribed). The influence of news agencies on reporting style was to prove immense. Because they were selling to papers of widely varying political stances, their stories had to be as shorn of overt bias as possible. As AP's leading Washington reporter Lawrence Gobright said in evidence to Congress in 1862:

My business is to communicate facts. My instructions do not allow me to make any comments upon the facts which I communicate… I do not act as a politician belonging to any school, but try to be truthful and impartial. My despatches are merely dry matters of fact and detail.

Fortunate, then, that it was an AP stringer, Joseph L. Gilbert, who was on hand at Gettysburg to take down Lincoln's three-minute speech, and not a passing polemicist.

Agency paragraphs apart, writing styles were still generally discursive, and the classic pyramid news lead ('More than 50 people were crushed to death by…' etc.) took many decades to become the norm. Partly this was a feature of the audience (leisured, educated and with no other source of news, they had no option but to wade through the dense text to find out what went on), partly it was a matter of prevailing fashion, and partly an inevitable consequence of paying correspondents by the line. Consider this from the *New York Times* of 1860:

Bristol, England, Dec. 17, 1860—An unusual degree of excitement was caused here this morning by an alarm of fire; and the consternation was not a little heightened when it became known that the conflagration had broken out amongst the shipping in the floating harbor. The ships' sea bow, on board of which the fire broke out, and in whose destruction it result, was a fine American-built ship, belonging to a New York firm, of some 1,400 or 1,500 tons of burden.

Or, as we would render the same set of facts today: 'A New York-owned ship was destroyed by fire yesterday as it lay at anchor in Bristol harbour.' But then, if you're paid a penny a line, brevity is not your friend.

Design also had (and has) an influence on writing style, and one of the things that held back the pyramid news lead were the multi-decked headlines that then sat atop major stories. It may, for example, seem risible to us that Gobright should begin his account of Lincoln's shooting thus:

President Lincoln and wife, with other friends, this evening visited Ford's Theatre, for the purpose of witnessing the performance of the 'American Cousin.'

But in the papers of the day, these words would only have come after the headline writer had all but exhausted the main points of the story in deck after deck of pithy headlines ('Horror at theatre – President shot by assassin – Mortal injuries sustained…' etc.). The *Philadelphia Inquirer*, for example, carried 18 decks of headline on the Lincoln assassination story, and it was only after absorbing this PowerPoint presentation that the reader would get to the reporter's words. A pyramid lead, after all that, might have seemed distinctly repetitious.

Easy access was the other great feature of Victorian reporting, and would linger in some fields (such as crime and sport) until the last decades of the twentieth century. Gobright, for instance, was in the Presidential box at Ford's Theatre within an hour of Lincoln's shooting, examining the scene for himself (and noting the rent in a flag caused by assassin John Wilkes Booth as he leapt from the balcony); and, in 1881, National Associated Press reporter Franklin Hathaway Trusdell was able to update his report on the dying President James Garfield by tip-toeing into the White House sickroom, listening to the great man breath, and then making his notes on White House-headed paper. War reporting, unsurprisingly, was the first arena to see restrictions (the British Army devised its rules for correspondents largely in response to Russell's free-range activities), although even in the first years of the twentieth century gentlemen reporters like Richard Harding Davis were treated as equals and confidantes by senior officers. The First World War put paid to all that – for good.

The gradual formalising of the relationship between reporters and the official world was a response to two things. First was the professionalising of the press as it catered to a mass market. Second – and provoked by the importance of media in democracies – was the need, perceived by big business and officialdom, to keep the so-and-sos under some sort of control.

The professionalising (symptomatic of which, trivial though it may seem to an outsider, was the starting of the first newspaper 'morgue' or cuttings library by the *New York Herald* in 1860) often went hand-in-hand with technology. The 50 years before the First World War saw: the spread of typewriters (the QWERTY keyboard came in 1873, and three years later Mark Twain's *The Adventures of Tom Sawyer* was the first novel to be typed); the first portable (1892); the telephone (50,000 in use by 1880, and long-distance calls four years later, although even in 1901 the *New York Times* still only had two); the improvement of agency services (AP issued its first 'FLASH' – a cablese message as short as possible to denote news of the first rank – in 1906); the gradual – and it was gradual – infiltration of women into reporting (the *Washington Post* hired Calista Halsey, its first female reporter, in 1878); the progressive improvements in printing and photographic processes that meant mass-produced, illustrated papers were possible; the spread of railways and, in America, Rural Free Delivery, meaning more and more readers could be reached speedily and cheaply.

The period 1890–1920 saw the establishment of three ruling aspects of a reporter's work: the news (or, in the US, city) editor, the inverted pyramid style of news writing, and, a by-product of it, the news lead (or, in the UK, intro), which packed the essentials into the first paragraph in a way that, as Paul O'Neill put it, would 'grab the reader by the throat'. Behind all this lay that great catechism of reporting ('Who? What? Where? When and How?'), whose first recorded use was in Chicago in 1892 but which is still drummed into trainees today. And spanning this 30-year era when reporting became recognisably modern was one of the most influential figures in all journalism history: Charles Chapin, city editor of the *New York World* for 20 years from 1898. Histories of journalism rarely acknowledge the power and influence of news editors, mainly because such books are generally written by people who have never worked in a newsroom. But reporters' lives are ruled by the quality and ferocity of their news editors, and no one typifies the flint-hearted news editor of fact and fiction more than Chapin. He presided over the *World's* newsroom with the absolute and capricious authority of a medieval monarch; terrorised reporters on an hourly basis; fired them for the merest transgression (108 in all, according to his own boasts, among them his proprietor's own son); and positively wallowed in tragedy (as his staff assembled their coverage of the sinking of pleasure boat the *General Slocum* with the loss of 1,021 lives, many of them wept and some vomited as they took down details of children flung into the wheels of the paddle steamer. Not Chapin: he fairly danced around the newsroom, humming in satisfaction at so big a story, and pausing periodically to read aloud the more lurid bulletins).

But this monster knew his business better than most have ever done. He was the first editor to appreciate the potential of the telephone for reporting, and he had his 'leg-men' spread around the city under instruction to phone with hot news as soon as it broke. He employed desks full of rewrite-men to turn these bare facts into gripping, if sometimes not entirely accurate, stories, and he insisted on a high story count per page, forcing reporters to write fast-paced stories with the best angles contained in what we have since learned to call the summary news lead. By the time Chapin left the *World* in 1918 (which he did in handcuffs, having murdered his wife Nellie), the way of writing a news story was recognisably modern, especially its start. The only major change since has been the amount of detail packed into it. (In 1932, for instance, the *New York Times* reported: 'Charles Augustus Lindbergh Jr, 20-month-old son of Colonel and Mrs Charles A. Lindbergh, was kidnapped between 8.30 and 10 o'clock last night from his crib in the nursery on the second floor of his parents' home at Hopewell, near Princeton, NJ.' Thirty years later the police notebook detail had gone from the first paragraph; the same paper reporting from Dallas in a mere 12 words: 'President John Fitzgerald Kennedy was shot and killed by an assassin today.')

Around this time – coinciding with the advent of radio and the movies – was also born the widespread use of wisecracks to open certain types of stories. It was a style of writing that owed as much to music hall and vaudeville as literature, but, happily, it stuck and has provided much, not entirely innocent, pleasure ever since. (A famous example was written about Richard Loeb, one of a pair of University of Chicago graduates who murdered a boy in 1924. They were sentenced to life and, 12 years later, Loeb was killed by a fellow prisoner after making advances to him. Legend has it that Edwin Lahey of the *Chicago Daily News* began his story: 'Richard Loeb, the well-known student of English, yesterday ended his sentence with a proposition.')

The final element in the professionalising of reporters was journalism training. The first J-school opened in Missouri in 1904, and, ten years later, no fewer than 39 universities offered journalism courses and more than 2,000 students attended them annually. Enter, in 1918, the Pulitzer Prizes, and you had the apparatus for self-conscious striving among reporters to achieve what the trade deems to be excellence.

Faced with the demands of – and liberties taken by – newspapers, both business and government responded with what became known as 'public relations', a term first used in 1897. The same year General Electric started a publicity department, within a short while President William McKinley's administration was the first to distribute press releases, and an industry that combines helpfulness and obfuscation in equal measure began to evolve. It took, from its very invention, a mere 17 years to produce the first of what would prove the bane of many a reporter's life: the stage-managed photo-opportunity.

(A strike at a Rockefeller mine in southern Colorado climaxed in the Ludlow Massacre, when several miners, two women and 11 children were shot. John D. Rockefeller was scathingly criticised, and so, in an effort to counter this, was advised to tour the mining camps, exuding concern, and thus publicising his charitable giving, hitherto a secret.)

Thus, by 1920, was the world of the reporter a recognisably modern one – save in one vital respect: newspapers were the sole mass carriers of information. The change in that was the shock the twentieth century had in store for journalists. First newsreels and radio, then television, and, finally, the Internet arrived. Each represented two things: an alternative source of information, and a rival way for people to spend time. Coupled with an increase in incomes, car ownership and leisure possibilities, electronic media gave people so much more to do with their time than simply spread the paper out on the porch or in the parlour and read it from cover to cover. And no longer would papers be the fastest way of finding out about the world.

Whatever the responses to these changes by proprietors (buy a TV station, start a dotcom) or editors (fluff out the features sections, hire three more columnists), the impact on reporters has been debatable. The conventional idea is that editors started saying: 'TV has already reported that, we must look "behind the news" for the story.' Hence, we are told, the increase in backgrounders and colour pieces. But when the town hall burns down, the paper's lead is pretty much how it would have been 50 years ago. The real reason for the proliferation of backgrounders, colour stories and sidebars is probably the huge increase in available space. In the age of multi-sectioned papers every day, there is more of everything in newspapers. And, on the assumption that the number of reportable events has not increased faster than the population has grown, you fill that extra news space with sidebars, backgrounder, panels, display and a bit more of the 'why' to go along with the who-what-where-whens. And, in many papers, more 'say' stories – disagreements, presented as 'rows', which are often a pure confection of the news desk or reporter.

What television has changed is the news agenda. If a story, however flimsy, is on television, and seen by large numbers of readers, then, for all but the most serious paper, a follow-up is almost obligatory. Look no further for one of the main reasons behind the rise of celebrity culture. For mass-market papers in Britain, TV pretty much *is* the agenda. Most American newspapers, because they are local ones, are less prone to this, although they have been subject to a process just as insidious: the erosion in the number of two-newspaper cities. This, whatever the annual roll-call of Pulitzer finery and investigations might suggest, has undoubtedly led to flabbier papers, and less slick reporting. After all, if you are the only paper in town, who's going to show you up if you're late on a story? Very few US newspaper executives spend press night as I do: anxiously scanning the pages of seven rival newspapers when they arrive at about 9.45pm, lest they have a better angle on one of our stories, or, even worse, a good tale that we haven't got. (The rise of the monopoly paper has also dealt a fatal blow to the kind of ra-ra local patriotism that used to keep more sophisticated metropolitan types amused. Gone are the days, I fear, when papers would find an absurd local angle on an international story in the way they used to. The best example of this was probably the *Bronx Home News* headline from 1917 on a story that Leon Trotsky once lived in the borough for three months: 'Bronx Man Leads Russian Revolution'.)

The other great change in the last few decades has been the growth of what Daniel Boorstin called 'pseudo-events' – press conferences, photo-ops, stunts, 'surveys', lobbyings, non-spontaneous demonstrations and all the other transparent tricks of government, business, politics, pressure groups and causes. The average reporter is confronted daily with all this before he even gets to the spin-doctoring, which, you can't help but think, is sometimes just a contemporary phrase for a process of lily-gilding and defect-bandaging that has always gone on. The difference now, apart from an undoubted increase in it, is that the fees commanded by decent spinners, and the hunger of their egos for attention in their own right, demand 'profile' where previously they had none – and reporters invariably oblige.

But journalism training at its best (and that includes virtually nowhere in Britain) has been trying to catch up with the other side in the information arms race. Reporters now start work in the US lacking perhaps a certain way with a cigarette, or facility at a craps game, but, in compensation, have a knowledge of computerised data (how to build spreadsheets, where to find online information etc.) that would positively appal their louche predecessors. And they have PCs (launched 1981); mobile or cell phones (where once they had to scramble for pay phones); satellite phones; and the Internet – the means to research any subject, trace and contact sources, pool knowledge via story archives, and file from anywhere in the world. No longer will Dorothy Parker's excuse for missing a deadline ('somebody was using the pencil') wash.

In return for this kind of kit, reporters have to tolerate working in a far more structured environment. Gone are the days of the 1960s when Roy Thomson could arrive at *The Times* and find to his horror that its newsroom provided sheltered accommodation for a collection of registered eccentrics. Too many papers are run by accountants for that sort of thing to happen these days, or for the kind of staffing levels that allowed general reporters to routinely spend entire days (or, in spectacular cases, whole weeks) out of the office. These days, a movie accurately depicting the work of most reporters would show him or her permanently seated at a computer in what appeared to be a call-centre. The scope for seeing life close-up, for meeting people (as opposed to merely your sources), romance, drinking, nonsense, mayhem, gambling, adventure and getting into scrapes is now much reduced. How different, how very, very different, from the lives of the great reporters...

William Howard Russell

1
William Howard Russell
1820–1907

The year is 1854, and Britain is unchallenged as a world power. It rules an empire that includes Canada, India, the West Indies, Australia, and it will soon begin annexing large parts of Africa. The majority of its people believe in God, country and the right of the monied and well-born to buy their way into, and out of, the officer class of the army.

A threat is perceived. It is several thousand miles away from the homeland, but, if unchecked, the government fears it will jeopardise the prosperity and security of the nation. So old obligations and new alliances are invoked, flags are waved, and the army is sent off to deter an ambitious empire. This is Russia, a land ruled by a royal dictator where serfdom still exists and which seems, in some indefinable way, a challenge to the civilised, democratic values of the homeland. The battleground is the Crimea, a place few back home could find on the map. But nevertheless, they wave their flags, and wait for news of the victories that they, being citizens of the most powerful nation on earth, expect as of right.

Into these circumstances there came a bearded, dishevelled figure called William Howard Russell. He was the correspondent for *The Times*, and the stories he wrote from that conflict shocked Britain as no reporting has done since. Middle- and upper-class readers read his despatches and were shaken to their complacent roots to learn that the army sent into the field by their own pre-eminent nation was poorly supplied, woefully organised, led by incompetent aristocrats, managed by an inefficient government and, worst of all, was so careless of its soldiers' welfare that thousands of them died not in battle but in the filthy hovels that passed for hospitals. Russell's reporting was, in every sense, a shock to the system for Victorian England; and, not least, because no one had ever written like this before. It was small wonder. To uncover these shortcomings, Russell had to endure nearly two years of fending for himself in the field without any assistance, face almost constant hostility from military authorities unused to the very concept of a meddlesome reporter, and throughout all this he knew that, back home, his honesty and patriotism were being vilified. But, as every line he wrote was picked over for faults by the highest in the land, he held his nerve. That took skill and care, but most of all, it took the guts, after learning awkward truths that conflicted with popular orthodoxies, to report them, and go on reporting them in the face of public attacks. This is the reason why a man born almost a generation before the Victorian age began, and who wrote in a leisurely prose that seems now like a foreign language, can stand comparison with the sharpest of modern operators, and be in this book.

However, he nearly didn't make it into anyone's book. In 1844, on his first major reporting assignment, Russell made such a fearful hash of it that only the charity of The Times editor saved him from the sack. He had been sent by the paper to Dublin to cover the trial of Irish leader Daniel O'Connell for sedition, one of that year's big stories. Since this was the days before the telegraph, the only way news of the verdict was going to get speedily back to London was if someone took it there in person. Thus the two big papers, The Times and the Morning Herald, had made elaborate arrangements to get reporters to the mainland, hiring steamers, special trains and cabs. These conveyances were all standing by when, late one August Saturday, the jury retired. The rest of the press, anticipating a long wait, left to get refreshments, and Russell was sitting outside the court, thinking what best to do, when his messenger boy rushed up and told him the jury was returning. Russell went back into court, heard the foreman deliver a verdict of guilty, and dashed off determined to be first back to London with the news. He jumped in a carriage, then on a special train to the port of Kingstown, boarded the *Iron Duke*, the boat hired by *The Times*, and, within half an hour it had got up sufficient steam to start heading for the Welsh coast. As it left, Russell noted that the *Herald*'s steamer was still lying peacefully at anchor. He arrived at Holyhead, caught the special train to London, tried to sleep but couldn't because of his tight boots, took them off, reached London after seven hours, flung himself bootless into the waiting cab, and finally, with one boot on and the other under his arm, ran lopsidedly into the precincts of *The Times* building. Years later, he described what then happened: 'As I entered Printing House Square, a man in shirt sleeves I took to be the *Times* printer came up and said: "So glad to see you safe over, sir. So they've found him guilty." "Yes, guilty my friend," I replied.'

Unfortunately the man he met was not a *Times* printer, but a reporter working for the *Morning Herald*. Thus did the young Russell present the paper's rival with a scoop on a plate, which it duly published. Something of the kerfuffle that ensued within *The Times* can be judged from the two angry notes sent him by Moberly Bell, the paper's manager. The first read, ominously: 'You managed very badly... This must be enquired into.' The second, penned after the editor saved his young reporter's neck, began: 'You have very nearly severed your connection with us by your indiscretion,' and went on: 'Let me warn you to keep your lips closed and your eyes open... We would have given hundreds of pounds to have stopped your few words last night.' Admonished, but spared,

Russell went on to cover pretty much every major story of
the high Victorian age: the railway mania, the Irish Famine,
the Great Exhibition, Wellington's funeral, the Crimean War,
the Indian Mutiny, the American Civil War, the coronation of
Czar Nicholas, the Paris Commune, the Franco-Prussian War,
the first attempt to lay a trans-Atlantic cable, the Sudan and
the Zulu Wars.

The man who was to have this ringside seat at the nineteenth
century was born the son of a manufacturer's agent near Dublin
on 28 March 1820. He was fascinated as a child by the soldiers
drilling near his home, and, while attending Trinity College,
Dublin, toyed with the idea of either the military or the law
as a career. But then, when he was 20, his cousin asked him to
help cover the Irish elections for *The Times* of London. Having
some knowledge of what passed locally for public debate,
Russell thought a good place to cover Dublin's elections might
be not the hustings or meeting rooms, but the casualty ward
of the hospital, where candidates would be brought when the
brickbats began to fly. Sure enough, as a procession of bloodied
electoral hopefuls were wheeled in, there was Russell stepping
forward to interview them. *The Times* was impressed, invited
him to London, and signed him up as a seasonal member of
the paper's parliamentary staff at £5 5s a week. The job often
involved staying at the House until debates finished at four
or five in the morning, and then walking the two miles back
to *The Times* offices to file his reports. But he excelled, and
was soon in charge of the reporters covering the blizzard of
railway bills then going through Parliament. There were so
many that, had they all been successful, their financing would
have required all the available capital in the country. It was,
of course, a classic speculative frenzy, always easier to see in
hindsight than at the time. But *The Times*, led by Russell, was
never fooled. He rejected the bribes on offer to puff various
schemes, correctly identified many of them as worthless, and

the paper more than made up in enhanced prestige what it lost in advertising revenues.

In 1846, with marriage looming, he accepted a better-paid post at the *Morning Chronicle*, and it was for them that he covered the Irish Famine. But he was soon back at *The Times*, covering Parliament, and beginning to prove himself the best 'colour' writer on the paper. He was sent to report on the Great Exhibition and, even though it meant having to be recalled from holiday in Switzerland (not a quick return trip in 1852), Wellington's funeral. So when war against Russia loomed in 1854 and *The Times* obtained permission to send a correspondent with the army, Russell was the man selected to go. 'You'll be home in two months,' editor John Delane assured him in February. Not for the last time, a desk man's assurance was to prove worthless. Russell would be gone for two years.

After a farewell dinner given for him at the Garrick Club, by Dickens and Thackeray, Russell made his way to Southampton, sailed with the Guards to Malta, and thence to Gallipoli, Bulgaria and the Crimea. He arrived there on 14 September, and found the stage set for Britain, and her allies France and Turkey, to go to war with Russia. Although he was not the first war correspondent (these were mainly serving soldiers who had reported battles as if they were sporting fixtures), Russell was the first journalist of stature to cover a major conflict.

What he gave the newspaper reading public (and at the time his paper sold more than four times its rivals' combined sales) was nothing less than its first true picture of war. From its gallantry (the Heavy Brigade charging at the Battle of Balaclava, October 1854):

> ... As lightning flashes through a cloud the Greys and Enniskilliners pierced through the dark masses of Russians... There was a clash of steel and a light play of sword blades in the air, and then the Greys and the redcoats disappear in the midst of the shaken and quivering columns.

From its moments of fortitude (at the Battle of Inkerman, 1854):

> ... A shell came right among the staff – it exploded in Captain Somerset's horse, ripping him open... struck down Captain Gordon's horse and killed him at once, and then blew away General Strangway's leg, so that it hung by a shred of flesh... The poor old general never moved a muscle of his face. He said merely, in a gentle voice, 'Will anyone be kind enough to lift me off my horse?...'

To its chaos (from the battle for Sebastopol, June 1855):

> ... The men of the different regiments got mingled together in inextricable confusion. The 19th did not care for the orders of the officers of the 88th, nor did the soldiers of the 23rd heed the commands of an officer who did not belong to the regiment. The officers could not find their men – the men had lost sight of their own officers.

Its house-keeping (after the Battle of Inkerman in November 1854):

> ... Litter-bearers dotted the hillside... hunting through the bushes for the dead or dying. Our men had acquired a shocking facility in their diagnosis... One of the party advanced, raised the eyelid if it was closed, peered into the eye, shrugged his shoulders, saying quietly, 'He's dead, he'll wait,' and moved back to the litter; others pulled the feet, and arrived at equally correct conclusions by that process...

Its squalor (from the Russian hospital he entered after the fall of Sebastopol in early 1855):

> In a long, low room... dimly lighted through shattered and unglazed window frames, lay... the rotten and festering corpses of the soldiers, who were left to die in their extreme agony, untended, uncared for, packed as close as they could be stowed, some on the floor, others on wretched trestles and bedsteads or pallets of straw, sopped and saturated with blood... Many lay, yet alive, with maggots crawling about in their wounds... Many, with legs and arms broken and twisted, the jagged splinters sticking through the raw flesh, implored aid, water, food, or pity...

Its futility (after the fall of Sebastopol – an event watched by sightseers in yachting caps):

> ... Tired armies, separated from each other by a sea of fires, rest on their arms, and gaze with varied emotions on all that remains of the object of their conflicts.

And its legends. In late October 1854, Russell stood on a ridge overlooking Balaclava and witnessed one of history's most famous feats of war. Three weeks later (his letters took that long to reach London), *The Times* published his account of the Charge of the Light Brigade, in which 673 horsemen set out and fewer than 200 returned:

> ... At 11:00 our Light Cavalry Brigade rushed to the front... They advanced in two lines, quickening the pace as they closed towards the enemy... At the distance of 1200 yards the whole line of the enemy belched forth, from thirty iron mouths, a flood of smoke and flame through which hissed the deadly balls...
>
> With a cheer which was many a noble fellow's death cry, they flew into the smoke of the batteries; but ere they were lost from view, the plain was strewed with their bodies and with the carcasses of horses... At the very moment when they were about to retreat, a regiment of lancers was hurled upon their flank. Colonel Shewell, of the 8th Hussars, saw the danger and rode his men straight at them, cutting his way through with fearful loss... The Russian gunners, when the storm of cavalry passed, returned to their guns. They saw their own cavalry mingled with the troopers who had just ridden over them, and to the eternal disgrace of the Russian name, the miscreants poured a murderous volley of grape and canister on the mass of struggling men and horses, mingling friend and foe in one common ruin... At 11:35 not a British soldier, except the dead and dying, was left in front of those bloody Muscovite guns... ·

Not surprisingly, the army never knew quite what to make of Russell. Lacking any official status, he was reliant on his ability to make friends with officers, and prise from them information he could not collect with his eyes. His Irish charm even worked with some senior officers. Early in the war, for instance, he was brought before General Pennyfeather, who demanded to know his business. When Russell told him he was a reporter, the general replied: 'By God, Sir. I had sooner see the devil!' Russell, however, replied with a little Dublin banter and the old general was won over. This did not, however, apply to the army as a whole. There were times when he was denied rations, returned to camp to find his tent taken down and flung outside the camp, refused information such as casualty figures, and warned that, if he valued his safety, he would leave. Embedded he was not.

In these circumstances, other reporters might have been inclined to take their foot off the honesty pedal. Not Russell. One of his first reports told of a serious cholera epidemic and the shortcomings of the medical service in dealing with it, and he continued to reveal the chaotic truth about the army. He laid bare the inadequacy of supplies that led to too few wagons, beds for the sick or medicines; he wrote of the fussy uniforms with their stiff high collars that were suffocating in summer and afforded no warmth in winter; the lack of sanitation and water filtration in camp; the poor, often contaminated food that was frequently in short supply (in theory, it was a pound of beef and bread, plus a little coffee and sugar, per man per day); and the fact that each man had to forage for his own firewood and then cook his own meal. The miseries of this life, quite apart from the risks of combat, he captured in late November 1854:

> ... It is now pouring rain... the trenches are turned into dykes, in the tents the water is sometimes a foot deep, our men have not either warm or waterproof clothing, they are out for twelve hours at a time in the trenches... and not a soul seems to care for their comfort, or even for their lives. These are hard truths, but the people of England must hear them. They must know that the wretched beggar who wanders about the streets of London in the rain leads the life of a prince compared with the British soldiers who are fighting out here for their country, and who, we are complacently assured by the home authorities, are the best appointed army in Europe.

Nothing hit home with the Victorian public more than Russell's accounts of the treatment of the sick and wounded. Although it was the reports of *The Times* Constantinople correspondent, Thomas Chenery, from Scutari that inspired Florence Nightingale, Russell had been reporting medical failings from the outset, and, six months into the expedition, things were even worse:

> ... The commonest accessories of a hospital are wanting; there is not the least attention paid to decency or cleanliness – the stench is appalling – the foetid air can barely struggle out to taint the atmosphere, save through the chinks in the walls and roofs, and, for all I can observe, these men die without the least effort being made to save them. There they lie, just as they were gently let down on the ground... The sick appear to be tended by the sick, and the dying by the dying.

And, a few weeks later, he reported on the effects of this lack of care, which eventually meant that fully 80 per cent of the war's casualties were caused by disease:

> ... The 63rd Regiment had only seven men fit for duty on the 7th January. The 46th had only thirty men fit... A strong company of the 90th had been reduced by the week's severity to fourteen file in a few days, and that regiment, though considered very healthy, lost fifty men by death in a fortnight. The Scots Fusilier Guards, who had had out from beginning 1,562 men, mustered but 210 men on parade...

The initial response of the government to such reports was flat-out denial, and Russell and *The Times* were vigorously condemned in Parliament, with at least one member wanting the correspondent's rations withdrawn. But, with *Times* editor John Delane holding back some of Russell's strongest criticisms and circulating them privately to the Cabinet, and with the paper's influential readership ever more convinced of the truth of Russell's reports, the denials had diminishing effect. Thanks largely to *The Times*, the government of Lord Aberdeen fell in February 1855, Palmerston became prime minister, and a commission of inquiry was appointed into the war. Four months later, it vindicated nearly all of Russell's work, and led directly to a series of reforms, some of which had been enacted by the time the war was won in mid-1856. The other legacy of Russell's Crimea reporting is not hard to guess: never again did a British army go into the field without a system of press censorship in place.

The Russell who returned home in August 1856 was now famous and, also, rather better off than he expected. He had, in laying down the foundations of war reporting, not neglected to start one of its more trivial, but persistent, traditions: being unable even remotely to account for the expenses he had received. *The Times* generously agreed to wipe the slate clean (a tradition among employers that has not endured), and awarded him a salary of £600 a year. He barely had time to celebrate. Ten days after he returned, he was off again, sent to report on the coronation of Czar Alexander II in Moscow. He then went south to revisit the Crimea, came back to London, and undertook a series of lectures. It was now late summer 1857, and there started to come from India tales of a rebellion and atrocities against the British colonials that became known as the Indian Mutiny. The worst of the tales concerned the butchering of hundreds of British women and children at Cawnpore by Indian troops formerly in the service of the Crown. Herded into the 'house of women', they were, it was said, slaughtered without mercy, but not before they had time to scrawl on the walls, in their own blood, such messages to posterity as 'Oh! My child! My child! Countrymen, revenge!' Not a single journalist was present then on the entire subcontinent, and so Russell was despatched. Even before his arrival, he got an unpleasant whiff of the colonial mindset courtesy of a fellow-passenger on his ship:

> 'By Jove! sir,' exclaims the major... thickly and fiercely, with every vein in his forehead swollen like whipcord, 'those niggers are such

a confounded sensual lazy set... that you might as well think to train pigs...'

Russell added:

The fact is, I fear that... the civilisers of the world... are naturally the most intolerant in the world.

His mission, however, was the atrocities, not racism; and, in his first despatch, there was a note of scepticism:

Hideous massacres of men, women, and children, were reported to us with such seasoning of horrors, made by skilful masters in that sort of cookery, as the imagination has never before devised... I never doubted them, but I wanted proof, and none was forthcoming. All the stories we heard emanated from Calcutta, and the people of Calcutta were far from the districts where most treacherous and wholesale murder has been perpetrated.

He landed in India in late January, and, by mid-February, had made his way across hundreds of miles to Cawnpore, where he found proof of the basic facts, if not of the more lurid legends. 'It is clear enough', he reported, 'that one of the modes by which the leaders... determined to effect their end was the destruction of every white man, woman or child who fell into their hands...' Yet, he added, it was 'a design which the kindliness of the people... frustrated on many remarkable occasions'. As for the messages written on the walls of the slaughterhouse, he was able to establish these were not there when the relief column arrived 'and therefore were not the work of any of the poor victims'.

The revenge of the British, when it came, was unrestrained, and, for Russell, went far too far. He wrote of British and Sikh soldiers 'drunk with plunder' as they looted the palaces and temples of Lucknow; of a British officer who, when a boy ran to him for protection, levelled his pistol at the youngster's head and made four attempts to shoot him before succeeding; and of the fate of one captured mutineer:

... he was pulled by the legs to a convenient place, where he was held down, pricked in the face and body by the bayonets of some of the soldiery whilst others collected fuel for a small pyre, and when all was ready – the man was roasted alive! There were Englishmen looking on, more than one officer saw it. No one offered to interfere! The horror of this infernal cruelty was aggravated by an attempt of the miserable wretch to escape when half burned to death. By a sudden effort he leaped away, but was... put back on the fire again, and held there by bayonets till his remains were consumed.

Russell wrote of the British occupation of India:

... That force is the base of our rule I have no doubt; for I see nothing else but force employed in our relations with the governed... the grave unhappy doubt which settles on my mind is whether India is better for our rule...

Most of his long despatches (and they were long – 2,500 words was brevity in those days) concerned the efforts of the British to retake Lucknow, the suppression of the revolt, sudden attacks (in one of which an injured Russell was rescued by the swift action of his servant), and meetings with high-ups. He enjoyed these hob-nobbings, for, despite his advanced views, Russell could never be described as anti-establishment, an inclination he proved the year after he returned from India by founding the house journal of the Victorian officer classes, the *Army and Navy Gazette*. It was hardly the act of a subversive, but he had barely begun to establish the new publication when *The Times* asked him to go to America, where tensions between north and south were bringing the country ever nearer a civil war. He arrived on 16 March 1861 and, within days was taken by Secretary of State Seward to the White House to meet the newly elected president.

... There entered, with a shambling, loose, irregular, almost unsteady gait, a tall, lank, lean man, considerably over six feet in height, with stooping shoulders, long pendulous arms, terminating in hands of extraordinary dimensions, which, however, were far exceeded in proportion by his feet. He was dressed in an ill-fitting, wrinkled suit of black, which put one in mind of an undertaker's uniform at a funeral... and above that... rose the strange quaint face and head, covered with its thatch of wild republican hair, of President Lincoln... A person who met Mr Lincoln in the street would not take him to be what... is called a 'gentleman'... but, at the same time, it would not be possible for the most indifferent observer to pass him in the street without notice.

... Mr Seward then took me by the hand and said: 'Mr President, allow me to present to you Mr Russell, of the London *Times*.' On which Mr Lincoln put out his hand in a very friendly manner, and said: 'Mr Russell, I am very glad to make your acquaintance, and to see you in this country. The London *Times* is one of the greatest powers in the world – in fact, I don't know anything which has more power – except perhaps the Mississippi.'

A politician's flattery of course, but Lincoln may have been hoping that, by charming its most famous reporter, there was a chance he could reverse the influential paper's support for the secessionists. As it turned out, there wasn't; and this, plus Russell's honesty in a land then going through one of its periodic fits of prizing partisanship more than truth, was to cause him much trouble.

His first major act was to tour the south. He saw a slave auction, which revolted him, met Jefferson Davis, leader of the Confederacy, and, after two months, returned to New York distinctly attached, unlike his paper, to the Unionist cause. He soon had his first significant action to report: the Battle of Bull Run, a clash now firmly understood to be a Unionist rout. That, however, is not how some northern papers saw the battle. Although the *World* and *Tribune* of New York both reported a chaotic Unionist retreat, many papers were misled by the initial Federal advance into reporting a great victory. So when Russell's report of the north's flight from the field reached the city, initially by garbled account and then by extensive reprinting ('... a cowardly retreat, a miserable causeless panic...' – though he did warn readers not to attach too much weight to the defeat), he, the representative of a secession-supporting foreign paper, was vilified. The *Chicago Tribune* wrote: '... not one incident which he relates as happening in that stretch had any foundation in fact'. *Knickerbocker* magazine said that Russell actually led the retreat, and the *New York Herald* agreed. Despite the *New York Times* and General Sherman endorsing Russell's account, he was ostracised, sent death threats, and insulted and jostled in the street. He sought refuge in the British embassy, tried lying low in Illinois for a while (where he was arrested and prosecuted for shooting on the Sabbath), and took a break in Canada. But there was no let-up. Even seven months after Bull Run, the *Herald* was describing him as 'the smallest man, morally and mentally in the world', adding a week later that 'it was likely he would be shot or hanged if found smelling about our camps'. On 22 March, it even alleged that Russell used confidential information from the British embassy to speculate during the Trent Affair. Five generals denied him a pass for the front, and, fearing that, even if he succeeded he would be shot in the back, he decided to abort the mission. His wife's ill-health played a part (she was to die five years later), and so, despite pleas from London to remain, he sailed home in April 1862.

This sad episode marked the high-water mark of his reporting career. By 1870, and the Franco-Prussian War and Paris Commune, Russell was showing his age. A new breed of younger correspondents, like Archibald Forbes of the *Daily News*, were adept at making full use of the telegraph, and filing crisp, breaking-news copy from the first wire office they could reach. Russell, meanwhile, preferred his leisurely, hand-written accounts sent by mail. He could still contribute expert and evocative despatches (reminding his complacent readers from Alexandria that Egyptians were entitled to their nationalism), but he could no longer compete as a news reporter. So, within a few years, he ceased to be one full-time. He stood for Parliament, married a countess, contributed book reviews and colour pieces to *The Times* (touring the American West in his sixties), and continued editing the *Army and Navy Gazette*. He was knighted in 1895 for services to the army, and died 12 years later, a month before his 87th birthday.

Russell now seems a figure from a very distant age, but, as a teller of uncomfortable truths, and challenger of cherished prejudices, he has had few equals. His reports from the Crimea, India and the US are a reminder that the reporting that really matters is an act not only of research, precision and coolness, but, above all, of moral courage.

Edna Buchanan

2
Edna Buchanan
1939–

THE BEST CRIME REPORTER THERE'S EVER BEEN

Once upon a 1940s time in New Jersey there lived a little girl who loved stories. Not stories about princesses, ponies and fairies, but newspaper stories, about the kind of people who don't make for very happy endings. People like 'Mad Bomber' George Metesky, mobster 'Lucky' Luciano and Willie 'The Actor' Sutton, a bank robber with lots of style but no conscience. These were, she later wrote, the dark princes of her childhood, and it was just as well she found in their tales some romance and adventure because there was not too much of these in her own young life. Her father had run away when she was seven, leaving her and her mother scraping along; she was awkward-looking, too tall for her age and she wore hand-me-down clothes. Neither was she any good at adding up. 'You'll never amount to anything,' an elementary school math teacher once told her on front of the whole class, 'Not even a good housewife.' The class laughed, and the girl had to sit there, reflecting, perhaps, on what Mad Bomber would do to the teacher if he only knew how his young fan had been humiliated.

Fortunately there was another teacher. Her name was Edna Mae Tunis, and she taught English to the girl who loved stories. And one day, when she was 11, the girl wrote a story of her own. Mrs Tunis liked it so much she singled her out, and made her promise in front of the whole class that she would one day dedicate a book to her. Well, the girl grew up, and it began to look as if, of the two schoolmarms, the math teacher had been right. The girl was soon in trouble, making the front page of her home town newspaper in Paterson, New Jersey for running over an old man in her car. Dead-end job followed dead-end job, and, as time passed, she was, as per the prediction, amounting to absolutely nothing. But then, in her twenties, she went down to Miami and discovered a whole new city of dark princes. And this time, they would be her stories to tell; for the gangly girl chewed out in front of the whole class for being devoid of promise had become, through several unlikely twists and turns, first a journalist, and then probably the best crime reporter there's ever been.

Edna Buchanan's by-line on a story in the *Miami Herald*, especially if it was front-paged in the more leisurely Sunday paper, was a sign to readers that they could pour themselves a coffee, settle in a chair and enter a world where jealousy, lust, greed or all three invariably led to a trail of mayhem and bodies. For Florida's armchair thrill-seekers, Buchanan made sure the lip-smacking pleasures kicked in right at the top: 'Bad things happen to the husbands of the Widow Elkin' began a 1985 story; 'A 12-year-old schoolboy who had everything in the world executed his 9-year-old brother, then ambushed and shot to death his socially prominent mother...' (1983); 'They called it Operation Snow White because the drug was cocaine and the suspects included seven Miami police officers' (1982); 'Angel Aguada saw a stranger across a crowded room. Their eyes met. The moment was spoiled when her husband shot Aguada three times' (1985); 'There was a gold, diamond-studded Rolex watch on her wrist, and a bullet in her head' (1984); and, most famously in March 1985, on the ex-con shot by a security guard before he could order at a fast food joint: 'Gary Robinson died hungry.'

Not all her stories began like a novel, but enough of them did to convince readers they were in the company of a reporter armed not so much with a news sense as a ravenous eye for a promising plot. And, in Miami in the 1970s and 1980s, there was no shortage of raw material. There was the woman who planned her own murder, hired a hitman to do it, and planted clues to frame two youths who feuded with her son; the rape victim who, running in distress down the street, came across another rape victim running in the other direction; the man who filled the house with propane gas from a 50-gallon tank, waited until his wife came home, lit a match, blew up the house, his wife – and himself; the 72-year-old man who ran away from home because his 103-year-old mother wouldn't buy him a car; a man who murdered his neighbour in a dispute over hedge clippings; the man killed by a bullet fired eleven years before; the mother who framed her own two-year-old for the murder of his playmate; the naked man who hurled the severed head of his girlfriend at police; the Bible-reading high school student who mistook his grandmother for the devil and killed her; and Jacinto Roas, who murdered a man only to find that an iron security door had slammed shut and trapped him with the corpse.

She first saw the setting for all these stories as a vacationer in the summer of 1961. A place 'all pink, radiant and bathed in sunlight' she called it, and, for Buchanan, it was love at first sight. The wedding cake architecture and balmy climate could not have been more different from her chilly, unexotic New Jersey hometown. She had dropped out of high school at 16, and worked on the sock counter of Woolworth's, then another store, photo studio, mail-order house, dry cleaners, assembly line at Western Electric, and, finally, a small-time office job at the company's plant. For someone who dreamed of writing, it was a dull, marking-time kind of existence, enlivened only briefly in the unlikeliest way when a colleague at work told Buchanan she wanted to learn millinery at night school. The wearing of hats, much less design and manufacture of them, held little thrill, but, on hearing there was a creative writing course on offer, Buchanan agreed to go along. She listened, wrote her stories, and one was praised by the teacher to the class. The course ended and her life resumed, but it was the first indication as an adult that she might amount to anything.

In Miami, staying at an oceanfront hotel, she decided that, if her own story was going to be a drab one, she might as well live it in a warm climate. Returning to Paterson only to take permanent leave of it, she and her mother hastened back to Miami and made their home there. It wasn't long before she joined another writing course, and this time it led to something. Also on the course was an editor on a small paper called the *Miami Beach Daily Sun*, and, impressed either by her writing, her persistence or her blonde looks, he suggested she apply for the vacant job of society page reporter. She did so, they gave her a press release about a church social to rewrite, she turned it into usable copy, and was hired. The kind of paper that would hire an untrained former Western Electric clerk as a reporter was not liable to be the big time, and the *Sun* was certainly not that. It had a circulation of just 10,000, paid below any union minimum, and regarded overtime as something that only happened in sports fixtures. Neither was there any fancy specialisation at the *Sun*. You wrote, copyedited, made up pages, wrote headlines, and, if necessary, tipped greyhounds and composed letters to the editor as well. In other words, for someone like Buchanan who knew nothing but was prepared to work like crazy, it was perfect.

Her first boss was Maude Massengale, a sort of Louella Parsons with a conscience who, as society editor, presided over the coverage of lunches, charity balls, soirées, dinners, and receptions. It was a world where the local ladies of leisure would drop by the paper and invite Maude to a dinner party with the words: 'Just come as a friend. Leave your notebook at home. We want you there because we love you.' And, if Maude told them she had a prior engagement, the crest-fallen party-giver would reply: 'Couldn't you at least send a photographer?' Often she did, which was one of the reasons why the city's most astute jewel thieves told Buchanan years later that they regarded Maude's column and its informative illustrations in the same way as gift-givers viewed a store catalogue.

In the mid-1960s Buchanan moved to general reporting – and politics, and crime, and interviews, and movie reviews. For one eight-month period she was the entire reporting staff of the paper. Hence, the following:

> One night, at 1 a.m., my editor, Ted Crail, a gentle but driven man, stood over my desk wearing the face of a man with a desperate need [she later wrote]. He wanted what they all want. More copy. More news. More stories. He still had blank space to fill. I had been working since 7 a.m. I hadn't had any dinner. I had to be back at 7 a.m. 'I can't, I can't,' I wailed. Exhausted, I slumped over my battered old Remington typewriter and began to cry. He did not go away. 'One more story,' he urged, 'one more story.' His pudgy fists clenched tight, his knees flexed, he was cheering me on as if I were a punch-drunk fighter on the ropes. 'One more story, one more story.' Wearily I sat up, leafed numbly through my notebook, and found – one more story.

Her enthusiasm, however, was never in question. When Calvin Trillin was researching his 1986 *New Yorker* profile of Buchanan, a woman who once worked at the *Sun* told of the day when a body had washed up on the beach: 'I had a camera... The managing editor said, "Go take a picture of the body." I said, "I'm not taking a picture of a washed-up body!" Then I heard a voice from the other end of the room saying, "I'll do it, I'll do it." It was Edna.'

As the 1960s wore on, Buchanan was more and more ripe for a move to a paper where the filling of holes in the news pages did not depend entirely on her. She had made inquiries

before about moving to the *Miami Herald*, and in 1970 she
wrote to its editor George Beebe:

> Dear Mr. Beebe,
>   Five years ago I called *The Herald* to ask how to apply for a
> job as a reporter. I was told not to bother unless I had a degree
> in journalism or five years experience at a daily newspaper. As of
> August 14, 1970, I have five years experience at *The Miami Beach
> Daily Sun*. How about it?
> Edna Buchanan

For weeks she heard nothing, except that the decision belonged
to city editor Steve Rogers. So she wrote him:

> Dear Mr. Rogers,
>   Obits?
> Edna Buchanan

The next day he called to ask when she could start.

The *Herald* she joined in the late summer of 1970 had, it
seemed to her, a fifth-floor newsroom the size of Carnegie
Hall. Buchanan, however, took the habits of a two-bit paper
with her, rapping out story after story, writing so many that
some of her new colleagues regarded her as a threat to their
own, less ferocious, productivity levels. Gradually, the one-
woman newsroom learned to pace herself. An early success
was a story about that old dark prince of her childhood, Willie
'The Actor' Sutton, who had, in the 1940s, posed as anything
from a window-cleaner to a florists' deliveryman to relieve
banks of their cash. Jailed in 1952 for a minimum 30 years,
the once-jaunty stylist had been released in Christmas 1969 on
health grounds, and was borne from jail in a wheelchair, white-
haired and wracked, it was said, with emphysema. Word came
he was living with his daughter in Sarasota, and Buchanan
learnt from a gabby TV reporter that Sutton had agreed to
an interview being filmed in a local hotel. This was where
her old reading material kicked in. Buchanan remembered
Sutton was an habitual early bird, door-stepped the hotel in
good time and, sure enough, when a car pulled up, out of

it bounced Willie Sutton in plaid jacket, having apparently made a miraculous recovery. He allowed himself to be led by Buchanan to the coffee shop and there told all, including plans to make television commercials for credit-card companies. She wrote the story on an old typewriter behind the hotel's front desk, filed it, and it was on the news-stands long before the TV station had broadcast their 'exclusive' interview.

She was gradually building a reputation for quality persistence, something she only appreciated when a reporter strolled into the *Herald* newsroom, said he'd just seen a Volkswagen in flames on the expressway, and casually wondered if someone might like to call to see if there were any casualties. The editor erupted, and, in the tirade that followed, was heard to say that if Edna Buchanan had witnessed the burning car 'she would be on that phone right now to Germany, talking to the assembly-line worker who put it together!' In her second year, she started covering court, interviewing, among other memorable miscreants, a lesbian Satanist who had stabbed her sugar-daddy 57 times. Jobs like this made Buchanan realise that the paper, lacking a full-time crime reporter, was only getting the legal conclusion of such stories, not their often tantalising beginnings. So, in 1973, she suggested to the city desk that someone should make daily calls on police departments, check the reports, drop in on the morgue and catch up with the latest arrivals. 'Sounds good,' said city editor Steve Rogers, hardly looking up, 'why don't you do it?' Thus Buchanan became the crime reporter in a city that was, in the next few years, to become an ongoing, 24-hour-a-day festival of serious felonies.

Her first murder was of Edward Beecher, a retired dealer in religious books whose vacation from New Jersey was crudely and terminally interrupted when he was battered to death on the sidewalk as he left his parked car. The killings were to get a lot more senseless and numerous than that. Among her stories were the Rastafarians driving along at 65mph when one sitting in the back decided it was sensible to shoot the driver in the head; the man killed while on his way to consult a clairvoyant about his future; the father who shot his daughter dead over a phone bill; the bridegroom on honeymoon who, when his wife was asleep, slipped off to see a prostitute, was robbed and fatally shot; the boy of five who deliberately pushed his three-year-old playmate to his death from the fifth floor; a young woman who 'felt used' by her date and so clubbed him to death with the dumbbells he used to keep fit; and the shootings of umpteen innocent bystanders, rival drug dealers, robbery victims and redundant spouses. And her adopted city held new dark princes, some of them very dark indeed. The worst was Robert Carr, a tousled-haired, freckle-faced psychopath who, with the aid of a car rigged so the passenger door could not be opened from inside, abducted, raped and tortured 15 victims, four of whom (three children and a mother of three) he also murdered. He was, she said, 'the most evil creature I've ever met', a judgement that carries some weight, since it was made after spending 120 hours in his cell interviewing him both for her paper and her first book, *Carr: Five Years of Rape and Murder*, published in 1979.

By 1981, Dade County's murder rate, which only four years before been 211, had risen to 621. The girl who couldn't count certainly had to now. 'Dade's murder rate hit new heights this week,' she began a story in June 1980, 'as a wave of unrelated violence left 14 people dead and five critically hurt within five days.' Within a year, things reached the stage where, as Buchanan reported in a story that ran around the world, Dade County's morgue was so stuffed full of corpses that officials had to hire a refrigeration truck from Burger King to cope with the overflow. Even when the mayhem was at its worst, in the immediate aftermath of the 1980 boatlift from Cuba, Buchanan was determined to record every murder. She told Teresa Weaver of the *Atlanta Journal Constitution* in a 2003 interview: 'My editors would say, "just cover the major murder of the day". But how could I pick the major murder of the day? I thought all of these people should be in the newspaper of record – in black and white, on our consciousness forever. We owed the victims that much.' It meant arguing with editors (her three rules of reporting are: 'never trust an editor, never trust an editor, never trust an editor'), and it meant shoe-horning six or seven or more homicides into each story; but she did it. And it meant calling hundreds and hundreds of relatives, a task she did not relish, but nevertheless did, with a sense that, often, she was giving the family a chance to see their loved one had a life worth recording, as well as a newsworthy death. Her technique, copied since by a generation of young reporters, was simple. She would call, and if someone slammed down the phone or chewed her out, she would wait 60 seconds, then call again and say: 'I think we were cut off.' The intervening time had allowed the person to think again, or for another, more talkative relative to answer the phone.

Many of the murders were related to drugs, a subject that runs through her cuttings like a poisoned stream. When Buchanan first went to Miami, drugs meant a few funny cigarettes. But other substances crept in, big money started to be made, and business rivalries were soon being settled with something more than a sharp exchange of letters. By the early 1970s, coverage of the crime beat took her out on her first drugs raid. It was at a poolroom in Opa-Locka, a small area of north-west Dade, and, before she went, the night editor arranged for a young intern called Herb to monitor police radios and tell the desk if anything untoward happened. So while Buchanan lurked with officers in bushes outside the poolroom, waiting for the moment to swarm in, there was Herb back at the office listening in on the radio. And hearing nothing. Afraid he'd missed his cue, he rang police to check if the raid had taken place. 'What raid?' they understandably replied. So Herb, being anxious not to miss anything, rang the poolroom. 'Have the police arrived yet?' he asked. Cut immediately to Buchanan and her uniformed friends, who, from the confines of the bushes, saw people hurling themselves out of the doors and windows of the poolroom like they'd just been scalded. And, from inside the premises, the unmistakable sound of toilets being flushed again and again.

By 1979, the drug gangs were involved in such murderous rivalry that Buchanan could more properly be described as the *Herald*'s war correspondent. Witness a story she wrote in July of that year about the cocaine gang who drove their armoured van into Dadeland Mall at noon, and from the gun ports that opened on its sides, sprayed the place with sub-machinegun fire, leaving not only several dead and wounded, but also their truck behind. It contained bullet-proof vests, more than a dozen guns, and thousands of rounds of ammunition, including shotgun shells adapted to carry ball bearings. And, on the side of the van, was, in jolly lettering, 'Happy Time Complete Party Supply'. Buchanan, never one to rely on police press statements for her stories, was quickly at the scene, noted the dealer's sticker on the side of the van, returned to the office, called him before police did, and traced the Colombian who had recently paid cash for the vehicle. Drugs stories such as this reverberated through the 1980s: the all-woman narcotics ring that included Rosie Ruiz, hailed as winner of the 1980 Boston Marathon until it was realised she had slipped into the field a mile from the finish; the drugs mule who died when some of the 82 condoms of cocaine he swallowed leaked ('his last meal was worth $30,000 and it killed him', began her story); from 1983: 'Enough of a powerful hallucinogen to alter the minds of a million people was seized Friday...'; and, January 1985, a story that opened: 'He helped set up a major cocaine deal, using fluent English and Spanish. He spotted the undercover detectives outside and shouted a warning, setting off gunfire between suspects and police. He is 6 years old.'

And then there were the city's rapists: the Bandanna Rapist, the Flashbulb Rapist, the A/C Rapist, the Coral Gables Rapist, the Silver-Toothed Rapist, the Umbrella Rapist, the Pillowcase Rapist. The activities of some of these were regarded as akin to a state secret by Miami police, a point of serious conflict between them and Buchanan. Take the Bird Road Rapist, whose 16 attacks on women came to her notice not as a result of an official appeal for witnesses, but as word she'd picked up on the police grapevine. When she started digging, police objected, and a senior officer even called her editor asking him to suppress the story. It ran, women came forward with witness statements and the culprit was in jail before the week was out. Ditto the Coral Gables Rapist, of whom police had a composite drawing, Buchanan learnt. She asked for it. No can do, she was told. Buchanan reported this, women's groups protested and police were forced to release the drawing, plus a description of the man's distinctive T-shirt which had JOU JOU printed on the front. That morning, a young man walked into a police station miles from Coral Gables and confessed he had stolen a girl's purse the night before. He wore a T-shirt with JOU JOU on it. The desk sergeant took the details and then went off shift. When he got home, he opened that day's *Herald*, and saw Buchanan's story with its description of a T-shirt. Within the hour, the Coral Gables Rapist had been charged.

Although the beat reporting job Buchanan did was recognisably the same as that done by old-time reporters with press cards tucked in their hat-bands, she operated very differently. She might spend time schmoozing with cops, badgering them for a look at their reports, hanging out at their stations and the morgues, but Buchanan also dressed listening to police scanners, was constantly working the phones ('Hi, this is Edna, what's going on over there?'); and, crucially, she had no desk in the corner of the station house, with all that this implied for hushing things up when some of the boys in uniform got involved in a little jiggery-pokery themselves. If Buchanan got hold of the beans, she spilled them, whether it was revealing the case of a trooper who had molested an 11-

year-old girl in his squad car and got only probation and no criminal record in the hushed-up aftermath (her story, much criticised by the judge, was later vindicated by an independent investigation and the officer jailed), corruption among the new breed of designer-clothed homicide squad ('I learned never to trust a man with a better manicure than mine'), or her investigation that led, indirectly to Miami's worst race riot.

That story began on 21 December 1979 when Buchanan's phone rang and she was tipped off that white Public Safety Department officers had chased, caught and cornered Arthur McDuffie, a black insurance salesman riding a motorcycle. He was rushed to hospital, but died soon afterwards. The officers would insist he died in a road accident. But he hadn't, said Buchanan's source. He had been beaten to death with the officers' heavy metal flashlights, and they had then faked the scene to make it look as if he had died in a crash.

Buchanan called the morgue, the PSD internal affairs section (just a simple accident, they said), and the morgue again. Then she went down to PSD and listened to the tapes of the chase, and read the officers' reports. A few of them she recognised as being the subject of brutality claims in the past. She also noted the towing firm that had removed the wreckage, and went round. They showed her McDuffie's bike, and she noted how every single piece of glass (instruments, lights etc.) was shattered. She also went down to the morgue for the post-mortem. She was not permitted to watch, but she waited for the results, which were ambiguous: either a bad collision with a 'solid object' or flashlights could have shattered McDuffie's skull. She drove to the crash scene. No sign of a 'solid object' McDuffie could have hit. She visited the McDuffie family. She rang all the officers involved. None returned her calls. She spoke to police chiefs she knew. None had yet been informed of the case.

Then she wrote her story. It was nearly neutered by a jumpy editor, but enough of it survived to suggest to anyone in the know that it was written by a reporter whose curiosity was unlikely to go away. It was published on Christmas Eve. Within hours, an officer was seeing his chief to say he had witnessed the beating. The following day, McDuffie's bike was seized as evidence and some of the officers were suspended. Then the officer who wrote the accident report confessed to his captain that it was false. The dam broke. A full murder investigation began, and so did the racial and political investment in its outcome. Four months later, in Tampa, four officers went on trial, three for manslaughter, one for second-degree murder. An all-white jury acquitted them. Within hours, the feelings aroused by the case and then inflamed by the outcome of the trial erupted into a fever of violence on Miami's streets. When it was over, 18 people were dead, more than 350 injured and 600 arrested. No one was ever indicted for the death of Arthur McDuffie. He is remembered today by an annual candlelight vigil, and a family enrichment centre that bears his name.

The police may have escaped the law, but Buchanan kept on their case. Four years later she reported the suspension for brutality of the officer who stopped Arthur McDuffie that night, and she went on investigating aspects of the riot. On the front page of 28 August 1983, her story on the shooting of one innocent bystander appeared:

Somebody shot Michael Johnson. He says it was a Miami policeman. Police say it was a Miami policeman. And under oath, some officers even say that 'it is common knowledge who shot Michael Johnson'.

... Evidence disappeared. A document vanished. Officers quit. No one was ever charged. Now there are accusations of cover-ups and talk of a 'reconstructed' report...

Police partners, side by side at the scene, fail to recollect the same events. One swears he heard no gunshots; an officer with him says he heard about 10 gunshots... State Attorney Janet Reno will not discuss the matter. Her staff, she says, also still is investigating. That is not what Reno's deputy chief assistant, Abe Laeser, advised police months ago...

The story continued, a 3,250-word forensic using reports, statements and depositions in police files. Small wonder that Lloyd Hough, a Metro-Dade homicide detective, told the *New Yorker*: 'If I had done something, I wouldn't want Edna investigating me. Internal Affairs I don't care about, but Edna...' Emmett R. Miller, police chief, said simply: 'Edna is the finest interrogator I ever met.' Miller was, very briefly, her second husband, the first being a *Sun* editor called Buchanan. The swift end to both relationships, she has admitted, was the result, in part, of her round-the-clock immersion in her beat. 'I realised sometime in the late '70s or early '80s,' she said in a 2003 interview, 'that the only thing that ever brought me real pleasure was my work.'

By the early 1980s she was at her peak, and in the next few years there followed a succession of prime Edna Buchanan stories. From December 1982:

> As a fat schoolboy, Gerald Eugene Stano stole money to pay his track team to run behind him. As a young bridegroom, he choked his wife's poodle. As a convicted murderer, he is not eligible for parole until he is 103 years old.
>
> If Gerald Eugene Stano is what he claims to be, he is America's most prolific killer. Now 31, he says he has murdered 39 women since 1969...

Using reports from four psychiatrists and a psychologist, plus Stano's own statements to police, she pieced together the story of the adopted child who showed no feelings for people, only things. He threw tantrums if so much as a stick of furniture was moved from what he thought was its rightful place, set off fire alarms at school, wrecked the family car at 16, made a retarded teenager pregnant, was repeatedly fired for lying or stealing, married, killed his father-in-law's horse, beat a hitchhiker to death a month after his wedding, and carried on a murderous spree that ended only when he was arrested. Her story ended – and Buchanan was nearly as ready with a smart last paragraph as she was with an opener – with a quote from a police officer: 'For Gerald, killing is a need. If he was free tomorrow he would go right back to it. He is not insane. He is a mean person. His hobby is to kill.' By the time he was executed in 1998, Stano had confessed to 41 killings.

From March 1983, the story of a deadly female:

> She is pretty, friendly and eager to go home with new male acquaintances. She is a knockout. Police want to find her before she kills somebody.
> She could be Angie, or Jeannie, or Debbie or Marie. Those are the names she used with four of her victims. She accompanied each of them home and furtively slipped a slightly bitter white powder into their drinks. Suddenly they collapsed, unable to move, then fell into deep, dreamless sleeps. They all awoke nine to 14 hours later, with throbbing hangovers – and without their money, jewelry and other valuables…

Less than a week later, Marie Gonzales was arrested for the crimes, together with boyfriend, Richard Carrero. And someone had indeed died: a woman of 76, strangled by Carrero when the couple tired of waiting for the drug to work.

From May 1984, a near-brilliant conspiracy:

> Except for a single slip-up, it was 'the perfect crime'… A wealthy man and his elderly mother, murdered and buried deep in his own front yard. One of the killers, posing as the dead man, takes over his business, sells his yacht, his stocks, his bonds, his house and his property, police said. No one misses the victims. The killers are home free, it seems…

Except that a conspirator talked to a friend, who talked to a friend, who talked to a friend, and someone then called the police. They moved in, arrests followed, and so, shortly afterwards did Buchanan with the full story.

And, from November 1984, a gay murder:

> They were an odd couple: the expert hairdresser with a following of devoted women customers, and a man with unkempt dirty blond hair, clipped straight across the back in an amateurish-looking cut that would horrify a professional.

It was a classic Edna Buchanan intro, using detail to hang a story that first tantalised and then delivered. The detail was not something she was spoon-fed by police handouts, but culled by her with obsessive questioning that bordered on the pernickety. What was the victim wearing? What was in their pockets? Any tattoos? What was playing on the radio? What was the movie he'd just seen? Did he wear a watch? Any inscription? She did it mainly for the sake of writing an intriguing story, but also believed passionately such detail can help solve cases. In July 1983, for instance, she opened a story: 'He wore a flower tattoo on his shoulder and he died violently. That is all police know about a man whose murder they are trying to solve.' Five weeks later she was reporting: 'The unknown tattooed man, dumped by his killer into a drainage ditch just off a rutted and remote dirt road, had been identified by relatives who recognized a newspaper description of the intricate flower design on his right shoulder.' And, in March 1985, she started another story about a mystery destined to be swiftly solved: 'The double feature was *Public Affairs* and *American Desires*. It was the last picture show for a mystery man found dead in an aisle at the X-rated Pussy Cat Theater shortly before Fifi Royale's exotic dance act.' Buchanan's story told his medical history (double heart by-pass, brain surgery and indigestion sufferer), what was in his wallet ($62.37), his age, height, weight, clothes, his posture (round-shouldered), brand of smokes (Salem), favourite chewing gum (Wrigley's spearmint), the number of keys on his ring (five), arrival time at the cinema, and, intriguingly, a medicine bottle in someone else's name. Not surprisingly, the man was identified within a day.

There was more, much more: the millionaire racing driver who turned into a serial killer, the Glades skeleton mystery of 1986, the four-times married millionaire garrotted in his suite at the Fontainebleau Hilton, and many of these stories with that trademark one-liner intro. January 1985: 'Who is the man

in black and why did he ambush the human cannonball?';
February 1988: 'Vincenzo Quinto's first marriage lasted for 62
years. His second ended after six days'; and, from July 1985,
perhaps the definitive Edna Buchanan story, a 2,952-word
Sunday morning special that began:

> Bad things happen to the husbands of the Widow Elkin. Someone
> murdered husband No. 4, Cecil Elkin, apparently smashing his
> head with a frying pan as he watched *Family Feud* on TV. Husband
> No. 3, Samuel Smilich, drowned in a weedy South Dade canal.
> Husband No. 2, Lawrence Myers, cannot be found... Husband
> No. 1, Wayne Wise, was divorced about 25 years ago. He is alive
> and well.
>
> The woman they married is Margaret Lucille Livingston Wise
> Myers Smilich Elkin. Now 46, she is a prim, Methodist churchgoer
> from South Carolina. She bakes apple pies, sews and works out
> at the Vital Lady exercise club in Homestead... To astonished
> housewife friends, she tells stories of kinky sex and violence. To
> one friend, she implied that the Ku Klux Klan is responsible for
> the deaths of her third and fourth husbands.

It would require more strength of character than most of us
possess to resist the temptation to read on. The story ended with
a quote from hubby number one: 'She is a very affectionate,
charming, Christian, almost bashful-type lady, emphasis on
the lady,' he said. 'She couldn't hardly kill a fly.'

And still those dark princes cropped up, except that now
she knew enough to no longer find much romance in them.
There were men like Jack, 'Murph the Surf' Murphy, the
former child prodigy violinist with the Pittsburgh Symphony
Orchestra whom she first came across in the early 1960s when
he dressed as a court jester to entertain tourists with his stunt
diving act. Then he went to the bad, stole the Star of India
sapphire from New York's Museum of Natural History, and
was jailed. When he was released, Buchanan was there for the
Sun to cover the triumphant homecoming of the jokey jewel
thief. She was also there, a few years later, when the one-time
funster was arrested, tried and convicted of armed robbery

and first-degree murder of two young women who had got in
his greedy way. And she was there, too, in the mid-1980s to
report his imminent release from an initial two-life terms in
jail. As she later wrote: 'Murph the Surf found Jesus in prison.
They usually do.'

While Murph was coming on with the piety and finding a
theological basis for an early release, the world beyond Miami
was starting to discover Buchanan. Calvin Trillin profiled her in
the February 1986 *New Yorker*, and Random House signed her
to write a book on her experiences as a crime reporter. Then,
in April 1986, came a Pulitzer Prize for general reporting.
Buchanan said it was a tribute to all beat reporters, but this was
one statement of hers not to be relied upon. The award was,
instead, a recognition of an eat-sleep-and drink the job reporter
whose relentless collection of detail ('Ask one more question,
knock on one more door, make one last phone call, and then
another. It could be the one that counts…') and ability to grab
the reader by the lapels in the intro was allied to a rare gift
for story-telling. It is a skill she has since put to use in writing
crime fiction, producing eleven novels by Spring 2004.

The book that started this career as a full-time author (she
still writes the occasional crime piece for the *Herald*), was her
first volume of reporter's tales. She called it *The Corpse Had A
Familiar Face*, an intro she had used on the killing of prostitute
Leola Covington in March 1986. And, with this book, she kept
a promise she had made nearly 40 years before. For the math
teacher had got it wrong, and the English teacher was right.
So there, on the leaf after the title page, was the dedication to
Edna Mae Tunis, who encouraged her to write, and who died
at the age of 48 shortly afterwards. It is a touch altogether
typical of Buchanan, a reporter who always knew how stories
should end as well how they should start.

3
A.J. Liebling
1904–1963

THE MOST QUOTABLE WIT EVER BY-LINED

Inside the side drawer of every reporter, goes the cliché, there is a half-written novel. Most never get finished, lodged in the desk (and the reporter's mind) like an old admonition. Some are published, and a few of these achieve a kind of immortality: *The Postman Always Rings Twice* (James M. Caan, late of the *New York World*); *Gone With the Wind* (Margaret Mitchell, once a reporter on the *Atlanta Journal*); *The Snow Goose* (Paul Gallico, sports columnist with the *New York Daily News*); the James Bond series (Ian Fleming, one-time foreign manager of the *Sunday Times*); and tales by Damon Runyon (reporter for the *New York American*), Jack London (for *Collier's*, among other magazines) and Tom Wolfe (reporter for the *New York Herald-Tribune*).

But whether these half-formed manuscripts are eventually completed or not, what lies behind reporters striving to scramble on to even the lower slopes of literature is not so much the thought of making money but the idea that fiction is a higher form of writing than journalism. Those who can, write; those who cannot, merely report. In Britain, a life spent reporting is regarded as almost an admission that, when it comes to words, you couldn't quite raise the puff to go book-

A.J. Liebling

length distance. And even in America, where you can at least attain some sort of intellectual profile with non-fiction, the idea persists that making stuff up is a classier act than trying to capture reality.

It's an odd concept for democracies to embrace so persistently, and an even odder one for those of us who have always preferred trying to get a handle on life as it is lived, as opposed to life as it might be imagined. Neither has it any intellectual foundation, the difficulty of attempting to investigate and describe actuality being a challenge at least the equal of rearranging 'facts' or 'characters' that the writer has dreamt up. Novelists, after all, only have to conform to their own truths, and they rarely have to issue corrections. Anyone trying to argue that the literary ability on display in the average novel is superior to the average newspaper article has clearly not visited an airport bookstore lately, nor read the scores of reporters who every day demonstrate a skill with words that most novelists would find a positive encumbrance.

And yet, many journalists persist with their inferiority complex. Consider this, from the *New Yorker*'s Saul Steinberg, describing an especially talented, but fiction-avoiding, colleague: 'He was like a ballerina who chooses to walk.' In other words, he took the easy way out; he didn't put himself to the test; he strolled rather than learnt all those difficult steps. Hokum, of course, especially as the man Steinberg was writing about was A.J. Liebling, not far short of the best pen in press history. 'Why don't you write a novel?' people would ask Liebling. 'What?' he replied, 'And make things up?' And when invited to comment on his friend Albert Camus, he shook his head and said: 'His energies were dissipated in creative writing and we lost a great journalist.'

Unable to conceive that any imaginings of his could possibly equal the absurd people and events in the real world, Liebling therefore spent his talents describing what he found there: New York low-life, war, the flotsam and jetsam of show business,

Paris, would-be demagogues, charlatans, boxers and their hangers-on, and heaped platefuls of appallingly rich food. And he did so with perhaps the most quotable wit ever by-lined. He called, for instance, the University of California 'the biggest magnet for neurotic adolescents since the Children's Crusade'; wrote that the hearings of the House Committee on UnAmerican Activities were 'reminiscent of a group of retarded children playing detekative'; famously wrote that 'the freedom of the press is limited to those who own one'; and dismissed Adolf Hitler in three lines: 'No ascetic,' he wrote, 'can be considered reliably sane. Hitler was the archetype of the abstemious man. When the other Krauts saw him drink water in the Beer Hall, they should have known he was not to be trusted.'

Liebling understood that it is not that reporting requires no imagination compared to fiction, it's that it requires a different kind. And, since his mind worked that way, reporting is what he wrote. Hence, there was no half-finished novel in Liebling's drawer; instead, reporting of such quality that, to date, an output confined by an early death to less than 30 years has been collected in no fewer than 16 separate books. As the man said himself, in a line that every reporter wishes they'd thought of first: 'I can write better than anybody who can write faster, and I can write faster than anybody who can write better.'

Abbott Joseph Liebling was born in New York on 18 October 1904 into considerable prosperity. His father was a furrier whose readiness to have the skin off the back of mammals extended, in his business dealings, to humans as well. He hired gangsters to break up strike meetings, and, when he saw the potential of a block of property on West 26th Street inhabited largely by prostitutes, became a patron of an anti-vice society, tipped it off about the dens of iniquity down at 26th, and watched his investment rocket in value when the cops moved in and the hookers were moved out. The result was a large home on the Upper East side, a clutch of German servants, trips to Europe, regular visits to the opera, and Liebling junior wanting for very little. The only son repaid this generosity by wolfing down whatever books and culture came his way, and becoming a model student at the public schools he attended. By the age of 16, he was at Dartmouth, and by 17 had the distinction of being sent away twice for non-attendance at chapel, on the second occasion permanently so.

Within a year Liebling was at the Pulitzer School of Journalism at Columbia. When he signed on, short story writing was his ambition; but by the time he left, two years later, he had discovered reporting. This was not through any inspirational teaching (he once titled a book chapter on Columbia 'How To Learn Nothing'), but to hitting the streets and getting the whiff of a story in his nostrils. He later wrote:

> I liked to pound up tenement stairs and burst in on families disarranged by sudden misfortune. It gave me a chance to make contact with people I would never otherwise have met, and I learned almost immediately what every reporter knows, that most people are eager to talk about their troubles and are rather flattered by the arrival of the *World* or the *Journal*.

His tutor, both in the ways of the slums and the men who covered them, was legendary police reporter Max Fischel of the New York *Evening World*.

Liebling finished the two-year course, and immediately took a job that could not have been less suited to his talent. The good news was that it was in the sports department of the *New York Times*, the bad was that it was copyediting – what Liebling regarded as journalism at second hand. He found himself, as he later wrote, 'among frustrated reporters who know exactly how a story should be covered because they have never covered one'. He enlivened the tedium in two ways. The first, when college basketball reporters failed to provide the name of a referee, was to invent an official named 'Ignoto', Italian for unknown; the second, when a pompous reporter called in with a paragraph about his election to a minor post with the boxing writers' association, was to send it for setting with the man rechristened with a grand-sounding, and entirely fictitious middle name. The sports editor was unamused. 'God knows what you will do next young man,' he told Liebling one night in March 1926. 'You are irresponsible. Not a *Times* type. Go.'

Providence, Rhode Island was where he went, as a $40 a week reporter on the *Evening Bulletin*, and, hours after stepping off the train to his new posting, he'd found the story of a property speculator who hanged himself in his cell, traced the man's family, interviewed them and filed his first big story. After a few more weeks of news hounding, Liebling wrote the line that set the direction for the rest of his career. He was covering the trial of Sigmund Rand, a German bootlegger whose home, when raided, turned out to have a still in the cellar. Rand, who had been cutting down a tree in his front garden when arrested, claimed, somewhat unconvincingly, that he knew nothing of the distillery. 'He may have chopped down a tree,' wrote Liebling, 'but he was no George Washington.' That wisecrack got him picked out as a writer with a light touch, and he was transferred to the *Bulletin*'s sister daily, the *Journal*, where there was a little more time and space to polish his stories.

He was still only 22, and his next move was thanks to his father's providence, rather than Rhode Island's. Liebling senior offered his son $2,000 to study in Europe. The reporter would later claim, half-seriously, that he had persuaded his father to cough up by telling him he was about to marry a kept woman ten years older than himself, but the truth was probably that Abbott Joseph remained the spoiled only son of a man of means and was simply collecting what both regarded as his dues. So he took the cash, spent $800 of it before his ship even sailed, twisted the old man's arm for a $200 a month allowance and headed for Paris. He investigated history, architecture,

French medieval literature, fine food and obliging women, not necessarily in that order. Ever after he was in thrall to Paris, and its morish cuisine.

By early summer 1928 he was back at work for the *Journal*, writing a mixture of investigations, news and features. 'I oozed prose over every aspect of Rhode Island life,' he later wrote, and, according to Raymond Sokolov's excellent biography *Wayward Reporter, the Life of A.J. Liebling*, he exposed a pathologist with phoney credentials, toured fortune-tellers collecting ever-more absurd predictions, and covered the visit to Providence of Zaro Agha, a Turk who kept a straight face while claiming to be 156 years old. Under the headline '156-year-old arrives seeking wife, teeth, cash', Liebling began: 'Spry as a lad of 90-odd, Zaro Agha, who has a nice new certificate giving his birth date as 1774, arrived in Providence from Turkey yesterday.'

Then, in the summer of 1930, came three turning points for Liebling: he resigned when his room-mate was fired to make way for the son of a local big-wig; he met his future wife, cinema ticket office girl Ann McGinn; and he moved back to New York.

He soon discovered, as have many before and since, that large by-lines on small papers are a currency with a pretty poor rate of exchange in big cities. Liebling was rejected by editor after editor, most memorably by Stanley Walker of the New York *World*. 'I have been informed', wrote Liebling, 'that you are looking for a good reporter. I am one.' Walker responded firmly, but ambiguously: 'You have been misinformed.' He tried buttonholing city editors in bars, and paying hopeful visits to offices, until, finally, he went to a Hungarian sign painter, commissioned a sign reading 'Hire Joe Liebling' in large orange letters, and paid an old Norwegian seaman to parade it up and down outside the *World*'s offices. It was not, as it turned out, Liebling's best-researched piece of work. The city editor used the back entrance, and so never saw the bearded old salt and his sandwichboard. Liebling did, however, sell the story of his gambit to *Editor and Publisher*, and the Sunday *World* Metropolitan section, and he began putting together a limited freelance practice writing about nightlife, show-business, boxing, cycle races, and interviewing hopeful writers and performers eager for publicity, like a young Ogden Nash. Some of these articles were for the Sunday *World*, where he had the fortune to have two editors who, in his words, 'did a lot to get the superfluous scroll-work out of my writing and make me "pack things tight"...'

Liebling had barely got into this particular stride when the *World* was sold to Roy Howard, who merged it with his *Telegram*. This, wrote Liebling, was 'a ludicrous rag. Written for the most part in an idiom I once described as Oklahoma Byzantine, to the specifications of an owner who had placed on the bulletin board a notice saying: "Remember, New York is Baghdad on the subway!"' But this was 1931, and fastidiousness about proprietors was a luxury, especially for a man whose new wife's mental problems were running up the doctors' bills. Liebling joined the *World-Telegram* as a reporter at $75 a week, and began writing features that soon showed his trademark fascination with misfits, scamps, scallywags and oddballs. In 'Back Where I Came From', a collection of pieces written at the *World-Telegram* and in the first couple of years on the *New Yorker*, there is to be found: I. Berkovitz, the leech dealer ('The leech...is a social barometer. If prohibition had been a success then there would have been less drunks, less black eyes, less demand for leeches. But no, the leech business was good'); Captain Louis Van Dycke, gnu trainer with Barnum & Bailey's circus; Samuel J. Burger, the cockroach race promoter who rented monkeys out to the city's neurotics so they could tell their problems to sympathetic primates rather than expensive psychiatrists; and the self-styled Mayor of Mulberry Street who took it upon himself to monitor the number of trips people took to Coney

Island because, he believed, an uneven number of dips in the sea would cause rheumatism. Liebling had a great eye for such charming fruitcakes, a God-given talent for phrase-making, but, most of all, he listened. Colleague after colleague noticed that: he knew when to shut up and let his subject talk.

The result was that his features were inhabited by people who sound real, not extruded through a reporter's idea of how they should speak:

> The least assuming world champion I ever met was a young man named Rubin Fisher of 214 Broome Street who had at that date read 146,444 gas meters without a mistake. He had been invited by officers of the Consolidated Edison Company to give a seminar course for other meter readers. I always covered those big stories.
> 'The first point in meter readings,' the champion said, 'is to find the meter. This is very easy... A meter reader sees a lot of things, but it is none of his business.' He is not a playboy. 'When I get home,' he said, 'I just like to sit quiet.'

There was the last elephant leaper with Ringling Bros Greatest Show on Earth, whose employers had abandoned the act in 1908 owing to the number of broken necks:

> Charlie Bell sat on a trunk by one of the entries to the circus ring, watching the elephants. 'Ain't nobody leaped over 'em for twenty-four years now,' he said pityingly. 'I don't see how they handle 'em. Nothing keeps an elephant in place like being leaped over. Makes 'em feel they ain't so big.'

There was Tom Wilson, tugboat master:

> 'I'm seventy-four years old and I can jump out of that window and jump back again. When they put me together, they put me together right... I went tug-boatin' when I was 18... Tugboat captains was the cream of society in them days. They wore high hats and gold watch chains and Prince Albert coats and striped trousers, and they never touched the wheel without kid gloves.'

And there was Ben Green, the professional faster:

> He is not a mere passive non-eater. He fasts for fifty days at a clip... to advertise swimming pools and department stores, on the

same principle as a flagpole sitter... 'At the age of 38 I weighed 278 pounds,' he told me once. 'I was in a fair way to becoming a laughing stock. I tried dieting and then I tried exercise. Neither seemed to help, so I decided to try both together. One day when my wife called me to dinner I put on my hat. "Instead of eating further viands," I told her, "I am going out for a nice nourishing twelve-mile walk." I went, and I went to bed afterward without having eaten. The next day I got up feeling fine, and instead of breakfast I took a five-mile walk. For lunch I had a juicy eight-mile hike, and for dinner I ran a luscious marathon on the Rockaway Broadwalk.'

The only exceptions to this authenticity were Asa Wood and Elmer Chipling, two wholly fictitious characters who appeared in several pieces as a kind of Greek chorus uttering homespun man-in-the-streetery. Thankfully, Liebling grew out of the habit as speedily as he learnt another secret of quality features: extensive, even what some would deem excessive, research. Collecting many times more material than he knew he'd ever need for the final piece gave him the assurance not only that what remained would be good, but that his questioning of the subject would be that much sharper. He once, for instance, began an interview with jockey Eddie Arcaro by asking him why his left stirrup was longer than his right – a question that has been famously contrasted to the one another reporter opened with when faced with actress Vivien Leigh. 'Tell me, Miss Leigh,' he began eagerly, 'what part did you play in *Gone With The Wind?*' The interview was terminated on the spot.

By 1934, Liebling thought he was worth more than the *World-Telegram* were paying him, asked for a raise, was refused and so left. The bills to treat his wife's schizophrenia were pressing down, and Liebling had also glimpsed a different, sweeter kind of journalistic life when he contributed occasional pieces to the 'Talk of the Town' section of the *New Yorker*. Within a couple of months, during which he scampered around for a Hearst syndicate, he had negotiated himself on to Harold Ross's magazine. He was to stay with it, one tiff apart, for the rest of his working life.

His first piece for the magazine was very nearly a disaster. It was an investigatory profile of Father Divine, a black evangelist and early civil rights campaigner who, for all his good works, used the donations of his working-class followers to subsidise a lifestyle not noted for self-denial. Liebling had research that cast considerable doubt on the size of Divine's following, including interviews with some of his hapless donors. Then he sat down to write, and produced what he later described as 'a million-word book on comparative religion'. Even allowing for Liebling's interest in the subject, it seemed like a classic case of the new boy on the heavyweight publication being overwhelmed by the thought of all those egg-head readers. The piece was rescued by St Clair McKelway; and Liebling's editors, who included the legendary William Shawn, steered him into more familiar territory than salvation and the meaning of life.

For the next three years, Liebling scanned the horizon for sharp-talking quirky characters, followed them to their home turf, and got them to talk their way on to the pages of the *New Yorker*. There was Augustine J. Grenet, oddsmaker at racecourses ('The average bookmaker has as much idea of horses as a hog has of heaven'); Mrs Selma Braatz, champion lady juggler, whose skills were the result of 12 hours' practice a day ('Sometimes, when I sit down in a restaurant, absentminded I begin to juggle the knife, the fork, soon a plate – it's very embarrassing...'); Whitey Bimstein, said to be the best cornerman in boxing; Dr Martin A. Couney, who exhibited premature babies in their incubators at Coney Island; an artist called Achille, who painted Biblical scenes for churches, taking as his model for the Madonna the distinctly unvirginal actress Merle Oberon; Professor Alexander Meyer, the Rockerless Chair Rocking Champion of the World (and inventor, also, of the one-piece four-piece suit, a garment that, in the end, proved no more popular than wobbling on two chair legs); Hymie Katz, ex-singing waiter and promoter of deliberately short-lived nightclubs, who believed the investment of his own money in these schemes would be somehow unethical ('Hymie is unmarried at present. Wives, with Hymie, are symptoms of prosperity, like tailored shirts'); circus clown Bluch Landof ('It is as hard to be an outstanding clown in an American circus as it is to be a distinguished artisan in an automobile factory'); and George A. Hamid, a Syrian former acrobat who booked on to the county fair circuit such deservedly forgotten acts as aerial artistes Albino Sensation, Pallenberg's Wonder Bears, Weir's Elephants, and Alf Loyal's Performing Dogs.

And then there was Izzy Yereshevsky and his famous Broadway cigar store, populated by customers like Three-To-Two Charlie, a betting man who disliked long odds:

> Most of Izzy's evening guests – their purchases are so infrequent it would be misleading to call them customers – wear white felt hats and overcoats of a style known to them as English Drape. Short men peer up from between the wide-flung shoulders of these coats as if they had been lowered into the garments on a rope and were now trying to climb out...
>
> In Izzy's store, as on the East Indian island of Buru and among certain Australian aborigines, it is considered bad form to speak a man's real name lest one unwittingly give an enemy power over his future. It is also bad form in addressing a customer who has been away to ask him where he has been. He may have been in Hollywood or he may have been in jail. If he has been in Hollywood, he will say so.

But Liebling was not just good for oddball character studies. Shawn called him 'a master in journalistic terms', and when war broke out in 1939, the *New Yorker* had no hesitation in sending him to Europe. He was in Paris by 12 October, and for the next seven months filed pieces on the life, people and theatre of a city bracing itself for German attack. It finally came in May 1940:

> The new phase of the second World War was announced to Parisians at daybreak Friday. People had gone to bed Thursday night in their habitual state of uncertainty... With the dawn came

the air-raid sirens, startling a city that had heard no alert during the daytime since the first week of the war. At once, each of the innumerable residential squares in Paris took on the aspect of an Elizabethan theater, with tiers of spectators framed in the opened windows of every building. Instead of looking down at a stage, however, they all looked up. All wore nightshirts, which, since the prosperity of tenants in a walk-up is in inverse ratio to their altitude, appeared considerably dingier on the sixth and seventh floors than on the second and third.

The French government soon abandoned Paris, trailing a reluctant Liebling in their wake, and by late June he was back in New York. As a magazine writer whose job was to capture atmosphere and characters rather than news, his war consisted of a series of sorties mounted from Manhattan to where the action was. In July 1941 he was sent to London to cover the Blitz, used that as a base for other pieces around Britain, and then returned five months later. Half a year later he was back in London, from where, in November 1942, he sailed with the First Infantry Division to report on the invasion of North Africa. In May 1943 he returned to New York, hung around for six months, and then left for London again. His task this time was to get himself on the Normandy invasion fleet, which he duly did, crossing the Channel in Landing Craft, Infantry, Large No. 88, and coming under considerable fire as the troops on his boat were landed on Omaha Beach. He wrote, in typical self-deprecating terms:

> … I looked down at the main deck, and the beach-battalion men were already moving ahead, so I knew that the ramps must be down. I could hear Long shouting, 'Move along now! Move along!,' as if he were unloading an excursion boat at Coney Island. But the men needed no urging; they were moving without a sign of flinching. You didn't have to look far for tracers now, and Kallam and I flattened our backs against the pilot house and pulled in our stomachs, as if to give a possible bullet an extra couple of inches clearance. Something tickled the back of my neck. I slapped at it and discovered that I had most of the ship's rigging draped around my neck and shoulders, like a character in an old slapstick movie

about a spaghetti factory, or like Captain Horatio Hornblower. The rigging had been cut away by bullets...

Liebling did not go ashore that day. He returned to London, filed, and then, on 24 June, crossed to France to follow the drive towards Paris. He was one of the first correspondents into the city, and he went straight to the same hotel he had left four years before. 'Mlle Yvonne was sitting behind the desk,' he wrote, 'going over her accounts. "Bonjour, Monsieur Liebling," she said, barely looking up. It was as if I had just stepped out for a walk.' Her reaction was more understated than the rest of Paris. 'For the first time and probably the last,' he wrote, 'I have lived for a week in a great city where everybody was happy.'

So may have ended Liebling's war, but the private conflicts that afflicted him were to have no such neat denouement. Almost from the start of their marriage, his schizophrenic wife's behaviour had been erratic. As the 1930s wore on, it got worse, and her husband never knew when she would turn from a laughing companion into the jumpy woman who would suddenly bolt out of bars or restaurants and not be seen again for days. Neither did he know if she would come back herself, hair or clothes in a mess, or be found and taken to Bellevue Hospital, from where he would have to retrieve her. The hospital stays got longer, the intermittent bouts of normality grew less frequent, and the medical bills mounted. By the late 1940s, Liebling wanted out. He divorced Ann, married again, left the *New Yorker*, went freelance, and moved to Chicago to research a profile for *Collier's* of *Tribune* publisher Robert McCormick. It never happened. Instead, he wrote a three-part series on Chicago called 'Second City', which still rankles with some of its more protective citizens. He described it as 'plopped down by the lakeside like a piece of waterlogged fruit', and ripped into what he saw as its inferiority complex, glorification of gangsterism, and ugliness.

In matters of appearance, Liebling in his late forties was in no position to cast stones. Although it was never likely he would be accosted in the street by artists in search of an Adonis to immortalise, Liebling had now passed from youthful plumpness to corpulence. He weighed in at around 246 lb, and was a martyr to kidney stones and gout. The cause was a fondness for rich, cream-smothered food that was not far short of an addiction. His *New York Times* obituarist wrote of him 'he bore the marks of a gourmet', but the truth was that he was as much a glutton as a connoisseur. 'I used to be shy about ordering a steak after I had eaten a steak sandwich,' he wrote, 'but I got used to it.' He wrote about this hobby with creditable lack of shame in a series of articles titled 'Memoirs of a Feeder in France', and these became the basis for a book called *Between Meals*, an interval that, for Liebling, was never long. It is entirely typical that when, in the mid-1950s, Liebling went to the famous Bircher-Benner fat farm in Switzerland, he returned home heavier than when he left.

Whatever state he was in personally (and his second marriage broke up in 1955), Liebling was now at his peak as a writer. He wrote several major pieces on the Middle East and Palestinian internment camps (and did so with such balance that he upset the ever-ready-to-be-offended Jewish lobby); wrote for the *Observer* of London on sport and politics; covered the Algerian War; researched in great detail a profile of Henry Wittenberg, the Olympic wrestling champion who became a New York detective (he tore the piece up when the NYPD insisted on the right to review the finished article); and then tackled a character so outlandish and convoluted that the articles became a book. This was Earl Long, brother of legendary populist Huey, whom he followed, after a gap of a decade or so, as governor of Louisiana. Politics was not Liebling's favoured subject, but when Long was manhandled mid-speech out of the state legislature, into a waiting car, and thence to a Texas asylum for the insane where his wife Blanche duly certified his instability, the reporter scuttled south.

Louisiana, wrote Liebling in the finished piece, was 'the westernmost of the Arab states', with politics 'of an intensity and complexity that are matched, in my experience, only in the republic of Lebanon'. That much didn't surprise him; what did was Long himself. Nominally a corrupt bigot ('Don't write anything you can phone. Don't phone anything you can talk. Don't talk anything you can whisper. Don't whisper anything you can smile. Don't smile anything you can nod. Don't nod anything you can wink…'), the governor came across to Liebling as a closet progressive: mad, but some of his heart in the right place. Pleased to be able to write of Long against the grain of near-universal derision, Liebling instead had his fun writing about southern ways and northern reactions to it, as here at a dinner at the Louisiana governor's mansion:

> One of the women guests, a Northerner, inadvertently sat on a jacket a political gent had laid aside. It was a silvery Dacron-Acrilan-nylon-airpox miracle weave nubbled in Danish-blue asterisks. She made one whoop and rose vertically, like a helicopter. She had sat on his gun, an article of apparel that in Louisiana is considered as essential as a zipper. Eyebrows rose about as rapidly as she did, and by the time she came down she decided that comment would be considered an affectation.

Earlier in the piece, he had described Long's antics as his running mate spoke at a campaign meeting:

> … Earl, seated directly behind him, was mugging and catching flies, monopolizing attention like an old vaudeville star cast in a play with a gang of Method actors.

In 1959, Liebling married again. She was Jean Stafford, a novelist and short story writer good enough to win the Pulitzer Prize. Her literary antecedents were mixed to say the least. Her first husband was the poet Robert Lowell, while her father had written Western stories with titles like 'Smoother Moody's Last Round', 'Forced to Fight', and 'Panhandle Nemesis' under the pen names of Jack Wonder and Ben Delight. His late father-in-law would have made an excellent feature for the *New*

Yorker. Liebling met Jean in England, and wooed her with a tour of provincial race courses in a hired Rolls-Royce, copious champagne and the contents of a permanently replenished hamper. There was ever a touch of romance about Liebling's bon viveuring.

His other great love was boxing. There was a two-part series on his beloved Stillman's Gym, titled 'The University of Eighth Avenue', and no fight could be described as major until Liebling had arrived to cover it. Two pieces stand out. The first is on the Archie Moore–Rocky Marciano fight in 1955. In the course of setting the scene, he describes a fight in London between Cuban heavyweight Nino Valdes and the overwight Englishman Don Cockell, which ended thus: '... the fat man settled in one corner of the ring as heavily as suet pudding upon the unaccustomed gastric system'. Thence to the main event, at the beginning of which, Liebling observed, Marciano, 'resembled a Great Dane who has heard the word "bone"...' He went on:

> ... At this point Marciano set about him. He waddled in, hurling his fists with a sublime disregard of probabilities, content to hit an elbow, a bicep, a shoulder, the top of a head... The crowd, basically anti-intellectual, screamed encouragement. There was Moore, riding punches, picking them off, slipping them, rolling with them, ducking them, coming gracefully out of his defensive efforts with sharp, patterned blows – and just about holding this parody even on points. His face, emerging at instants from under the storm of arms – his own and Rocky's – looked like that of a swimming walrus. When the round ended, I could see that he was thinking deeply. Marciano came back to his corner at a kind of suppressed dogtrot. He didn't have a worry in the world.

The second was on the rematch between clean-living Floyd Patterson and the good-time Charlie who deprived him of his title, Sweden's Ingemar Johansson:

> Patterson had no time to think about the rewards of virtue – he was too busy reaping them. He hit the hedonist with a left hook to the body and then switched it to the head. The Swede was in the same place when the punch landed as when it started. He went

down like a double portion of Swedish pancakes with lingonberries and sour cream. He got up, though. There was no quit in him; he was still, in spirit, disputacious. Patterson swung his left again, like a man with a brush hook clearing briars. It hit the champion's chin, his head went back on a loose neck, and he struck the mat with a crash that I swear I heard at a distance of at least three hundred yards.

By now Liebling was in his late fifties and his body was so furred up by gout that he could barely move without excruciating pain. This did not stop him travelling – even in the summer of 1963 he went collecting material in Algeria, France and London – but it eventually slowed his article production to a crawl. His ill-health meant he was now a sitting target for any passing infection, and, in late December, he developed viral pneumonia. He was taken first to New York's Doctors' Hospital, then, as his condition deteriorated, to Mount Sinai. But there was little that could be done, and he died there on 28 December. He was 59. A few months later, his first wife Ann, whom he had always loved and had always loved him, drowned herself in the Providence River.

Liebling left behind more than most journalists. There was his reporting, progressive amounts of it cast between hard covers, and much of this still in print decades after his death. And there was something else, too: the critical writings on journalism that he maintained for nigh on thirty years through his 'Wayward Press' column. No other reporter of his class has written so much about his own trade, and the result is more wisdom than in an entire library of textbooks. He poured elegant scorn on stories that were hyped; those that were biased, especially if against unions or welfare recipients; those that reporters just plain missed; and the kind of foreign reporting that affected an authoritative voice for no very good reason. In 1953, for example, he wrote:

Within a week after Stalin's announced demise, the American public knew that he had died of natural causes or been murdered subtly, either on the date named by Pravda or several weeks earlier; that the people of Moscow had demonstrated grief but (a *Journal-American* scoop) the demonstration had been a carefully organised fake; that his death portended either a hardening or a softening of policy toward the West, which, in turn, would lessen or increase the chances of open war; and that his death would either precipitate an immediate struggle for power among the surviving leaders or impel them to stand together until they got things running smoothly...

He attacked newspaper executives ('... the reign of these non-writers makes our newspapers read like the food in the *New York Times* cafeteria tastes'), and used good writing to point out bad, as when, in a profile of New York *Telegram* owner Roy Howard, he said the paper's readers: '... had developed hallucinations from reading its prose and were dragged from subway trains slapping at adjectives they said they saw crawling over them'. And he bequeathed, for those who want to comb his collected 'Wayward Press' columns, a lot of straightforward tips, such as this:

> The best way to describe how dull a dull event is, is to tell it straight; the trouble with writing ominously about this sort of thing is that you make it sound ominous, and the trouble with being amusing about it is that you make it sound amusing.

Liebling left behind one more thing. A few days after his death, a *New Yorker* colleague entered his chaotic lair of an office and found its desk almost submerged in piles of books and papers he had been consulting. They included the collected works of Albert Camus, a manual on beer-making, the New York Historical Society's *Annual Report*, three books on boxing, a month's back numbers of the *Las Vegas Sun*, a travel guide to Tunisia, and a copy of the *American Racing Manual*. It is a snapshot of a wide-ranging, inquiring intelligence interrupted by illness in his search for that nugget, statistic or juxtaposition of facts that would bring alive the piece he was working on. What the office did not contain, even in its bottom-most desk drawer, was a half-written novel. Liebling left the world plenty of stories; they just happened to be real ones.

George Seldes

4
George Seldes
1890–1995

In the long, and not entirely wasted history of journalism's awkward squad, one reporter stands out as having caused more trouble to more big-wigs, fat cats, charlatans, poison peddlers and members of the world domination league than any other: George Seldes. He made a career out of presenting the high and mighty with inconvenient and embarrassing facts. On his very first paper, while barely out of his teens, he seriously got up the noses of local big business, and, for the rest of his long life, he went on adding names to those irked by his reporting: First World War censors, the Soviet state, Harvard University, Benito Mussolini, oil companies, General MacArthur and the entire army general staff, right-wing radio commentators, the *New York Times*, General Motors and other firms that traded with fascism, the *Chicago Tribune*, William Randolph Hearst, the FBI, the House Committee on UnAmerican Activities, *Reader's Digest*, Edgar Hoover, the Communist Party, Republican Party, evangelists and the tobacco industry. His opponents might harass him, threaten him, smear him and call him, to quote just one, 'a rotten little scare-mongering louse', but for nigh on 70 years they couldn't shut him up.

And he did it, mostly, on his own. Not for him, after he turned 38, the protection of a big name publication. Instead, he worked as a freelance, and, for ten years, the writer and publisher of a newsletter that charged at the brick wall of corporate America with revelation after revelation. He was, as A.J. Liebling said, 'about as subtle as a house falling in', but, as the press critic went on: 'He is a useful citizen. In fact he is a fine little gadfly.' That is putting it mildly. Between the eras of the Muckrakers and Watergate, Seldes kept the tattered flag of investigative journalism flying, at times almost single-handedly. And, as if that was not enough, he also met or interviewed a virtual who's who of twentieth-century life, from Teddy Roosevelt, Sarah Bernhardt and Charles Chaplin, through Lenin, Mussolini, and Picasso, Hindenberg, Einstein and Marlene Dietrich, to Ford Maddox Ford, H.G. Wells, Errol Flynn, Joe McCarthy and President Tito. He appeared in a Hollywood film at the age of 90, and a documentary on his life made when he was 104 was nominated for an Oscar. Few, if any, journalists have led such an extraordinary life as George Seldes.

The story of his youth would alone be worthy of a movie. He was born on 16 November 1890, his mother died when he was six, and he spent his childhood shuttling between his grandparents and father. Seldes senior was postmaster and leading light of Alliance, New Jersey, the kind of liberal community where no one turned a hair to see Mr Bailey, farmer and town philosopher, using one hand to lead a cow, while, with the other, he held an open volume of Kant or Spinoza. Seldes's father blended perfectly with these saintly cranks, being described by his son as 'a libertarian, an idealist, a freethinker, a Deist, a Utopian, a Single Taxer, and a worshipper of Thoreau and Emerson'. Neither did his selection box of causes stop there. They also included being secretary to the Friends of Russian Freedom, in which capacity he once gave bed and board to a visiting Maxim Gorky, and also carried on a busy correspondence with Prince Kropotkin and Count Tolstoi. Their lengthy letters back to him sadly perished one chilly morning when a laundry-maid used them as fuel for the Seldes family stove.

The ideals and interests of Father Seldes kept the family permanently short of cash, but in the early years of the century, modest prosperity beckoned. He was offered a drugstore on Center Avenue, Pittsburgh which, he was assured by its seller, was good for a profit of $50 a day. With the help of some doctors, he secured a mortgage and, at 6am on the first day of trading, opened the doors, and in trooped a dozen or more shabby characters. The first of them slapped a silver dollar on the counter, pointed to a drawer marked 'SOD.Bicarb', and waited expectantly. Inside the cabinet, Seldes found two rows of packets already prepared. The first was marked 'Heroin 50 cents', and the second 'Cocaine $1'. The old Utopian slammed the drawer shut, drove the addicts out of the store, and with them went any prospect of serious profit.

By the age of 18, young George was ready to earn both a living and some liberal stripes. So, impressed by the buzz generated by the reporters who occasionally swarmed into his father's store in search of a local angle on events in Russia, he walked into the offices of the *Pittsburgh Leader* on 9 February 1909 and asked for a job. He was told that, if he wanted to learn reporting, he could hang around, make himself useful, and in return be given $3.50 a week 'lunch money'. He accepted, and so began his apprenticeship under perhaps the most splendidly named city editor in newspaper history: Houston Eagle. It wasn't long before Mr Eagle handed his protégé one of the newsroom's more hapless assignments: asking has-been celebrities insolent questions with an air of utterly genuine innocence. His quarry was three-times presidential candidate William Jennings Bryan, a man always better at electrifying party conventions than voters, and, by then, a good few years after his heyday, more a figure of fun than stature. Off went Seldes to the great man's hotel, tapped on the door, and, when it was opened by Bryan – still, at 11am, in his underwear – popped the question: 'Seldes, the *Pittsburgh Leader*. Mr Bryan, do you intend to run for President a fourth time?' Before the query was even fully put, Bryan flushed with anger. 'Out! Out! You impudent cub!' he cried, and rushed at his interlocutor. Seldes fled. Back at the office Eagle listened with rising pleasure. 'Did he hit you?' he asked, imagining the story that might then be constructed. 'No,' said Seldes. 'Just shoved me through the door.' 'Great,' came the reply. 'Write it. And don't forget the one-piece woollen underwear.' Seldes wrote, and the following day, there was his very first front-page story under the headline: 'Bryan Assaults *Leader* Reporter.'

It wasn't long before Seldes had the first encounters with an issue that was to become one of the themes of his life: the indecent speed with which many American papers (of that time, and for many decades afterwards) gave in to pressure from business interests, whether implied, anticipated or actual. In 1910 there came to a Pittsburgh court the divorce of billionaire Andrew W. Mellon, then one of the richest men in America. Despite this, Seldes found himself the only reporter present – a mystery that eluded him until he saw the city's papers minus any report of the proceedings, but liberally favoured with plenty of ads from Mellon-owned banks. Not long afterwards Seldes covered another case involving a local department store owner's son who felt it was his right to assault – and in one case, rape – his father's salesgirls. The young reporter filed, but the story was never printed. Instead, the paper began taking twice as many ads from the store at a higher price. Seldes's story had simply been used for commercial blackmail.

His escape was the theatre, reviewing the likes of Sarah Bernhardt and Dame Nellie Melba, and stringing for *Variety*.

There wasn't a lot of competition for the week's hot tickets. 'The word culture', he later wrote, 'was pejorative... Not one evening paper in my time ever mentioned a book. If there was a college graduate among my hundred or more fellow reporters, he kept his sin a secret.' In 1912 he moved, at the sprauncy salary of $20 a week, to the *Pittsburgh Post*, and it wasn't long before his taste for telling it like it was, and his paper's inclination to take a rather more commercial view, threw up problems. They came in the fiery shape of Billy Sunday, famed evangelist, peddler of theological certainties and, unbeknown to Seldes, canny business operator. Into Pittsburgh on a mission to convert the immoral masses came Sunday, along went Seldes to his rally and, as the preacher raved against sin and Charles Darwin, the son of the Freethinking druggist sat taking his notes. Finally, Sunday reached his climax: an appeal for sinners to come forward, and repent. Up stood a number of men, and, as they began making their way forward, Seldes recognised them. Far from being Pittsburgh's most dedicated debauchees, they were church members, YMCA stalwarts and the like – plants in the audience whose role it was to trigger an avalanche of converts. It never came. Those inspired from their seats by the prime movers, were, instead, mostly drunks.

The following morning, Seldes not only had the front-page lead but what was then the rarest of accolades: a by-line. His satisfaction, however, was short-lived. Soon after arriving for work, he was told he had been fired as a reporter and transferred to copyediting, where, it was felt, his incorruptible nature would cause less trouble. What he only later learnt was that Billy Sunday was not quite the gauche Pied Piper for Jesus he might have appeared to be. Before agreeing to come and work his religious mojo on a city, his finance men would cut a deal with local banks: Billy's magic will convert feckless sinners into thrifty bank customers, went the spiel, and in return we'd like a donation. Seldes's paper was owned by the Farmer's National Bank, one of Sunday's sponsors. Bad for business,

this Seldes, they decided. And, when he went to Harvard for
a year, not all that much better for academia, either. Working
for the *Harvard Illustrated Monthly*, he uncovered the story
of how a Professor Nolan ensured athletes got degrees with
minimal study by coaching them to learn by rote the answers
to pat questions. Seldes filed the story, it was rejected, and so
he sold it to a Boston magazine.

Back in Pittsburgh, it wasn't long before he met the woman
who was to change his life: a little pack of cutesy trouble
named Peggy Keith. He met her when he covered the story of
a theatre manager who'd skidaddled with his show's takings,
leaving behind a penniless bunch of performers, among whom
was a doe-eyed soubrette. She had, she sobbed, not a penny
in the world, had been thrown out of her hotel, had her trunk
seized, no one to turn to, and she didn't know what a poor girl
was to do in a big, bad city like Pittsburgh. The Betty Boop
performance worked. In an instant, Seldes fell for her, ripped
half a week's wages from his wallet, gave it to her, took her
to his apartment and set up home. Soon he was night editing
the *Post*, leaving at 5pm, and not returning to the beguiling
Miss Keith until 6am. After a few months of physical bliss, he
opened a drawer and found it brimming with cash. He realised
that while he had been putting the paper to bed, little Miss
Keith had been doing the same with some lucrative clients.
Seldes withdrew his $200 savings from the bank, gave half to
her, bought a train ticket and headed for New York.

He freelanced, for the Sunday *New York World* among
others, and was beginning to exorcise the memory of Peggy
Keith when, one day, there was a knock on his door. It
was her, trunk in tow and copious tears at the ready. 'She
looked beautiful,' he later wrote, 'I told her to unpack.' The
reconciliation lasted until a writer asked her to a hotel for the
weekend, and she accepted without a second's thought. Fearing
that if she returned another time he'd be weak enough to take
her in, Seldes decided to go where even she couldn't follow.

He packed his bags and headed for London. It was 1917, and there was a war to cover.

He found work in London with United Press, writing war news for syndication to South America, and interviewing leading figures such as Joseph Conrad. By the end of 1917, Seldes was hired by the army edition of the *Chicago Tribune*, and moved to its Paris office, handily placed two flights above Maxim's and next door to the equally legendary Harry's Bar. His job was to write 14 columns of war news every day, a task not eased when, after only a few weeks, the managing editor ran off with a French countess, taking the *Tribune* car and all the paper's funds with him. Seldes had no option but to promote himself. A few weeks of that, and he gratefully accepted an offer to join the Marshall Syndicate, which supplied papers such as the *Atlanta Constitution, Detroit Free Press* and *St Louis Globe-Democrat*.

Seldes was now an official war correspondent. He was 27, a short, sharp-faced man who, with his slick-backed hair and neat moustache, looks, in pictures taken with roustabout colleagues, less like a journalist than a bureaucrat sent along to monitor their expenses. No one who met him, however, was liable to mistake him for a timid pen-pusher for long. He shared a tent with air ace Eddie Rickenbacker, met a young Colonel Douglas MacArthur (whom he saw leading a German prisoner back to the US lines by the ear), and, for a Sunday paper feature, was taken for a bone-shaking drive in a tank by one Colonel George Patton, even then famous for his brace of pearl-handled revolvers. His greatest adventure, however, came at the war's end when he and three other correspondents ignored the ban on travel to Germany, tracked down the defeated Hindenburg and interviewed him. Germany, he told them, was beaten not by starvation at home or a withering of domestic will, but on the field, largely because of the American infantry. At the end of his explanation, Hindenburg muttered 'Mein armes Vaterland, mein armes Vaterland...', bent his head and wept.

It was a considerable scoop, but no one ever read it. Instead, when the US army authorities got to hear of the reporters' trip into Germany, they threatened them with court martial if they wrote the story. This suppression rankled with Seldes until his death, not because it deprived him of a famous exclusive, but because, as he later wrote, it fed the great myth of interwar Germany: that of the *Dolchstoss*, the-stab-in-the-back from 'socialists, Communists and Jews', which deprived the Fatherland of a deserved victory. Seldes wrote in his autobiography: 'If the Hindenburg interview had been passed by Pershing's (stupid) censors at the time, it would have been headlined in every country civilised enough to have newspapers... I believe it would have destroyed the main planks on which Hitler rose to power...' The experience was a powerful one for Seldes. Never again would he submit to threats to shut him up.

After a brief interlude in the States, Seldes was back in Paris, on the staff of the *Chicago Tribune*'s Foreign News Service. This was set up by the paper's owner, Colonel Robert Rutherford McCormick, a man who once explained his choice of chief roving reporter with the words: 'Larry doesn't speak any foreign languages. I do not want my fine American boys ruined by these damned foreigners.' Seldes covered British politics, the negotiations that set up the Irish Free State, and the seizure of Fiume by Italian poet and poseur Gabriele d'Annunzio, the man who did much to pioneer the trappings of Italian fascism: the black-shirted followers, the Roman salute, gaudy leader's uniform, balcony appearances and even the novel assassination technique of pouring large amounts of castor oil down opponents' throats. In late 1919, Seldes was made roving Europe correspondent. One of his first assignments was to interview D'Annunzio and the doddery, puppet president of Fiume, Dr Grossich. When pressed by Seldes about the fairness of recent elections, the latter said: 'It was fair and honestly conducted. All the good citizens were allowed to vote – we cleared out all the undesirable elements – all the socialists, the working men who were troublemakers – we deported some five thousand of them.' They just happened to be ethnic Yugoslavs, and when Seldes pointed this out in the story he managed to smuggle out, he was warned to leave the country. He did so on the next available train, but, halfway to Trieste, three members of D'Annunzio's Dalmatian League entered his compartment and beat him up.

He had hardly got back to Paris before he was ordered to Turin, where, by all accounts, Italian car workers were staging the beginnings of a communist revolution. Hearst's papers had shown picture of workers armed to the teeth with swords, guns and bayonets, standing in front of walls on which was daubed 'Viva Lenin'. When Seldes arrived, however, he immediately bumped into the author of this picture, Hearst International Newsreel photographer Ariel Vargas. He explained that, since the relative quiet of Turin contrasted with what his office had instructed him to find, he had paid a man to paint the slogan on the FIAT factory walls, toured antique shops buying up every old weapon he could find, handed them out to the lads, and told them not to laugh while he took their picture. In the absence of genuine news, Seldes went off to see an Italian journalist who had once stringed for him: one Benito Mussolini.

In 1920, Seldes moved to the Berlin office, and took up residence in the Hotel Adlon, a rococo confection that proved an excellent look-out post on the Weimar Republic. Marlene Dietrich took tea in the lobby, a sinister multi-millionaire lived on one floor dining off peasant food, and through its doors there passed the likes of Prince Yusupov, who called round to tell Seldes of his part in the killing of Rasputin, and the Tsarina's jeweller Aron Siminovich, who said he had proof Rasputin was a German agent. Both wanted large cheques for their stories, but Chicago refused to pay up; as they did whenever Einstein, in response to Seldes's phone calls for a quote on the latest controversy, asked for a small donation to Jewish causes in return. Some things, however, the office was prepared to pay for, such as $25,000 for Sigmund Freud to comment on the great American murder trial of the day (he wisely declined), or $5,000 for the love letters of dancer Isadora Duncan. Seldes had found her living in a cheap tenement in Friedrichstrasse, too poor to go out and too fat to perform. She accepted the Chicago cash, and dictated a chapter, but the stenographer was so shocked by its content that she went to Seldes and said she could no longer listen to such carryings-on. By the time he had hired a replacement, Isadora had changed her mind. There was lunch with Arnold Bennett, the absurdities of German inflation (4.2 marks to the dollar rose inexorably towards 4.2 billion by November 1923, rates that enabled Seldes to buy a Van Gogh for 25 cents, and a colleague to buy a castle for $10,000), and there was dinner with Charlie Chaplin. Wanting to make an impression on Pola Negri, the comic furtively asked the German for 'You are the most beautiful woman I have ever seen.' Given what he took to be the correct words, he bowed and said to her: 'Madame Negri, du bist ekelhalft' – at which the actress rose, slapped his face and left. It was understandable; the hapless Chaplin had told her she was disgusting.

The big story of the early 1920s was the Russian famine, and, after Floyd Gibbons's scoop (see chapter 9) the Russians, in return for American aid, allowed reporters in to cover it. Seldes was among them, and, when the starvation in the south began to subside, he was told to remain in Moscow. Thus it was that he found himself, while taking pictures of Trotsky at a Red Square parade, involved in an argument with another photographer. In a move hard to imagine being repeated by any of his successors, Trotsky broke off from inspecting the masses, and asked what was going on. Seldes said his adversary had told him he had a monopoly on Red Square pictures, which was odd, since he thought the Revolution had abolished monopolies. Trotsky agreed, sent the other snapper packing, asked Seldes how he wanted him posed, and duly puckered up. The pictures were sold around the world. Lenin required more connivance. Seldes had heard him speak (describing him as having 'a clever motion of the hand by which he could emphasize a point and yet steal a look at the time on his wrist watch...'), and interviewed him briefly. But, when he and a colleague heard that an American artist was making sketches of Vladimir Ilyich, they primed him with questions and so conducted by remote control a long-running interview with the Soviet leader. Such stories as this, and the revelation that some 50,000 'traitors' had been executed by the Soviets (extracted from a secret police chief by the old technique of putting various numbers to him until he agreed with one), were either kept in the notebook to be written after leaving Moscow, or slipped past the censor as letters in the diplomatic pouch by the simple expedient of adding a 'Dear John ... best wishes George'. In August 1923 the ruse was rumbled and Seldes and three others were expelled.

He returned to the Chicago office for the intellectual detox then obligatory for all *Tribune* foreign staff. Every three years they had to return to base for a spell of police court reporting, or 're-Americanisation' as it was called. Seldes underwent his under the watchful eye of Alfred 'Jake' Lingle – the *Trib*'s main man with police, and also, as it turned out, on the payroll of Al Capone. The diamond-studded money belt he wore was something of a hint, but it was not until Lingle was gunned down some years later that the truth about the reporter whom the *Trib* had initially described as a 'journalistic martyr' emerged. Seldes, meanwhile, was back in Italy, now being run by his old stringer, Mussolini. Almost as soon as he arrived, he began hearing rumours that Il Duce had ordered the murder of Socialist Party leader Giacomo Matteotti. Despite warnings of the dangers of doing so, Seldes and his assistant Camillo Cianfarra began poking around and soon came across the proof. An added bonus was an American angle: the thug who had done most of the stabbing was Amerigo Dumini, a native of St Louis.

Seldes sent the story out with a plea that it was not to be carried by the Paris edition. Sure enough, the next day, there it was in the Paris paper together with a prominent by-line. The furious Italian authorities marched Seldes on to the first train out. Sure enough, when it stopped at Modena, on got a gang of armed blackshirts calling his name. Seldes managed to find sanctuary in the compartment of four British Royal Navy admirals, who sent the fascists packing with a flea in their ears. Seldes's assistant, Cianfarra, was less fortunate. He was badly beaten and never recovered, one of a long line of largely nameless helpmeets, interpreters, fixers and, occasionally, ghost-writers, who have died or suffered terribly for the sake of reporters' stories – without any of the compensating glory, awards or subsequent plum assignments. While Cianfarra lay permanently disabled, for instance, Seldes was, within a year, handed the ultimate job: roving correspondent for Eastern Europe, tasked with visiting every country on the Orient Express route twice a year, all expenses paid. Plus, of course, diversions by car to Baghdad and Damascus. There is, at least, a kind of justice in Seldes's contracting malaria, albeit a mild form, and being invalided home to the US. He was almost immediately sent to Mexico, and there he found the story that brought his career with the *Tribune* to a bitter and premature end. He had been passed documents suggesting that the American embassy was complicit in the assassination of the Mexican president in 1913, and filed a story that began: 'The US ambassador to Mexico, Henry Lane Wilson, had prior knowledge of a plot by a general named Huerta to overthrow the government and imprison its president, the liberal leader, Madero.' The *Tribune* declined to publish, Seldes quit in disgust, and he never worked regularly for newspapers again. He was 39.

Seldes went to Paris to work on a book, met the woman who was to become his wife, and mixed, via the contacts of his brother Gilbert, who edited a leading arts magazine, with Aldous Huxley, H.G. Wells, Picasso, Rebecca West, Kerensky, Theodore Dreiser and Cole Porter (only the protests of Seldes and other partygoers on whom Porter was testing the lyrics of his latest song prevented it containing the line: 'You're the top, you're Mussolini'). Sinclair Lewis became an especial friend, lending Seldes $5,000 towards the cost of his first home, thus enabling him to claim that his savings and loan company was run by a Nobel Prize winner. Thus domestically settled but professionally something of a dissident, he began to get the truth out the only way now available to him: in books. His first was *You Can't Print That!*, based on pieces he had never managed to wangle past his editors, and there followed: *The Vatican: Yesterday-Today-Tomorrow*, a history of the Roman Catholic Church sufficiently objective to be both chosen by the Catholic Book Club as a read of the month, and widely thought to be a left-wing demolition job; *Iron, Blood and Profits*, an investigation of the armaments industry; *Sawdust Caesar*, on Mussolini; *Freedom of the Press* and *Lords of the Press*, both charting how little of the former was permitted by the latter; *You Can't Do That!* and *Witch Hunt*, which looked at restrictions on civil liberties, and red baiting; and *The Catholic Crisis* on the Church's links to fascist groups.

Few of these efforts were reviewed by the mainstream press, and, in the case of the two press books, even advertisements for them were rejected. On some papers, his very name was unmentionable, especially the *New York Times*. In 1934 he had given evidence at the National Labor Relations Board for the Newspaper Guild, then trying to win recognition at the *Times*. Afterwards, the paper's managing editor approached him and said: 'Well, George, I guess your name will never again be mentioned in the *Times*.' And, for decades, it wasn't. Fortunately for him there was at least one liberal New York paper, the *Post*, owned by David Stern, and in late 1936 he persuaded it to send him and his wife Helen off to Spain to report the civil war. He interviewed captured Italian infantrymen, and was thus able to prove, in the face of denials by the fascists, that complete divisions were being sent in by Mussolini. And he reported on the bombing of Guernica and Barcelona, where air-power flattened entire areas as if a giant had stamped on them in a tantrum. In one raid on Barcelona, for example, 2,000 people died in a single block. Seldes returned, convinced he could hear the approaching march of a world war.

His eye for the slightest sign of a jackboot at home had been sharpened, too. In 1938, he discovered a pamphlet written by General MacArthur called 'Military Aid in Civil Disturbances', which was the standard manual for army or National Guard when confronted by strikers. It advocated, among other remedies, that machinegun fire from aircraft could keep rioters off roofs, and, according to *Basic Field Manual*, Volume VII, Part 3, 'Domestic Disturbances': 'Driving the mob into or through the district of the city where looting is the least profitable and where destruction of property incident to military operation will be reduced to a minimum and preferably fall on the rioters or the class of people composing the rioters...' Seldes quoted extensively and devastatingly from MacArthur's works, his article was followed up by the *New York Post* and *World-Telegram*, and the War Department was forced to withdraw the pamphlet.

Seldes was thus a natural recruit for *Ken*, a radical magazine then being planned by David Smart, owner of *Esquire*. It was to be 'one step left of centre', as its owner put it, and among the editors recruited were Seldes and Ernest Hemingway. Seldes immediately got to work on a column called 'Nail That Lie', pointing out falsehoods peddled by mainstream media, and started an investigation into the American Legion and its role in strike-breaking. But while he was building up this radical head of steam, other forces were at work. Not only would no advertiser take a single column inch of space, the big agencies also informed Smart that if *Ken* was in any way left-of-centre, then full-page ads would start disappearing from *Esquire*. Smart caved in, told Seldes to lay off the Legion, at which the reporter resigned, and *Ken* was shorn of all liberal content when it launched. It struggled for a while and then died. Not long afterwards Smart was found guilty of finagling his company's stock, and jailed.

After this debacle, Seldes knew that there was probably only one way he could get his kind of awkward-squad journalism printed, and that was by publishing it himself. Finance for a conventional magazine or paper was out of the question, and so was born the idea of a four-page weekly newsletter, along the lines of *The Week*, a mimeographed news-sheet produced by Claud Cockburn, cousin of Evelyn Waugh, that proved so inconvenient to the British authorities it was banned. Seldes's newsletter was to have a less international focus, but, like *The Week*, it would by financed by sales alone. His friend, communist Bruce Minton was tasked to solicit labour unions for subscribers; he duly reported back with 6,000 names and $3,000 in the bank, and *In Fact*, as Helen Seldes christened it, was all set. It was to be Seldes's most enduring contribution to journalism, would break one of the most important stories of the twentieth century and be cited by a host of later activists, from I.F. Stone to Ralph Nader, as their inspiration.

The first issue appeared on 20 May 1940 with the slogan 'An Antidote for Falsehood in the Daily Press', and for once a publication lived up to its own billing. The first item was headed 'Sworn to Secrecy' and began:

> Eighteen prominent figures met secretly on April 29th in downtown New York and decided to do their utmost to abrogate existing neutrality legislation. America, they resolved, must be in a position to give whatever aid – even armies – is required of the Allies.
>
> The gathering was apparently called by Frederic R. Coudert, legal adviser to the British Embassy in 1915–20. Attending were a number of leaders from church and peace organizations and: Henry L. Stimson, Secretary of State under Hoover, Wendell Wilkie, utility

magnate and Republican dark horse; Thomas W. Lamont, Morgan partner...

The issue also included items on the newly formed Consumers' Union, race and anti-Semitism. Soon Seldes was revealing 'The Truth About Wendell Wilkie', itemising, on 15 July 1940, the Republican's far-right views expressed in off-the-record speeches; exposing a US fascist organisation called the White Shirts; and the reactionary campaigns and lobbying of the National Association of Manufacturers. His supporters and sources included Harry Truman, Vice-President Henry A. Wallace, Eleanor Roosevelt, Secretary of the Interior Harold L. Ickes, several dozen senators and representatives, and scores of journalists who plied him with stories they knew their own papers would find too hot to handle. In all, Seldes reckoned, some 200 reporters passed him stories, including members of the Hearst White House staff, two Scripps-Howard editors and editors of Hearst papers who sent him originals of their boss's 'The Chief Says...' internal memos that they thought deserved a wider audience. They certainly got one. Soon, the circulation of *In Fact* was 100,000 and rising.

Most of Seldes's stories were not media tittle-tattle, but solid reports that the mainstream press would not touch for fear of offending advertisers. Only Seldes and a few other small liberal papers, for instance, would fully cover Truman's Senate Committee on War Profiteering. This revealed the agreement that General Motors, Standard Oil and the Ethyl Gas Corporation had with I.G. Farben of Germany, which was responsible for supplying Hitler with the secrets of making tetra-ethyl lead for petrol (essential for his air force), and handed him the technique for making synthetic rubber. In 1943, such a scandal, which would nowadays keep reporters and columnists fuelled with indignation for months, went largely, and deliberately, ignored – as did the links between Nazis and Pratt & Whitney, Douglas Aircraft, Alcoa, General Electric and Du Pont, all charted in Seldes's book *Facts and Fascism*.

Suppression of uncommercial facts was at its most blatant on the story that Seldes made a personal crusade for more than ten years: the link between cigarette smoking and cancer. In February 1938 Dr Raymond Pearl of Johns Hopkins University presented the result of a four-year study of smokers, which concluded that smoking reduced life expectancy – in particular that between the ages of 30 and 60, 61 per cent more heavy smokers died than non-smokers. His audience was the New York Academy of Medicine, and present were press and wire reporters. As Seldes later wrote: 'Of the eight daily New York newspapers of the time, six did not run the story. The *World-Telegram* and the *Times* each ran a few paragraphs. A wider search showed that the only other major metropolitan daily newspaper that covered the story was the *Washington Post*.' At the time, cigarette advertising was worth more than $50m a year.

Seldes published his first *In Fact* item on cigarettes on 13 January 1941, under the heading 'Tobacco Shortens Life'. He didn't let up. Over the next decade, he ran more than 50 stories on the subject, battering away at what he regarded, with justification, as the scandal of 50 million American smokers being kept ignorant of the dangers of their habit. He carried reports from experts like Dr Edwin J. Grace, one of the first to cite smoking as a cause of lung cancer, and to warn of the effects on the unborn child. He ran extensive stories on the American Medical Association's 1944 report 'The Effects of Smoking Cigarettes', which, save for six inches in the *New York Times*, was generally ignored by the press. And he reported in detail on press censorship of the smoking story. In 1948, for example, Dr Alton Ochsner, professor of surgery at Tulane University, presented new evidence on the direct relationship between cigarette sales and lung cancer deaths. AP reporter Elliott Chaze covered the story, and began his file: 'The cigarette companies won't like this, but a man who ought to know thinks a lot of citizens are digging their graves with their own lungs.' An hour after this went out on the wires, AP sent a 'kill' message, saying the story was 'controversial'. *In Fact* revealed: 'The story which followed 90 minutes later eliminated the references to citizens "digging their graves with their lungs," to the "dim view of cigarette advertising," to the "increase in cancer among women" and to women smoking more and more heavily, to the incidence of death, and the concluding line to "think it over".' It was not until December 1952, 11 years after Seldes's first story, that *Reader's Digest* (ironically, a frequent Seldes target) published its article 'Cancer by the Carton', *Time* and *Newsweek* followed it up, and the truth about cigarettes was finally delivered to a mass audience.

Seldes also had the courage to expose the House Committee on UnAmerican Activities, its chairman Martin Dies, and its witch-hunting successor Senator Joe McCarthy. The latter, especially, got it with both Seldes barrels for tricking up baloney evidence, for his relentless policy of character assassination and for bent income tax returns. On 14 February 1948, for instance, *In Fact* reported:

> US Senator 'Neglects' To Report $43,000
> Profit In Stock Deals,
> News Services Kill Tax Scandal

The reluctance of the mainstream press to carry such stories was even more apparent two years later. Dr Leon Birkhead, of the Friends of Democracy, found that some information in McCarthy speeches bore a startling resemblance to that contained in a pamphlet written by Joe Kamp, co-publisher of *The Awakener*, the first openly pro-fascist magazine in the US, who in 1948 was jailed for contempt of Congress. Dr Birkhead wrote to McCarthy requesting an explanation, and, when none arrived, circulated his evidence to the press. Not one word was published; until, that is, the good doctor contacted Seldes. The result, on 17 April 1950, was an entire issue of *In Fact* devoted to the story, headlined:

McCarthy Data On State Dept 'Reds'
Lifted Verbatim From Anti-Semites' Smear Pamphlet

By this time, the enemies of Seldes were doing more than merely circling. They were now out to get him. He attracted death threats, and splenetic attacks from right-wing radio commentators such as Westbrook Pegler (once a friend, but who ended his days as too right-wing even for the John Birch Society), George Sokolsky and Fulton Lewis Jnr. 'They were bastards,' Seldes said. 'They would write that a Russian agent stopped by my office each week to pay my salary. I didn't have the money to sue them for libel. My lawyer told me it would take years to reach a settlement and even if I won I would never see a dime. There was no way I could fight them.' Even *Life* described him as a communist, along with such other threats to civilisation as Einstein and composer Aaron Copland.

But more serious than any of these barbs were the attentions of the insidious bureaucracy of J. Edgar Hoover's FBI. They began not only to use the Post Office to monitor Seldes's mail, but to compile a list of *In Fact* subscribers. Seldes tried sending the newsletter out in plain wrappers, but once the word was out that *In Fact* readers were marked men and women, subscribers began at first to drift away, and then stampede. From a high of 176,000 in 1947, Seldes's subscription list disintegrated to 56,000. In October 1950, *In Fact* ceased publication. The red baiters had won.

It was only a matter of time before Seldes was summoned before the HUAC hearings. So it was, in 1953, that the reporter who had exposed McCarthy's tax evasion and hypocrisy sat facing the man himself and was asked: 'Are you now or have you ever been a member of the Communist Party?' The answer was no, and it still was when McCarthy's lawyer Roy Cohn tried again with questions that would not have fooled a student debater: 'What was the number of the Communist Party cell you belonged to in Connecticut?' Cohn and McCarthy went on to accuse him of being anti-Catholic, of attacking the American Legion (Seldes told him they were strike breakers, which he regarded as a pretty unAmerican activity), of being a fellow traveller by praising Tito (Seldes had to point out that Tito had defied Stalin), and of being unsupportive during the Korean War (Seldes referred him to his statement that he regarded the North as the aggressors). Getting nowhere, McCarthy dismissed Seldes, and, a while later, emerged to declare the reporter 'cleared', although of what was never explained.

Seldes was now approaching his mid-sixties, and in the illiberal atmosphere that long survived McCarthy's downfall was virtually a journalistic pariah. He devoted himself to books (*The Great Quotations*, which sold more than a million copies despite never being reviewed, was followed by *Tell the Truth and Run* in 1953, and *Never Tire of Protesting* in 1968. He watched the 1960s roll over America like a thunderstorm at a church outing, and saw with satisfaction the impact of I.F. Stone, whose newsletter putting Washington shenanigans under the microscope had been inspired by *In Fact*, and indeed inherited its subscription list (referred to by Seldes as 'the five dollar Liberals'). He lived to see the Surgeon-General's 1965 report on cigarettes and lung cancer vindicate the reporting he did decades before. He went on watching, surviving into his eighties to write *Even the Gods Can't Change History* when he was 85, and see Watergate and the triumph of his kind of journalism. In his nineties, he wrote his autobiography, *Witness to a Century*, and appeared as himself in Warren Beatty's film *Reds*, based on John 'Ten Days That Shook The World' Reed, whom Seldes knew both at Harvard and in Russia. He lived to see the best of his reporting revived and published in *The George Seldes Reader*, edited by Randolph T. Holhut. He even lived long enough to see his name in the *New York Times*.

Seldes eventually died in 1995, aged 104, which meant he missed, by a year, the release of Rick Goldsmith's documentary on his life, 'Tell the Truth and Run: George Seldes and the American Press', which was nominated for an Oscar. The *Times* saw him off with sniffy euphemism. '*In Fact* ceased publication in 1950,' it declared, 'when his warnings about fascism seemed out of tune with rising public concern about Communism.' Still, at least that was better than the *Chicago Tribune*'s smear. 'Mr Seldes', wrote his former paper, 'never publicly declared his Communist Party membership.' I.F. Stone, however, got it right: 'He was the dean and grandaddy of us investigative reporters.' George Seldes had lived to see the American newspaper change from the kind that, for commercial reasons, killed the story of a department store owner's son raping its staff, and suppressed news of cigarette smoking's links to cancer, into the mainstream press that exposed Watergate and Abu Graib, and the alternative media that acts as such a relentless watchdog. It was a transformation in which he played no small part.

Nellie Bly

5
Nellie Bly
1864–1922

THE BEST UNDERCOVER REPORTER IN HISTORY

In September 1887, a young woman was brought before Essex Market Police Court in New York. She gave her name as Brown, which may or may not have been the case, for, according to the evidence of a Mrs Irene Stanard, the poor girl was quite mad. She had been behaving so strangely that some of the other residents in her boarding house were convinced she would murder them in their beds. And she kept staring into space, and mumbling something about a missing trunk. The judge listened and felt he had no choice but to commit the girl to Bellevue Hospital, and thence, almost certainly to Blackwell's Island, the city's asylum for the insane.

Judge Patrick Duffy was, however, a kindly soul. He was convinced the girl was 'somebody's darling', as he chivalrously put it, and was likely to be claimed if only her case was publicised. So, before the confused girl was led away, he invited the gentlemen of the press (they were virtually all men in those days) to view the pitiful creature and write up appeals for her relatives to come forward. Next day, the New York papers buzzed with stories about the little girl lost. The *Sun* asked: 'Who is this insane girl?'; the *Evening Telegraph* told the tale, adding 'she is undoubtedly insane'; and the *New York Times* wrote about the 'mysterious waif... with the wild hunted look in her eye' who repeated over and over again: 'I can't remember. I can't remember.'

All the papers carried something like this, except one. This was the *New York World*, and the reason it didn't carry any such story was that it knew appeals were pointless. No one would be coming forward to claim their 'darling' for the simple reason that the girl even now being deemed mad beyond hope of recovery by the Bellevue doctors, was in fact Nellie Bly, their utterly sane reporter on her first assignment. She was attempting to feign madness and get herself committed to Blackwell's Island so she could investigate conditions there. It was all her own idea, an indication to her editor that this pale 23-year-old woman who had walked into his office just a week before was something extraordinary. After all, a woman reporter was rare enough in the 1880s, but one who went undercover, placed herself in physical danger and then wrote about it in straightforward language, was more like the heroine of a girl's adventure book than anything encountered in real life. And that, in a way, is appropriate; for Nellie Bly's life resembles nothing so much as the plot of a particularly far-fetched Victorian novel. An idyllic childhood spoiled by a sudden death, a wicked stepfather, strokes of outrageous fortune, fame as a reporter so great that one of her stories was turned into a board game, a bizarre marriage, a fortune made and lost, a betrayal, and, finally, a kind of redemption – it had the lot. We shall return to her bout of 'madness' in a little while, but her story is really too good to tell in anything other than the order in which it all happened.

She was born Elizabeth Jane Cochran, in Pennsylvania on 5 May 1864, the daughter of a moderately prosperous rural judge. Her first six years, in a rambling country house, were blissful, but came to an abrupt end when her father died suddenly at the age of 60. Only then did his family discover that, although he was a man of some charm and good humour, the judge was not much of a one for forward planning. He left no will, a disturbing enough turn of events for a man with one wife, but Judge Cochran had had two, and, between the pair, produced 15 children. The family home had to be auctioned, the proceeds divided more ways than the sum total could bear, and Elizabeth, her mother, brothers and sisters had to pack their pretty things and move to Apollo, where they ran a boarding house on the threadbare side of the tracks. It got worse. Enter, soon afterwards, the story's black-hearted villain, John Jackson Ford, who inveigled Elizabeth's mother into marrying him and rapidly proved himself a sour, drunken, violent wastrel. Divorce eventually saw him off, but the bad memories lingered, and money was perpetually short. When, at the age of 15, Elizabeth went away to Indiana State Normal School to train as a teacher, the family funds proved inadequate even for that and she was recalled after just a term. She returned to a life hemmed in by a lack of money on the one hand, and the restricted sense of what was respectable for a girl of her class on the other. She was, at 20, an imaginative young woman starring in her own melodrama of unfairness, and yearning for escape. It came, as it does in all the best Victorian stories, in the most unexpected way.

Among her regular reading was the *Pittsburgh Dispatch*; and there, in one of the first issues of 1885, was the 'Quiet Observer' column of Erasmus Wilson. He was not, even for the times, a man of progressive views, and he took as his text that week the 'alarming' increase in young women working in shops and offices – a threat, as he saw it, to the very nature of existence. To counter it, he urged the average Pittsburgh maiden to concentrate on making 'her home a little paradise, herself playing the part of angel'. It was headed 'What Girls Are Good For' and, to a young woman like Elizabeth, who felt herself almost suffocated by lack of opportunity, it could not go unchallenged. She sat down and wrote a letter describing the barriers to poorer women finding a role beyond the home. To preserve her anonymity and also add a touch of melodrama, she signed it 'Lonely Orphan Girl'. Its spelling and grammar were not perfect, but it was clear, original, to the point, and the editor of the *Dispatch*, George Madden, saw in it a raw talent. He wanted to commission an article from its author, a task that would have been easier had she included an address. How, then, to get in touch? Madden decided to place an advertisement in his own paper, and thus it was, on 17 January 1885, that the following announcement appeared in the classified section:

> Lonely Orphan Girl
> If the writer of the communication signed 'Lonely Orphan Girl' will send her name and address to this office, merely as a guarantee of good faith, she will confer a favour and receive the information she desires.

He half suspected the writer of the original letter to be a young man, and he was not put off that scent when a reply was received from someone signing themselves simply 'E. Cochrane' (the final 'e' was a Nellie embellishment). Madden wrote back, asking for a piece on 'Girls And Their Spheres of Life', and, on Sunday 25 January 1885, Little Orphan Girl's first article appeared under the heading, 'The Girl Puzzle – How The Average Employer Discriminates Against Petticoated Workers'. It was sufficiently good for Madden to write again, asking 'E. Cochrane' – whoever he or she was – for story ideas. The next day a young woman in a black silk dress and fur turban appeared at his elbow, telling him in a voice made breathless by excitement that E. (for Elizabeth) Cochrane stood before him. They talked and agreed she would write a second article. Its subject was divorce, and, published under the title 'Mad Marriages', was even more provocative than the first. A shoal of letters descended on the paper, Madden congratulated himself on finding this new protégée, and promptly signed her up at $5 a week to become the first woman on his paper's staff. With the job came a new name. Elizabeth Cochrane didn't sound quite racy enough for Madden's taste, so he asked for suggestions. Someone in the office came up with 'Nellie Bly' (the title of a popular song), and she used it in print for the rest of her life.

Her first project was 'Our Workshop Girls', an eight-part series on the city's factory girls covering not just their working lives, but social and romantic activities as well. In it, Bly unveiled what was to be one of her trademarks: the asking of questions other reporters might think of, but then wouldn't dare ask. Confronted with one factory girl who said she often went to bars and drank with strangers (behaviour that was regarded as almost unspeakable at the time), Bly asked: 'Why do you risk your reputation in such a way?' To which the girl replied with the kind of quote any reporter would cherish:

> Risk my reputation! I don't think I've had one to risk. I work hard all day, week after week for a mere pittance. I go home at night tired of labour and longing for something new, anything good or bad to break the monotony of my existence. I have no pleasure, no books to read. I cannot go to places of amusement for want of clothes and money and no one cares what becomes of me.

Factory owners protested to the paper, and despite, or – more probably – because of this, the paper was a sell-out. Bly's reward was a doubling of her wages, and 'promotion' to society editor and the, to her, dreaded ghetto of flower shows, home and beauty. She stuck it for a year, before persuading Madden to unleash her first on an exposé of prison conditions, and then, courtesy of a disguise, an undercover investigation of factory conditions. The response was as before: a sell-out of the paper, protests from advertisers and big-wigs, followed, after a pay rise as sweetener, with another dreaded stint as society editor. So when a visiting Mexican delegation casually invited her to their country, she jumped at the chance. In late 1885, she left the paper, collected her mother as a chaperone, and the next thing *Dispatch* readers knew of her was in February 1886 when the headline 'Nellie in Mexico' appeared. Her cheeky tone was evident before she'd even crossed the border, reporting from somewhere in the West: 'For the first time I saw women plowing while their lords and masters sat on a fence smoking. I have never longed for anything so much as to shove those lazy fellows off.' In her reporting from Mexico, she was initially more careful not to offend local sensibilities, but she gathered evidence, and finally filed a piece on the jailing of a newspaper editor for publishing criticism of the government. Threats followed, Nellie left with a suitcase full of notes, and, once home, began reporting what she'd been told of the real Mexico and its corruption.

Back at the *Dispatch* the only assignments on offer were theatre reviews and features, and so, lest she be offered a third shot at the society columns, she took the only way out and didn't show up for work one day. Colleagues came into the *Dispatch* to find an empty desk and a note: 'I am off to New York. Look out for me.'

She arrived in New York in May 1887, and soon found that the characters running papers there were rather less susceptible to her undoubted promise than was Madden. Days of job hunting turned into weeks, and the weeks turned into months. She filed the occasional story back to Pittsburgh, but made no impact until she had the idea of turning her experiences into a piece for the *Dispatch*. She would interview all the city's principal editors and put to them the question: 'What chance do women have in New York journalism?' The answer, predictably, was not much, especially if, like Bly, they had an ambition to write for Joseph Pulitzer's *New York World*. The idea of a woman news reporter there, according to the paper's editor, Colonel John Cockerill, was almost too far-fetched for words.

The resultant story created quite a stir. So stuffed-shirt were the editors' comments that trade papers like *The Journalist* picked up the story, as did syndicated columnists, and it became, for a few days at least, the talk of the media in-crowd.

What it didn't do was produce a job offer; and so finally, in something approaching desperation, Bly borrowed the cab fare from her landlady, rode down to the *World*'s offices on Park Row, bluffed her way into Cockerill's office, and demanded he listen to her story ideas. There were, as far as we know, at least two: to travel to Europe and return steerage class so she could report on what it was like to be an immigrant; and to pose as mad and get herself sent to the notorious women's asylum on Blackwell's Island. Cockerill must have been impressed, for he paid her $25 to retain her services while he thought the matter over. Within days, she was back in his office and given the go-ahead for the test assignment: Blackwell's Island.

It was a highly ambitious plan, but Bly prepared well. She went to the assistant district attorney to get immunity from prosecution, agreed with her editor how she would be liberated from the asylum if successful, and, the night before she was to 'go mad', stayed up reading ghost stories and practising in front of a mirror the catatonic expression that would accompany her apparent loss of memory. When everything was ready, Bly, dressed as poorly as pride would allow, made her way to the Temporary Home for Females on Second Avenue, and asked for a bed. Once admitted to the shabby house (60 cents a night, including dinner), she began behaving in a way she hoped would soon have the authorities sent for: confused, unable to say where she came from, muttering odd thoughts, assuming a far-away look and asking over and over again where her trunk was. By bedtime, some of the other residents were so disturbed that one feared the new resident would slit their throats while they slept and favoured the police being called out there and then. Kinder voices prevailed, and 'Nellie Brown' was put to bed. But, after a night in which she refused to sleep and sat staring at the wall till dawn, the assistant matron bustled off to fetch a couple of burly lawmen, lest the girl turn violent. On the pretext of helping her find her trunk, they escorted her to the station house, and thence to Judge Duffy's court. He ordered her detained and examined at Bellevue Hospital.

This was the first great test. Her main fear had been that somewhere along the line a doctor would have the wit to declare her a fraud. She need not have worried. The Bellevue doctor deemed her not only insane, but also, when looking into her eyes, mistook pupils dilated through shortsightedness for the symptoms of someone taking belladonna, and declared her a possible drug addict too. So, after a night in the cold hospital, she was conveyed via van and boat to her goal: Blackwell's Island, the city's repository for the raving and the simple, and those who, through misdiagnosis, a language problem, or merely because the courts did not know what else to do with them, ended up incarcerated in a place from which there was little likelihood of escape.

From the moment she stepped ashore and was marched into the cold, white, institutional hall of Hall 6, Bly was treated, as were all inmates, as a delinquent animal that needed corrective training. Bed was a hard, oilcloth-covered crib, from which inmates were roused at 5.30am, and then forced to sit in a freezing room, bolt upright and in silence, on hard wooden benches from 6am to 8pm. As she reported:

> I was never so tired as I grew sitting on those benches. Several of the patients would sit on one foot or sideways to make a change, but they were always reproved and told to sit up straight. If they talked they were scolded and told to shut up; if they wanted to walk around in order to take the stiffness out of them, they were told to sit down and be still. What, excepting torture, would produce insanity quicker than this treatment...

Bly was, however, more anxious about being detected than driven mad. When one enterprising rival reporter arrived one day to inspect the mysterious Nellie Brown, she begged him in a whisper not to give her away, and he didn't. Thus was she able to continue collecting the evidence of cruelty and neglect that, in a week or so, would shock the city. The people who might have been expected to rumble her – the doctors – were far too incompetent to do so. Once on the island, she had dropped all pretence of madness, behaved rationally, and answered all questions honestly, saving those about her identity. But three times these 'experts' examined her, and three times they declared her insane. 'Positively demented,' said the first of them. 'I consider it a hopeless case.' Only one showed her kindness, allowing her after five days to move into a ward for the quieter inmates, where the discipline was a little less ferocious. And it was here, a week and a half after she was admitted, that 'friends' came forward to claim her. She was freed into the tender care of the *New York World*, and five days later the paper's Sunday feature section led with a report headlined 'Ten Days In A Madhouse'. Mental health care in the city – and Bly's career – was never the same again.

Her two-page report – with the same again the following week – laid bare the conditions in which 1,600 women were held on the island. The strict regime of sitting still on the freezing benches was the least of the torture. The food (insipid tea, hard bread, rancid butter, unseasoned meat and thin gruel) made all but veteran inmates gag, and they then had to watch as raisins, grapes, apples and crackers were brought to the nurses. Hygiene was minimal. At bathtime, inmates were stripped, sluiced with buckets of ice-cold water and then dried with communal towels. Soap was only available once a week, and dresses changed but once a month. This, however, was unlikely to be fatal, unlike the risk of fire. Bly reported:

> Every door is locked separately and the windows are heavily barred, so that escape is impossible. In one building alone... there are 300 women... Should the building burn, the jailers or nurses would never think of releasing their crazy patients... All would be left to roast to death.

The cruelty Bly witnessed was institutionalised in every sense of the word. It ranged from routine slaps meted out if patients would not get into line as they were marched into the dining hall to a beating so bad that a girl died. There was a girl called Urena Little-Page, whom the nurses teased constantly about her age:

> They kept this up until the simple creature began to yell and cry... After they had gotten all the amusement out of her they wanted, they began to scold and tell her to keep quiet. She grew more hysterical until they pounced upon her and slapped her face... This made the poor creature cry the more, and so they choked her. Then they dragged her out to the closet, and I heard her terrified cries hush into smothered ones.

There was an old, blind woman who found the sitting room too cold to bear:

> ... she would get up and endeavour to feel her way to leave the room. Sometimes the attendants would jerk her back to the bench, and again they would let her walk and heartlessly laugh when she bumped against the table or the edges of the benches...

There was Mrs Cotter, who told Bly:

> For crying, the nurses beat me with a broom handle and jumped on me... Then they tied my hands and feet, and, throwing a sheet over my head, twisted it tightly around my throat, so I could not scream, and thus put me in a bathtub filled with cold water. They held me under until I gave up every hope and became senseless.

And there was Bridget McGuinness, totally sane as far as Bly could judge, who was beaten, choked and, when she reported it, beaten again for telling. She was lucky to escape with just two broken ribs.

Perhaps most moving of all were those women who were as lucid as Bly, and yet were trapped in this Manhattan gulag: Mrs Louis Schanz, a German woman who understood little English and was so judged to be simple; Mary Hughes, Margaret, a young German servant girl, and Mrs McCartney, who also showed 'no obvious traces of insanity'; Josephine Despreau, a young French girl, 'perfectly sane' according to Bly, but choked by nurses for complaining that she should not be there;

Sarah Fishbaum, a young Jewish girl whose husband had her committed because 'she had a fondness for other men'; and, saddest of all, Tillie Mayard, rational when Bly first met her, but who, after begging repeatedly to be tested, was finally unhinged by her treatment. The doctors, unable to judge the sanity of patients, knew only how to subdue the more restless ones with repeated injections of morphine. Bly concluded her report:

> The insane asylum on Blackwell's Island is a human rat-trap. It is easy to get in, but once there it is impossible to get out.

The story – written in clear, simple language – was a sensation. It was by-lined (almost unheard of for a newcomer), and overnight Nellie Bly became a New York phenomenon. The rival *Sun* paid her the compliment of lifting large chunks of her story and publishing them as their own, she was offered lecture tours and parts in plays, her proprietor Joseph Pulitzer wrote her a handsome cheque, a Grand Jury investigation exonerated her findings, the city gave an extra $1 million for mental health care (today Blackwell's Island is known as Roosevelt Island, home to upscale apartments), and her reports were turned into a book. For Bly, however, the real prize was the job she had longed dreamed of: news reporter on a New York paper.

She responded by producing a cascade of stories in the next two years. Virtually every other week there was an exposé. She posed as a maid in search of work to show how employment agencies exploited women servants; as an unmarried mother with an unwanted child to reveal the trade in newborns; a lonely heart in search of a husband to investigate the shady ways of marriage agencies; a prostitute to report conditions in a home for 'fallen women'; as the wife of a jealous husband who wanted her followed to expose private investigators; and she managed to get herself arrested as a thief so she could tell the law-abiding readers of the *World* what it was like to spend a night in jail. She acted as an innocent country girl so she could uncover Charles Cleveland, who toured Central Park picking up girls fresh in from rural areas, pressing them into servitude as prostitutes; she was a penniless invalid to report on life (and death) as a charity patient at city hospitals; and, in April 1888, she acted as the wife of a businessman anxious to stop a piece of state legislation so she could unmask the corrupt lobbyist, Edward R. Phelps, who, satisfyingly, left town, never to return. In all these ventures, nothing aided her so much as the fact that no one ever suspected a woman would turn out to be a reporter.

She also got inside a paper box factory to write about the conditions of virtual slavery in which its young women workers toiled; learnt to fence, swim and cycle; joined a chorus line, covered graduation at West Point, spent a night in an opium den; exposed a mesmerist, an unlicensed money lender, gimcrack washing machine sellers; and she made a laughing stock of seven of the most prominent doctors in New York by presenting all of them with the same symptoms and getting from them seven different diagnoses, ranging from malaria to 'shattered nerves'. For the election of 1888, she interviewed the candidates' wives, every living First Lady, and all the wives of Benjamin Harrison's cabinet. And, assuming her flirtatious persona, she interviewed champion boxer John L. Sullivan, who told her: 'I have given you more than I ever gave any reporter in my life.'

The charm worked just as well on women, and when 1889's big story broke – a sex scandal involving the grandson of Alexander Hamilton – Bly inveigled her way into prison and interviewed the alleged scarlet woman at the centre of it. Eva Hamilton was a former good-time girl who had been kept by, among other men, Robert Roy Hamilton. The story went that she had tricked him into marrying her by claiming to be pregnant, a baby had been bought by an old associate of hers to play the part of their offspring, and that when the child's nanny blurted out the truth in Hamilton's presence, Eva went for her with a knife. The servant survived, and Eva duly got two years. Her side of the story, however, had gone untold, and so Bly took her sense of fair play and interviewing skills off to Trenton Penitentiary and got her to open up. The result was a front-page lead that put matters in a rather different light: far from sponging on Hamilton, he actually owed her money; there was no trickery, since the baby was hers; Hamilton had forced her to have two abortions during their relationship; and the baby procuress was not only buying infants for others, but had been blackmailing Eva. The scoop was another sell-out for the *World*.

She gave readers more than just straightforward, no-frills writing. They also knew, if they saw her by-line, that they would be in the company of a reporter who asked direct, even shocking, questions, was incurably nosy, and who also took risks. The illustrator on her paper, Walt McDougall, said: 'Nothing was too strenuous nor too perilous for her if it promised results'; and sometimes she had to be restrained because the project she wanted to attempt was too hazardous. Her edgy sense of adventure was partly driven by the need to constantly 'top' her previous efforts, and partly because her popularity inspired a raft of imitators, and therefore, in her eyes, competitors. The need to outdo the likes of Violet Roseborough and Meg Merrilies could never have been far from her mind. What they wrote was called 'stunt' journalism, a rather sneering phrase for reporting that not only shifted large amounts of newspapers, but at last gave female reporters a profile outside the ghetto of fashion and lifestyle. It also meant that women's lives, and the issues they raised, were covered widely for the first time. It was a world away from campaigns for equal rights, but it was a start, and Bly's next major project probably did more to advance the cause than anything else at that time. She wanted, she told executives at her paper, to travel around the world in less than 80 days.

They were appalled. It was impossible, they told her, for a woman to travel unchaperoned. If the venture was to be attempted, it would have to be by a man. Very well, she replied, I will go to another paper, get them to send me and I will beat your man. Confronted by the 25-year-old's determination, they gave in: Nellie Bly would try to circle the globe in less time than it took Phileas Fogg in Jules Verne's novel. Informed on a Monday evening that she would depart on the Thursday, she had just enough time to go to a seamstress and have made a dress that would stand three months' continuous wear, and throw the following into a trunk: two travelling caps, three veils, slippers, toiletries, ink-stand, pens, pencils, copy paper, pins, needles, thread, dressing gown, tennis blazer, small flask, drinking cup, underwear, handkerchiefs, and a large jar of cold cream. At 9.40am on 14 November 1889, Bly, armed with no more tickets than her passage to London, set sail on the *Auguste Victoria*. She was seasick before land was even out of sight.

As she crossed the Atlantic in heavy winds – in the company, among other bizarre passengers, of a man who constantly took his pulse and another who counted each step he ever took – the *World* announced her venture with considerable fanfare. It launched a competition for readers to guess the time the trip would take, and, almost immediately, thousands of entries flooded in – along with several marriage proposals. The intrepid Bly, meanwhile, had reached England after nearly seven days, and was about to take a detour that would place her entire schedule in jeopardy. Jules Verne would be delighted to meet her, she was informed in London; and so she risked a week's delay in dashing down to Amiens to shake the celebrated French novelist's hand. Then it was back to London, a hasty planning of her itinerary, booking passage on the relevant ships, and departure on the series of trains and boats she hoped would propel her speedily round the world via France, Italy, Egypt, Aden, Arabia; Colombo, Ceylon; Penang, Prince of

Wales Island; Singapore, Malay Peninsula; Hong Kong, Japan and the United States.

Back home, entries in the contest were arriving at the *World* by the hour, which was more than any detailed word from their heroine was. She could cable snippets of her progress, but detailed accounts of her adventures took weeks – her hand-written report of the mid-November Atlantic crossing, for instance, did not arrive in the office until 2 December. By this time she was in Asia, and facing a series of voyages, any delay in which could wreck her chance of beating the deadline: sailing to Colombo (where she was held up for five anxious days), six days to Penang, another two before she reached Singapore, and then a further week at sea before she gained Hong Kong. This last was a mixed trip for Bly. A smitten passenger trailed her round the boat at all times, finally plucked up courage to speak to her, and was promptly sick at her feet. A few days later he approached her again, and announced that he would die happy if they could but embrace, fall into the sea as one, and drift together into all eternity. And then there were the newlyweds who were under the impression that it was compulsory to sleep in their life preservers.

The crew of the steamship *Oriental* were mercifully less eccentric. The boat made record time to Hong Kong, and it was, perhaps, just as well they did, for a series of shocks awaited her. At the offices of the Oriental and Occidental Steamship Co., where she had gone to buy tickets for Japan, she was informed *Cosmopolitan* magazine had despatched Elizabeth Bisland around the world in the other direction, her rival was currently well ahead, the contest had been set up by her own paper (untrue), and, just to cap it all, there would now be a five-day delay before the boat could leave for Japan. Bly filled the enforced hiatus in search of copy by visiting the ancient city of Canton, and spending Christmas Day at a leper colony. Less than a week later she was in Yokohama, waiting for the (inevitably delayed) boat to San Francisco. Five days on that, and the west coast of America hove into view. She had 12 days to spare, and all was looking good.

Too good, of course. In the morning of 20 January, as the steamship *Oceanic* neared port, the ship's purser informed her that he had left the ship's bill of health back in Japan, and without this there would be no landing. There was, he said, no alternative but to wait for the next ship out of Yokohama to bring it over, which would take another 14 days. Bly's response was as calm and measured as any reporter's would be in the circumstances: she threatened to slit her throat. Thus inspired, the crew renewed their search for the papers, found them in the doctor's cabin, Bly hurled herself on to the waiting tug, the doctor shouted she could not go until he had examined her tongue, and, as the little boat sped off to Oakland Pier, she stuck it out at him.

She landed back on US soil to find she was the celebrity of the moment. The train rides across the States, completed in less than four and a half days, were a triumphal progress, past cheering crowds and bands of varying tunefulness; and hordes came to see her arrive at Pittsburgh, even though it was 3.10 in the morning. In Philadelphia, there were 5,000 waiting. The train then took her on to Jersey City, where she got off, made her way to the dock and, on the afternoon of Saturday 25 January, clocked in at her point of departure. For those keeping records, and more than a million who entered the *World*'s contest were, she made it in a time of 72 days, six hours, eleven minutes and 14 seconds. *Cosmopolitan*'s Miss Bisland was, as it turned out, beaten by more than a week. With this one story (headlined by the *World* 'Father Time Outdone!'), her paper's circulation soared to new peaks and Bly became the best-known reporter in America. Gun salutes, firework displays and a parade down Broadway were just the beginning. There followed a song about her, a board game ('Around The World With Nellie Bly'), dolls made in her likeness; a hotel, train and racehorse were named for her; and her image – resembling a Gibson Girl got up as Mary Poppins – was everywhere: on soap, dressing gowns, liver pills, cigars, sometimes even with her permission. Working undercover would never be easy again.

Bly had reached a kind of watershed, and, after a lecture tour, signed a $10,000-a-year contract with the *New York Family Story Paper* to write fiction. It was, to put it mildly, not her forte, and by September 1893 she was back at the *World*, interviewing murderesses in jail, exposing gambling dens, unmasking mind reader Maud Lancaster as a fraud, taking a critical look at the Salvation Army, and investigating on behalf of readers what it was like to spend the night in a haunted house. A much meatier assignment came in July 1894, when she went off to cover the Pullman Palace Car Company strike in Chicago, then in its eighth week. Her rivals were filing rumour-filled hype about riots and head breakings, but Bly, instead of relying on what company patsies told her, went off to see what life was like for the strikers and their families:

> I go into the quiet homes and I find the strikers nursing the babies... They are not firebrands; they are not murderers and rioters; they are not Anarchists. They are quiet, peaceful men who have suffered beneath the heel of the most heartless coward it has ever been my misfortune to hear of.

Subjective reporting it may have been, but it was a lot more accurate than any other paper was carrying.

She did a few more stories, including a tour of the drought-hit Midwest, but a permanent break with the *World* was looming. She was never popular with colleagues, her celebrity bred resentments, and the paper was a stew of jealousies, not so much by accident but by design. Its owner, Joseph Pulitzer, believed as a matter of policy in setting reporter against reporter and editor against editor. The result was an atmosphere that, according to its cartoonist Walt McDougall, 'drove at least two editors to drink, one to suicide, a fourth into insanity and another into banking'. In February 1895, Bly moved to the *Times-Herald* of Chicago and had barely time to expose conditions at Cook County jail, before she met, at a dinner at the city's Auditorium Hotel, an industrialist called Robert Seaman. Two weeks later they married. She was 31, and he was 69, thus inspiring the resident satirist at *Town Topics* to wonder if it was all another one of her investigations. 'Is Marriage a failure?' wrote the funster. 'Nellie Bly tries it with a good old man!! Her experience and his!!'

If only it had have been a stunt. But it wasn't, and after just six months, her husband's stick-in-the-mud ways, his jealousy and Bly's independent streak rendered the union so troubled that Seaman hired a private detective to follow her. A mere eight months after the wedding he drew up a will leaving her just $300. Inspired by this, or the presence of Seaman's drunken brother in their home, she fleetingly returned to work at the *World*, and more private eyes were hired. But then some sort of domestic deal was done. She gave up work, his will was changed, and she went to Europe and stayed there for three years. By the time she returned, Bly was 35 – middle aged for the period – and, with her husband having a controlling interest in the Iron Clad Manufacturing and American Steel Barrel companies, the conventional thing would have been to sit at home, spending his money and maintaining a modest salon for her fellow Manhattan matrons.

This, however, was Nellie Bly, and, shortly after she came back from Europe, the one-time scourge of the sweat-shop owners decided to try her hand at running her husband's ailing firm. She began by learning how to operate every machine at the Brooklyn factory, and then set about reforming the whole place. Working 12-hour days, she turned things round to such effect that, by the time Seaman died in 1904, the loss-making venture was doing four times the business and bringing in $200,000 a year profit. Once a widow, she went further, inventing new processes for the making of boilers, milk cans and kitchen sinks (she eventually held 25 patents), and providing worker benefits that ranged from a recreation centre and 5,000-volume library to health schemes and Saturday night lectures. She was the owner of a firm that was worth millions.

In a life like hers, so resembling a novel, it couldn't last, and it didn't. She had left the finances to a Major Edward Gilman, and after his death from cancer in 1911, his embezzlement, and that of his team, brought the company down like a house of cards. It went into receivership, Bly was barred from the factory, and, as the lawsuits flew, she edged ever nearer bankruptcy. At the age of 48, and 17 years after she last worked fully as a journalist, she returned to reporting for the *New York Evening Journal*. She was still enough of a name to be sent to cover the national conventions in 1912, and President Wilson's inauguration early the following year. But the legal fall-out from the collapse of her firm was pressing down on her, and in 1914 she went to Austria, partly to recuperate and also to see if she could find new sources of finance. She had not been there a month when war broke out, and Bly, the old instincts overcoming any need to butter up potential backers, immediately cabled the *Journal* to say that she was off to the front. Her most memorable story was filed from the American Red Cross Hospital in Budapest, where she watched a Russian soldier die while crying out for his children. Eventually she could stand no more and left the room:

> The low moan seemed to call me back, but I walked steadfastly toward the door and down the corridor.
> 'Could emperors and czars and kings look on this torturing slaughter and ever sleep again?' I asked the doctor.
> 'They do not look,' he said gently.

She spent the rest of the war hurling her still formidable energies into the relief effort. In February 1919 she returned to the US, the now hopelessly complex legal actions over her old firm, and a $100-a-week job at the *Journal*. She covered the Jack Dempsey–Jess Willard fight in Toledo, Ohio (the first woman to report on a big fight), once again wrung confessions from a murderer in his cell, and had a column which, in a way, brought her back full circle to where she began: writing about things so she could change them. It was not a column where she preached, but where she reported – on the individual lives of New York's most hard-pressed residents. People wrote to her about their problems, Bly reported them, others wrote with their advice, Bly saw needs, tried to do something about them, and the column became a sort of community noticeboard for those in distress and those who wanted to help. And it mushroomed from there. She told, for instance, stories of abandoned babies, people wrote in offering to foster or adopt, and she soon had so many babies needing homes (some were even found with notes pinned to their clothes reading 'Take me to Nellie Bly') that a nursery had to be set up to deal with them. And this, in turn produced a self-help group for needy mothers.

People wrote in with so many problems that, even with a small army of secretaries and volunteers handling the mail, the waiting list for a reply grew to eight weeks. Something of the flavour of her column can be gauged from the announcement at the head of it on 20 September 1919:

> IMPORTANT
> Dear friends – ... I need immediately address of 'L.M.', 'A Failure' (a disowned boy consumptive in hospital), 'Herbert's Mother', 'L.M.G.', 'M.R.A', 'P.Z.', 'M.L.D.', 'V.D.H.', 'Lonesome', 'F.S.', all those who wish to adopt babies, and those who have written about work.

Her answer to those who said she was being rooked by artful scroungers was 'Relieve immediately; investigate afterwards', a motto that did nothing to stem the tide of unkempt assistance-seekers who, instead of writing, simply turned up in the lobby of the hotel where Bly lived. They rarely found her at home. A reluctant user of the telephone, she bustled about the city doing all her researching, helping, collecting and lobbying in person, only pausing when she sat down and wrote her column two or three times a week. And then, suddenly, it all stopped. In January 1922, she developed pneumonia and was dead within three weeks. She was 57, and left an estate that contained less than $1,000 in cash.

Arthur Brisbane, editor of the *Journal*, called her 'the best reporter in America', and he may well have been right. Quite why might seem a mystery to the twenty-first century, but there is an answer. Nellie Bly wasn't a very imaginative writer (although she was a very clear one), but she had an incurable curiosity and an unshakeable faith in the power of reporting. If only the true facts could be uncovered, she believed, then people and authorities could be roused to act and make improvements. It's not a very fashionable kind of journalism these days, when many journalists think it more important to be thought smart or metropolitan than to do good. But that's because we seem to have mislaid the optimism about what reporting can achieve that she, for all the twists and turns of her novelistic life, never lost. All good Victorian stories must have a moral, and that is hers. Nellie Bly was the very antithesis of cynicism.

Richard Harding Davis

6

Richard Harding Davis
1864–1916

ONE OF THE BEST DESCRIPTIVE REPORTERS EVER

Journalism is probably not much more riddled with professional envy than any other cut-throat trade inhabited by the chronically insecure. But if there is one kind of person who sticks right in the narrow craw of its less successful practitioners, it is a man like Richard Harding Davis, the war correspondent whose seemingly casual success made him the twentieth century's first prince of reporters.

He was, to begin with, the son of two gifted writers, an advantage that nature had somewhat unfairly supplemented by making him also tall, fair-haired and good-looking. He dressed with the kind of classy sense of style that has never been exactly common in newsrooms, and the result was that he looked in his prime like one of those perfectly tailored and incorruptible heroes whom Edwardian boys' adventure books showed effortlessly cornering the villain before adjusting their white tie and heading for the theatre. The appearance was not deceptive. Not only did he have a habit of emerging from danger unruffled and smelling of rosewater, but also, like his fictional counterparts, he was an easy and elegant mover in rarefied social circles. When on assignment in England, this American was as likely to be staying with a milord as putting up at the Ritz. And, as if all this was not enough to make the tobacco-chewing toilers in the engine rooms of newspapers hate him, he was also a highly successful novelist and dramatist, could command huge fees for freelance articles, and was friend and correspondent of the famous. All in all, if you were the third copyeditor from the door on an early twentieth-century newspaper, with a grumbling ulcer nagging at you and pressing bills to pay, Richard Harding Davis was just the kind of big-name, fancy writer whose by-line would remind you most sharply of the young man you once wanted to be.

Genetics, you would have said; those and connections – that was the difference between Davis and you. He had them, you did not. His mother was the realist novelist Rebecca Harding Davis, and his father was Clarke Davis, managing editor of the *Philadelphia Inquirer*. Must have pulled strings. Got 'their boy' a head start. You know, pushed him, introduced him around and puffed him to editors. Eased his passage. Not like you, with your struggle to get in somewhere, and then the fight to work your way up to be the man who was sometimes allowed to handle to city page splash on a slow night.

Well, it wasn't quite like that. True, there was his good fortune to be born to a pair of writers, but Davis made his own way: to hometown titles other than the one his father edited; to New York and to being the most celebrated journalist in America by the time he was 30; to South America, England, Russia, Italy, and Hungary; to wars in Greece, Cuba, South Africa, Japan, Belgium and Turkey; and to a place in journalism history as one of the best descriptive reporters ever to file. What makes him special is not just the quality of his writings, but the driven way he pursued their raw material. Long after his books and plays had begun to earn the money that could have kept him in perpetual idleness, Davis was seeking out freelance assignments that involved the worst that foreign bureaucrats and their equally callous armies could throw at him. Never mind the three dramas he had running simultaneously on

Broadway, the fretting of his mother, the young wife he had
just married, the new house he had bought, or the birth of the
baby daughter he had always craved; never mind the chronic
sciatica that could, without warning, virtually cripple him for
days at a time, Davis would sign a new contract and exchange
the safety and cushions of home for the squalor of war. He
was, quite simply, addicted to being there. And if that meant
he was shot at, shelled, arrested or, as he was once, within an
hour of being executed as a spy by the Germans, then so be
it. How else to gather the experiences that fed his compulsive
need to explore, describe and explain?

This need to be where the action is was not something his
first editor saw in him. Davis joined the *Philadelphia Record*
in 1886, and within three months was sacked from his $7
a week post. It is entirely possible that this young man's
affected-sounding Anglicised vowels and well-heeled, literary
background – an unusual thing in an 1880s newsroom – had
already aroused the democratic instincts of his editor. But
when the impression of feyness was compounded one day
by his wearing kid gloves in the office to ward off the cold,
his editor decided that the namby-pamby college boy had
to go. The editor's instincts, although subsequently proved
spectacularly wrong in a professional sense, had something in
them. Davis was, for all his roughing it in war zones, something
of a Philadelphia mother's boy all his life. Even if he had been
absent from her company for only a few hours, he would,
when they met again, hold her in a lengthy, rocking embrace,
and if he was staying away from home, he would write to her
every day. These were not mawkish, sentimentalised billets-
doux to a clinging parent, more like the letters to a friend; but
still, even for the period, it was an unusual habit for a war
correspondent to have.

   Davis was not, however, to be defeated by the only editor
in history whose instruction to staff to take the gloves off
was intended literally, rather than merely metaphorically. He

joined the *Philadelphia Press*, settled down to a life of general reporting, interviewing (Walt Whitman found him 'unusually wholesome-looking' for a journalist), plus the odd reporting caper. In one, he disguised himself as a crook, inveigled himself into a gang of some of the city's worst desperados, and sufficiently gained their trust to join in planning a robbery. Having gathered the evidence, he went to the police, arrests were made, and Davis had the perfect ending to his story. He was no mean hustler in the newsroom, either, as this August 1888 letter to his family shows:

> I got a story on the front page this morning about an explosion at Columbia Avenue Station – I went out on it with another man my senior in years and experience, whom Watrous [the editor] expected to write the story while I hustled for facts. When we got back I had all the facts, and what little he had was incorrect – so I said I would dispense with his services and write the story myself... Next time Andy will know better and let me get my own stories alone.

It is the authentic voice of the journalist's idea of teamwork.

By 1889 the 25-year-old had been marked down as the man to send to the next big story. He didn't have to wait long. That May rainstorms had filled the dam above Johnstown in upstate Pennsylvania to bursting point – and, on the 31st on the month, beyond it. The dam burst, and the 20 million tons of water held 400 ft above the town crashed down onto it. Davis was sent to cover the devastation, and his first questions upon arrival were thought to be sufficiently silly to enter local newspaper lore. Where, he asked, can I find a restaurant, buy a boiled shirt, and rent a horse and buggy? These, as anyone who has ever covered a scene devoid of normal services and communications knows, were by no means as risible as his fellow reporters thought.

Davis's subsequent articles, telling how 2,200 people lost their lives, showed he could handle the really big story, and, since a tale like that was unlikely to come along in his home state for a long while, set him thinking that the time was ripe for a move to New York. In September 1889 he began touring newspapers in the city looking for work, drew a blank, and was about to take the train back to Philadelphia when he sat down on a bench in City Hall Park. Along came Arthur Brisbane, an acquaintance and, more to the point, the newly appointed editor of the *New York Evening Sun*. Brisbane offered him a job, and Davis started almost immediately on a salary of $30 a week. Within the year, his reporting, short stories and features, had attracted the attention of *McClure's*, who offered him $75 a week to join them. He turned that down, but in December 1890 went to *Harper's Weekly* as managing editor on the understanding that he could spend a certain part of every year travelling and writing for *Harper's Monthly*.

This job gave him two things. First was the lifelong habit of consuming prodigious amounts of newspapers and magazines every day. As his brother wrote:

> He subscribed to most of the English and French illustrated periodicals and to one London daily newspaper which every day he read with the same interest that he read half a dozen New York newspapers... When others, tired after a hard day's work or play, would devote the evening to cards or billiards or chatter, Richard would write letters or pore over some strange foreign magazine, consult maps, make notes, or read the stories of his contemporaries. He practically read every American magazine from cover to cover...

The second thing was a broad journalistic canvas. He now had the opportunity to write big pieces on big subjects, and he did not waste it. Articles on a rail tour of the West, 'Our English Cousins' (the research for which involved a surprising amount of country house living), on the Chicago World's Fair, on Paris, the Mediterranean, Central and South America followed. These, and the short stories he was now writing, rapidly made him the best-known, and best-paid, journalist of his day. By 1895, his by-line was in such demand that when Hearst asked him to report the Yale–Princeton football match, Davis, not really wanting to cover it, asked for an afternoon's work the sum of $500 – and got it. Yet having now reached the stage where he could name his price, and stipulate his assignments, he opted not for a life of top-dollar travel writing or penning thumb-sucking pieces from behind his own desk, but instead to be a roving correspondent. In the space of 12 months in 1896–97, he covered the Coronation of Czar Nicholas in Moscow, the Millennium celebrations in Budapest, the inauguration of President McKinley, the Greek–Turkish War, the Cuban revolt and Queen Victoria's Jubilee in London.

Moscow tested his ingenuity. He arrived after a journey of some weeks to find himself one of 90 correspondents each trying to obtain one of the 12 coronation tickets. The next few days were a frantic round of lobbying, cajoling, ingratiating and conniving to get one of the coveted passes. As he wrote to his brother Charles:

> There is not a wire we have not pulled, or a leg either, and we go dashing about all day in a bath-chair, with a driver in a bell hat and a blue nightgown, leaving cards and writing notes and giving drinks and having secretaries to lunch and buying flowers for wives and cigar boxes for husbands, and threatening...

Meanwhile, he also had to make sure his story, once written, actually got on the wire to New York. So he went to the head of the Telegraph Bureau, wrote a cable and added the words: 'Recommend ample recognition of special facilities afforded by telegraph official.' Then, on the pretext of checking if his writing was legible, he asked the man to read it. The official did so, smiled at its final sentence, and a day or so later Davis slipped him 200 roubles 'from my office'. Thereafter Davis's wires went to the head of the queue. And, of course, he duly got his coronation pass.

Six months later, in December 1896, Hearst commissioned Davis to visit Cuba, then in revolt against Spanish colonial rule. It was his first assignment as a war correspondent, and he undertook it in the company of Frederic Remington, the artist who was the alleged recipient of Hearst's infamous, and almost certainly mythical, 'You furnish the pictures, I will furnish the war' telegram. By late January, Davis's natural sympathy for the Cuban underdogs, together with his sense of a defining story, had prompted him to attend the execution of a young rebel. The story he filed, published by Hearst's *New York Journal* on 2 February 1897, and known to us now as 'The Death of Rodriguez', is one of the most anthologised pieces of reporting in newspaper history:

> ... With us a condemned man walks only the short distance from his cell to the scaffold or the electric chair, shielded from sight by the prison walls... But the merciful Spaniards on this morning made the prisoner walk for over a half-mile across the broken surface of the fields. I expected to find the man, no matter what his strength at other times might be, stumbling and faltering, but as he came nearer I saw that he led all the others, that the priests on either side of him were taking two steps to his one, and that they were tripping on their gowns and stumbling over the hollows, in their efforts to keep pace with him as he walked, erect and soldierly, at a quick step in advance of them.
>
> ... It was very quickly finished... The crowd fell back when it came to the square, and the condemned man, the priests and the firing squad of six young volunteers passed in, and the line closed behind them. The officer who had held the cord that bound the Cuban's arms behind him and passed across his breast, let it fall on the grass and drew his sword, and Rodriguez dropped his cigarette from his lips and bent and kissed the cross which the priest held up before him... The Cuban walked to where the officer directed him to stand, and turned his back to the square and faced the hills... As the officer gave the first command he straightened himself as far as the cords would allow, and held up his head and fixed his eyes immovably on the morning light which had just begun to show above the hills... The officer had given the order, the men had raised their pieces, and the condemned man had heard the clicks of the triggers as they were pulled back, and he had not moved. And then happened one of the most cruelly refined, though unintentional, acts of torture that one can very well imagine. As the officer slowly raised his sword, preparatory to giving the signal,

one of the mounted officers rode up to him and pointed out silently what I had already observed with some satisfaction, that the firing squad were so placed that when they fired they would shoot several of the soldiers stationed on the extreme end of the square.

Their captain motioned his men to lower their pieces, and then walked across the grass and laid his hand on the shoulder of the waiting prisoner... The boy turned his head steadily, and followed with his eyes the direction of the officer's sword, then nodded his head gravely, and, with his shoulders squared, took up a new position, straightened his back again, and once more held himself erect... The officer of the firing squad, mortified by his blunder, hastily whipped up his sword, the men once more leveled their rifles, the sword rose, dropped, and the men fired. At the report the Cuban's head snapped back almost between his shoulders, but his body fell slowly, as though someone had pushed him gently forward from behind and he had stumbled. He sank on his side in the wet grass without a struggle or sound, and did not move again... The figure was a thing of the past, and the squad shook itself like a great snake, and then broke into little pieces and started off jauntily, stumbling in the high grass and striving to keep step to the music.

... as I fell in at the rear of the procession and looked back the figure of the young Cuban, who was no longer a part of the world of Santa Clara, was asleep in the wet grass, with his motionless arms still tightly bound behind him, with the scapula twisted awry across his face and the blood from his breast sinking into the soil he had tried to free.

Ten days after the death of Rodriguez was published, an altogether different kind of story appeared under Davis's by-line. On his way back to the US on a steamer, Davis sat one night at dinner beside a young woman called Senorita Clemencia Arango. She told him that she and two other women were being expelled from Cuba on suspicion of rebel sympathies, but that, before their departure, the Spanish authorities had twice strip-searched them. His sense of chivalry aroused, and no doubt also mindful of Hearst's panting appetite for any Spanish outrage, real or imagined, Davis filed the story as soon as his boat reached Tampa, Florida. Two days later, it appeared in the *Journal* under screaming headlines. 'Does Our Flag Shield Women?' asked the top line, followed by 'Indignities Practiced by Spanish Officials On Board American Vessels – Richard Harding Davis Describes Some Startling Phases of the Cuban Situation – Refined Young Women Stripped and Searched by Brutal Spaniards While Under Our Flag on the Ollivette'. And centrefield on the page was a drawing by Remington showing a half-naked woman from the back being molested by leering Spanish officials. It was, as Hearst intended, an instant sensation. But not for long. A day or so later, Senorita Arango arrived in New York, and, interviewed by the rival *New York World*, insisted that things had been not quite as the *Journal* said. She was, she protested, stripped not by slavering Spanish men, but by two women police matrons. The *World* published its scoop with relish.

The explanation, when it emerged, has the ring of authenticity to anyone who ever filed an accurate story, only to find, upon publication, that the practitioners of the black arts of presentation back at the office have taken it up a notch or three. Davis had made no mention of the gender of the strip searchers. It was the fertile mind of Frederic Remington who had invented the sweaty-palmed men who presided over Ms Arango's disrobing, Hearst's headline writers had taken their cue from his fanciful pen-and-ink, and, as usual, it was the writer who copped most of the initial blame. Davis learnt from the episode. He never again worked for Hearst, and was permanently wary of Remington, who, in a letter to his mother, he had presciently described just a month before: 'he is an alarmist and exaggerates things'.

Two months later he was on his way to cover the war between Greece and Turkey for the London *Times*, and by mid-May he was getting his first taste of large-scale combat, on the front line at the battle of Velestinos. Here, in his reports, is evidence of Davis's eye for detail and ability to describe it in ways that are not just fresh, but strikingly simple. Like all seriously talented writers, his possession of the facility to show off on the page meant that he also had the sense not to do it. Here he is on one of his first days in the trenches:

> What impressed us most was the remarkable number of cartridges the Greek soldiers wasted in firing into space... The cartridges reminded one of corn-cobs jumping out of a corn-sheller, and it was interesting when the bolts were shot back to see a hundred of them pop up into the air at the same time, flashing in the sun as though they were glad to have done their work and to get out again. They rolled by the dozens underfoot, and twinkled in the grass, and when one shifted his position in the narrow trench, or stretched his cramped legs, they tinkled musically. It was like wading in a gutter filled with thimbles.

Neither did it take him long to rumble, and express in a memorable way, one of war's dirty little secrets:

> There was no selection of the unfittest; it seemed to be ruled by unreasoning luck. A certain number of shells and bullets passed through a certain area of space, and men of different bulks blocked that space in different places. If a man happened to be standing in the line of a bullet he was killed and passed into eternity, leaving a wife and children, perhaps, to mourn him. 'Father died,' these children will say, 'doing his duty.' As a matter of fact, father died because he happened to stand up at the wrong moment, or because he turned to ask the man on his right for a match, instead of leaning toward the left, and he projected his bulk of two hundred pounds where a bullet, fired by a man who did not know him and who had not aimed at him, happened to want the right of way. One of the two had to give it, and as the bullet would not, the soldier had his heart torn out.

Such cool observation was rather less in evidence a year later, when Davis was in Cuba to chronicle the brief Spanish–American war. His account of the Rough Riders' famous charge carried more than a tinge of cheer-leading, partly because he was an admirer of Lt-Colonel Roosevelt, and partly because Davis was rather more actively involved in the action than a bystander should be. The general flavour can be gauged by the following:

... Roosevelt, who had picked up a carbine and was firing to give the direction to the others, determined upon a charge... And so, when instead of retreating on each volley, the Rough Riders rushed at them, cheering and filling the hot air with wild cowboy yells, the dismayed enemy retreated upon Santiago, where he announced he had been attacked by the entire American army.

Still, modern criticisms of Davis as a PR man for Roosevelt are not borne out by reading his reports. (Neither does their bias seem especially outlandish compared to some pieces filed from the Iraq War in 2003.) Safe, perhaps, to say that although this was Roosevelt's finest hour, it was not Davis's.

But judging him by the standards of later eras is nonsensical. He was, for all his descriptive talents, as representative of his times as we are of ours. And in nothing is this more apparent than in the train of considerable luggage that Davis trailed around on campaign. He travelled in the grand manner; partly because he hated austerity, and partly because, as he once explained, those reporting for one of the great newspapers were required to maintain certain officerly standards. Thus, when in the field for *The Times*, he needed an enormous cart, two oxen, three ponies, one Australian horse and three servants to transport his four hundred pounds of supplies and baggage. And not just any old 400 lb, either. He was most particular about his kit, insisting not just on his trusty green tent, cooking gear, bed, table, chair, mosquito net and folding rubber bathtub, but also, as itemised in his book *Notes of A War Correspondent*, the following:

> Two collapsible water-buckets of rubber or canvas.
> Two collapsible brass lanterns, with extra isinglass sides.
> Two boxes of sick-room candles.
> One dozen boxes of safety matches.
> One axe. The best I have seen is the Marble Safety Axe, made at Gladstone, Mich. You can carry it in your hip-pocket, and you can cut down a tree with it.
> One medicine case containing quinine, calomel, and Sun Cholera Mixture in tablets.

Toilet-case for razors, tooth-powder, brushes, and paper.

Folding bath-tub of rubber in rubber case. These are manufactured to fold into a space little larger than a cigar-box.

Two towels old, and soft.

Three cakes of soap.

One Jaeger blanket.

One mosquito head-bag.

One extra pair of shoes, old and comfortable.

One extra pair of riding-breeches.

One extra pair of gaiters. The former regulation army gaiter of canvas, laced, rolls up in a small compass and weighs but little.

One flannel shirt. Gray least shows the dust.

Two pairs of drawers. For riding, the best are those of silk.

Two undershirts, balbriggan or woollen.

Three pairs of woollen socks.

Two linen handkerchiefs, large enough, if needed, to tie around the throat and protect the back of the neck.

One pair of pajamas, woollen, not linen.

Two briarwood pipes.

Six bags of smoking tobacco; Durham or Seal of North Carolina pack easily.

One pad of writing paper.

One fountain pen, SELF-FILLING.

One bottle of ink, with screw top, held tight by a spring.

One dozen linen envelopes.

Stamps, wrapped in oil-silk with mucilage side next to the silk.

One stick sealing-wax. In tropical countries mucilage on the flap of envelopes sticks to everything except the envelope.

One dozen elastic bands of the largest size. In packing they help to compress articles like clothing into the smallest possible compass and in many other ways will be found very useful.

One pack of playing-cards.

Books.

One revolver and six cartridges.

Absurd to our twenty-first-century eyes though this all may seem, as he explained to his pre-airplane readers:

A man's outfit is a matter which seems to touch his private honor...
On a campaign, you may attack a man's courage, the flag he serves,

the newspaper for which he works, his intelligence, or his camp manners, and he will ignore you; but if you criticise his patent water-bottle he will fall upon you with both fists.

Thus encumbered (although he was known sometimes to economise and travel with reduced needs strapped to his back), Davis went on through 1899, 1900 and 1902, to South Africa to cover the Boer War for the *New York Herald* and Northcliffe's new *Daily Mail* (he reported it first from the British side and then the Boer), Spain and London for the coronations, more books and plays, and, then, in 1904, to Japan for *Collier's Weekly* to cover the Japanese–Russian War. This proved the most frustrating assignment of his life: weeks of travel, followed by four months of waiting in Tokyo, then three more weeks of travel, only to be hoodwinked by the Japanese and shown nothing more exciting than the smoke rings of cannon at a distance of eight miles. Describing himself as a mere 'cherry blossom correspondent', he left in disgust shortly afterwards.

He was now 40, the marriage he had made in 1899 was failing, and there was a strange hiatus on the international conflict front. Davis, as ever, kept busy. There were his travels, novels and plays, party conventions to cover and his private life to repair. He divorced in 1910, the year that his mother died, and, two years later, made a match that he knew would have set his beloved mama's teeth on edge. His bride was born Miss Elizabeth Genevieve McEvoy, but Broadway stage-door Johnnies knew her as vaudeville performer Bessie McCoy, aka 'The Yama-Yama Girl', after a song she sang. She was considerably younger than Davis, and he was besotted, and would remain happily so until his death. So he went through 1913, writing plays, setting up the home in which his daughter would shortly be born, and, even – odd though it must have seemed to a man brought up in the mid-Victorian era – being at hand and on set when one of his books, *Soldiers of Fortune*, was turned into a film.

By 1914, he was 50, wealthy, and with a new wife heavily pregnant with their first child. Yet when the promise of significant gunfire could be heard rumbling in the distance, he was ready to go. In April, war between the US and Mexico loomed, and off Davis went, only to experience as frustratingly un-newsworthy a time as he had in Japan. Back in New York by late June, he barely had time to complete his Mexican writings when it became obvious to him that Europe's armies were marching towards a full-scale continental war. He made his arrangements, and on 4 August, the very day that war was declared between Britain and Germany, Davis and his wife sailed for Liverpool in a $1,000-a-day suite on the *Lusitania*. He could afford it; he was being paid $32,000 a year to report the war for the Wheeler Syndicate.

The British refused Davis credentials to cover their army, and he made his way across the Channel to Brussels, through which, shortly after his arrival, came the German army, trampling Belgian neutrality underfoot in their haste to get to France. The spectacle of the immense German forces was war as he had never seen it before, a display of military strength produced on an industrial scale. Thus did Davis, a man thought by some to be a figment of an age gone by, and of wars more sportingly fought, watch as this vision of global conflict rolled past the window of his room at the Palace Hotel. The piece he wrote (carried out of besieged Brussels to Ostend, and thence safety, by an old Flemish woman) is thought by many to be his greatest report.

> The entrance of the German army into Brussels has lost the human quality. It was lost as soon as the three soldiers who led the army bicycled into the Boulevard du Regent and asked the way to the Gare du Nord. When they passed, the human note passed with them.
>
> What came after them, and twenty-four hours later is still coming, is not men marching, but a force of nature like a tidal wave, an avalanche or a river flooding its banks. At this minute it

is rolling through Brussels as the swollen waters of the Conemaugh Valley swept through Johnstown.

At the sight of the first few regiments of the enemy we were thrilled with interest. After three hours they had passed in one unbroken steel-grey column we were bored. But when hour after hour passed and there was no halt, no breathing time, no open spaces in the ranks, the thing became uncanny, inhuman. You returned to watch it, fascinated. It held the mystery and menace of fog rolling towards you across the sea.

The grey of the uniforms worn by both officers and men helped this air of mystery... It is a grey green... It is the grey of the hour just before daybreak, the grey of unpolished steel, of mist among green trees. I saw it first in the Grand Place in front of the Hotel de Ville. It was impossible to tell if in that noble square there was a regiment or a brigade. You saw only a fog that melted into the stones, blended with the ancient house fronts... it is no exaggeration to say that at a hundreds yards you can see the horses on which the uhlans ride, but you cannot see the men who ride them.

For seven hours the army passed in such solid columns that not once might a taxicab or trolley car pass through the city. Like a river of steel it flowed, grey and ghostlike. Then, as dusk came and as thousands of horses' hoofs and thousands of iron boots continued to tramp forward, they struck tiny sparks from the stones, but the horses and the men who beat out the sparks were invisible.

At midnight pack wagons and siege guns were still passing. At seven this morning I was awakened by the tramp of men and bands playing jauntily. Whether they marched all night or not I do not know; but now for twenty-six hours the grey army has rumbled by with the mystery of fog and the pertinacity of a steam-roller.

On 24 August, a day after this was published in the London *News Chronicle*, Davis and a colleague started to make their own way to Paris. He got as far as the town of Hal when he was arrested by the Germans on suspicion of being a spy. 'I am Richard Harding Davis!' he protested, a plea that might have carried more weight had his captors been regular Broadway playgoers or subscribers to American magazines. But they weren't; instead they felt sure they were holding a British spy. A summary court martial was held, the evidence (such as it was) was heard, sentence passed, and he was told he would be shot in the morning. Luckily, and it was luck, the British attacked that night, and the Germans, with rather more pressing matters on their hands, accepted Davis's offer to go back to the American embassy in Brussels, reporting to each German officer he met en route. It worked, and the US ambassador Brand Whitlock speedily identified him. The reporter left Brussels on a train that took him through the burning remains of Louvain ('War upon the defenceless,' he called it, 'war upon churches, colleges, shops of milliners and lacemakers; war brought to the bedside and fireside; against women harvesting in the field, against children in wooden shoes at play in the streets'); and then he stood in Rheims Cathedral while German shells splintered the ancient roof and stained-glass windows. But, deprived of a permit that would allow him to cover the front and appalled at the restrictions placed on reporters, he sailed back to New York, declaring that the days of the war correspondent were over.

A year later he was lured back again. He arrived in Paris in late October 1915, went to the front at Amiens and Artois, and, two weeks later, left for Salonika, from where he covered the Balkan campaign. There were no rooms to be had, but despite sharing accommodation with five other correspondents, he was able to keep up some of the old standards, bathing each morning in his portable tub, and dressing formally for what passed for dinner each evening. This time, it really was the last hurrah for the old-style gentleman correspondent. In April 1916, shortly after returning to America from Salonika, he suffered a heart attack while dictating a telegram over the telephone, and died a week short of his 52nd birthday. He left a young widow and a one-year-old daughter called Hope.

Today, nearly a century after his death, Davis seems to some as he must have done to those tobacco chewers toiling away at the copyediting face in the newspapers to whom he filed: a playboy journalist recounting the ripping yarns of the Progressive Era. But the best of his writing is timeless in its sentiment and still fresh in the force of its descriptions. Partly this was a matter of talent, but mainly it was a matter of sweat. Davis was one of the great rewriters and fiddlers, and his method of describing something was to do so initially at length, and then question each line, eliminating any deemed inessential, asking himself at each turn 'Does the picture remain?' As a way of producing tight, pacy reporting, it has a lot of merit, especially if combined with that other great hallmark of the restless Davis, that of never being truly satisfied with anything he wrote. For all his money, aristocratic connections, hand-tooled luggage, portable bathtub and dressing for dinner, Davis was a pro. Like all great reporters, each story was, for him, not so much a stage on which to perform as a responsibility to be carried out.

J.A. MacGahan

7

J.A. MacGahan
1844–1878

PERPETRATOR OF PERHAPS THE GREATEST SINGLE
PIECE OF REPORTING EVER

Every year a small group of people gathers in the Ohio town of New Lexington to honour the memory of a reporter born more than 150 years ago. They congregate, among other places, across Main Street from the Perry County Courthouse, around a statue in reddish stone of the journalist. It is not the only monument to this man. Six thousand miles away, in Bulgaria, there are other statues; five towns contain streets named after him, portraits of him hang in schools and museums, children learn his name in class, encyclopaedias and history books tell his story, and there are churches where his name is regularly remembered in prayers by distant descendants of those who were alive when he came to their land. Journalism, however, has virtually forgotten him. No awards exist in his name, and there are no libraries, colleges, halls of residence or any other tangible sign that he is valued by his own trade. I doubt if one journalism student in 10,000 knows his name. This is unsettling, to say the least, because he is, quite probably, the perpetrator of the greatest piece of reporting of all time.

What makes this so is not the quality of its writing, research and attention to detail – high though they all are – but its impact. This series of stories uncovered a campaign of genocide by one people against another, proved two governments to have been systematically lying, provoked a tide of revulsion that swept the civilised world, and so led to the declaration of a war, the redrawing of the map of Europe, the creation of four new nations and the electoral defeat of a British prime minister. No other single piece of reporting comes close in its effect; and it was all the work of an Irish-American reporter born 32 years before in a place of otherwise empty insignificance called Pigeon Roost Ridge, Ohio.

He was Januarius Aloysius MacGahan, not a by-line that modern newspaper typography would welcome, but a name that was entirely typical of the time of his birth: June 1844. His father died when he was seven, and from then until the age of 16, the young MacGahan worked on the family farm in the summer and attended school in the winter. Whatever the shortcomings of an education confined to the colder months of the year, MacGahan was, by 1860, sharp enough to be employed as a junior teacher in Hartington, Illinois, where he learnt book-keeping and then turned it into his main occupation. That took him to St Louis, a course at a business college, and the gradual dawning of an ambition to be a lawyer. By the age of 24, he was in Europe studying international law, and perfecting a self-taught facility at German and French. He was about to leave for home when his linguistic ability attracted the attention of the *New York Herald*, and he was asked if he could act as the paper's special correspondent covering the Franco-Prussian War. The law was immediately forgotten; from now on MacGahan was to know no other life but adventure and war.

For the next six years, MacGahan reported from the battlefields of France, the Paris Commune (where he was arrested as a communist, condemned to death and only saved by the intercession of the US ambassador), the court of St Petersburg, Central Asia, London, Cuba, the Arctic, the Caucasus and Spain, where once again it needed a US diplomat to rescue him from a potential execution. In 1873 he defied a Russian embargo on reporters to make a remarkable ride over the Central Asian steppes. His goal was to catch up with a Russian military expedition on its way to Turkestan. Cossacks bent on his destruction pursued him for nearly a thousand miles but, after 29 days, accompanied by two attendants, sometimes forced to wade knee-deep in sand and several times lost, he reached the camp, joined the Russian forces and covered their subsequent campaign. His *Daily News* colleague Archibald Forbes described this ride as 'the greatest feat of war correspondence in history'. By way of an encore, he joined the crew of the *Pandora* and sailed through the Arctic's ice-choked waters in a wooden boat.

By the late spring of 1876, the 32-year-old reporter was in London with his Russian-born wife, Barbara, and their young son Paul. He was planning a book and some rest, but his relaxation was short-lived. News began to filter through to London that an uprising by the Bulgarians against their Turkish rulers had been put down with a brutality that beggared belief. The first word of these atrocities was published in the *Daily News*, a prominent liberal paper whose Constantinople correspondent, Edwin Pears, had sent telegrams speaking of 'dark rumours' that anything between 18,000 and 30,000 Bulgarian villagers had been butchered by the Turks and their mercenaries. The *News* published the first of these messages on 8 June, with small amplifications following on the 23rd and 30th. The British Foreign Office was furious. So, too, was the pro-Turkish Prime Minister, Benjamin Disraeli. Describing the reports as 'coffee-house babble', he flatly denied them and openly charged the paper with misreporting and, that old standard whine of politicians, 'irresponsibility'. The Turks, who had imposed a total censorship on events, dismissed the talk of atrocities as 'sensationalism'.

The *News* was now in some trouble. The paper either had to prove its charges, or humiliatingly climb down. So it sent for MacGahan (who had earlier tried – and failed – to interest both the *New York Herald* and London *Times* in the story) and commissioned him to go to Bulgaria and try to discover the truth. By early July he was on his way, and by the 23rd of the month he was there, investigating and interviewing hundreds of survivors. What he found was beyond even his hardened imaginings: the frenzied and wholesale butchery of at least 15,000 Bulgarian men, women and children. In the first of his despatches, published by the *News* on 28 July, MacGahan wrote in a preamble:

> I think I came in a fair and impartial frame of mind... I fear I am no longer impartial, and I am certainly no longer cool... I have already investigated enough to feel convinced that, except from a purely statistical point of view, further investigation would be unnecessary... The atrocities admitted... by those friendly to the Turks, and by the Turks themselves, are enough, and more than enough. I do not care to go on heaping up the mournful count... 60 or 70 villages have been burned... some 15,000 people have been slaughtered, of whom a large part are women and children...

MacGahan then travelled the countryside to see for himself if the survivors' tales were accurate. They were, and none more so than in the case of Batak, a village, before the Turk's mercenaries visited it, of 900 homes and 8,000 to 9,000 people. Despite his earlier remarks about impartiality and although his later despatches were full of bile for Disraeli and British policy, MacGahan's central account of what he found in the village is a model of how the cool collection of facts, rather than emotional grandstanding, is the most effective form of reporting. His story, written in haste on 2 August right after visiting the village, has the immediacy that his rewritten and collected accounts (published in pamphlet form a month later and which are quoted in some anthologies), somehow lack.

He began: 'Since my letter of yesterday I have supped full of horrors...,' and continued:

... At last we came to a little plateau or shelf on the hillside, where the ground was nearly level, with the exception of a little indentation, where the head of a hollow broke through. We rode toward this... but all suddenly drew rein... for right before us, almost beneath our horses' feet, was a sight that made us shudder. It was a heap of skulls, intermingled with bones from all parts of the human body, skeletons nearly entire and rotting, clothing, human hair and putrid flesh lying there in one foul heap, around which the grass was growing luxuriantly... We observed that they were all small and that the articles of clothing intermingled with them and lying about were all women's apparel... I counted about a hundred skulls, not including those that were hidden beneath the others in the ghastly heap nor those that were scattered far and wide through the fields. The skulls were nearly all separated from the rest of the bones... These women had all been beheaded.

... Now we began to approach the church and the school-house. The ground is covered here with skeletons, to which are clinging articles of clothing and bits of putrid flesh... The school-house, to judge by the walls that are part standing, was a fine large building capable of accommodating 200 or 300 children. Beneath the stones and rubbish that cover the floor to the height of several feet are the bones and ashes of 200 women and children, burned alive between these four walls. Just beside the school-house is a broad, shallow pit. Here were buried 200 bodies two weeks after the massacre. But the dogs uncovered them in part. The water flowed in, and now it lies there a horrid cesspool, with human remains floating about or lying half exposed in the mud. Nearby, on the banks of the little stream that runs through the village, is a saw mill. The wheel pit beneath is full of dead bodies floating in the water. The banks of this stream were at one time covered with the corpses of men and women, young girls and children... But... the little stream swelled and rose up and carried the bodies away and strewed them far down its grassy banks, through its narrow gorges and dark defiles, beneath the thick underbrush and shady woods, as far as Pesterea and even Tartar Bazardjik, forty miles distant.

... We entered the church yard, but here the odour became so bad that it was almost impossible to proceed. We take a handful of tobacco and hold it against our noses while we continue... The church was not a very large one, and it was surrounded by a low stone wall, enclosing a small churchyard about fifty yards wide by seventy-five long. At first we perceive nothing in particular... but we see that the place is heaped up with stones and rubbish to the height of five or six feet above the level of the street, and upon inspection we discover that what appeared to be a mass of stones and rubbish is in reality an immense heap of human bodies covered over with a thin layer of stones. The whole of the little churchyard is heaped up with them to the depth of three or four feet...

We are told that 3,000 people were lying in this little churchyard alone... There were little curly heads there in that festering mass, crushed down by heavy stones, little feet not as long as your finger, on which the flesh was dried hard by the ardent heat before it had time to decompose; little baby hands, stretched out as if for help; babes that had died wondering at the bright gleam of the sabres and the red eyes of the fierce-eyed men who wielded them; children who had died weeping and sobbing, and begging for mercy; mothers who had died trying to shield their little ones with their own weak bodies, all lying there together, festering in one horrid mass. They are silent enough now. There are no tears nor cries, no weeping, no shrieks of terror, nor prayers for mercy. The harvests are rotting in the fields and the reapers are rotting here in the churchyard.

We looked into the church, which had been blackened by the burning of the woodwork... An immense number of bodies had been partly burned there and the charred and blackened remains that seemed to fill up half way to the low, dark arches and make them lower and darker still were lying in a state of putrefaction ... We walked about the place and saw the same things repeated over and over again a hundred times... Here they show us a house where twenty people were buried alive; there another where a dozen girls had taken refuge and been slaughtered to the last one as their bones amply testified. Everywhere horrors upon horrors. Of the 8,000 to 9,000 people who made up the population of the place only 1,200 to 1,500 are left, and they have neither tools to dig graves with, nor strength to use spades if they had them.

... We asked about the skulls and bones we had seen upon the hill... These, we were told, were the bodies of 200 young girls who had first been captured and particularly reserved for a worse fate. They had been kept till the last; they had been in the hands of their captors for several days – for the burning and pillaging had not all been accomplished in a single day – and during this time they had suffered all that poor, weak, trembling girls could suffer at the hands of the brutal savages. Then, when the town had been pillaged and burned, when all their friends had been slaughtered, these poor young things, whose very wrongs should have insured them safety, whose very outrages should have insured them protection, were taken in the broad light of day, beneath the smiling canopy of heaven, cooly beheaded, then thrown in a heap there and left to rot.

MacGahan's reports, according to Edwin Pears, 'struck the British public like a thunderbolt'. Scores of public meetings were held, and, as indignation spread across the Western world, the British government was forced to concede the truth of MacGahan's reports. Pressure for military intervention built up, and, in the spring of 1877, Russia launched a war against Turkey. The British stayed neutral, an inconceivable state of affairs before MacGahan had reported. As he wrote to his mother just before the outbreak of war: 'I can safely say I have done more to smash up the Turkish empire than anybody else... except the Turks themselves.'

Eighty correspondents arrived to cover the Russian side but such were the rigours of the campaign that by its end, less than a year later, only four of the original reporters were still in the field. MacGahan, of course, was among them. He had gone off to war with one foot in plaster, after injuring it in a fall. He ignored this, and the fracturing anew of the half-set ankle bone when his horse fell on him meant that in the latter stages of the war he had to be carried to the touchline of the action on a gun carriage. Six months and two treaties later, the nations of Bulgaria, Serbia, Montenegro and Romania had come into being, Russia was enlarged and the British had Cyprus.

MacGahan, however, was not alive to report it. A few weeks after the end of the war, he was in Constantinople recovering from the campaign. A friend, Francis Greene, contracted typhoid fever, and MacGahan, despite his own debilitated state, went to nurse him. Greene survived, but MacGahan caught typhus, a more dangerous disease than typhoid, and on 9 June he died, three days short of his 34th birthday. He was buried, to the accompaniment of the uncontrollable weeping of his friend, the Russian general, Mikhail Skobelev, at Pera, masses were said for his soul in St Petersburg, and he was mourned, too, in London, Paris and America. Six years later his body was borne across the Atlantic by an American warship and brought to New York, where it lay in state in City Hall, and then again in the capitol building in Columbus, Ohio, before being carried to its final resting place in Maplewood Cemetery, New Lexington. His wife, who had become the Russian correspondent of the *New York Herald*, crossed the ocean with her husband's body, settled in America with her son, and wrote successfully for a wide range of American and Russian papers. Later that same year an official inquiry confirmed, in the cool calm of hindsight, everything that MacGahan had written from the killing fields of Bulgaria.

Nearly a decade later, according to Dale Walker's *Januarius MacGahan, The Life and Campaigns of An American War Correspondent*, a friend of MacGahan's widow went to the World's Columbian Exposition in Chicago, and, during his tour, came to the Bulgarian exhibition stand. Seeing an official standing there, he asked the man if he was Bulgarian and whether he had ever heard of Januarius MacGahan. 'I shall answer that', the man replied, 'by inquiring if you are an American and if so, if you have ever heard of Washington, Lincoln or Grant. What you think of these immortal heroes, we think of MacGahan.' If the forgetful trade of journalism had a conscience, those words should still sting.

8
James Cameron
1911–1985

THE DEFINITIVE FOREIGN CORRESPONDENT

Journalism training began more than a century ago, and there are now thousands of people in Britain and the United States fulfilling some sort of function in this field. It will, one hopes, come as a sobering thought to them, that of the 13 reporters in this book, only two have passed through their halls of learning.

This is recorded not so much as a comment on the quality of formal education and journalism training as on the futility of it when it comes to producing truly outstanding reporters. Although other characters in this book illustrate the point (fewer than half are graduates), no journalist better represents the baffling appearance in one relatively uneducated person of the mental equipment and talent required for greatness than James Cameron, widely considered as the wisest news reporter that Britain ever produced.

His formal education was almost shockingly haphazard. It ended at 16, and he then spent a dozen or so years working for publications about as far removed from mainstream news reporting as you can get. And yet, like some ugly duckling of the world of print, he emerged, after the interval of a few years copyediting in London, as the sharpest, most stylish and

James Cameron

thoughtful reporter of his day. In time, his voice became that of the definitive foreign correspondent – a magnificent instrument of scepticism, matured in the cask of years of serious whisky and tobacco consumption, but never so world weary that he stopped ferreting out revealing incongruities and telling absurdities, or finding fresh ways to describe what he saw.

Cameron was born, in Battersea, south London, in 1911 to a couple, the bread-winning half of which was a disillusioned barrister who had turned to serial and novel writing. He thus grew up in a household that held literature in greater esteem than the law, a judgement which, for the rest of his life, Cameron saw no reason to modify. That his home had a bookish atmosphere was perhaps just as well, so erratic was his schooling. For much of his childhood, his parents lived, not in England, but, for economy's sake, in Brittany, France. He therefore attended the local village school, giving him great fluency in a second language, but little by way of structured learning. His most vivid classroom memory was a traumatic one. A schoolmaster who had served on the Western Front would occasionally harangue his little charges about the horrors he had seen. Unbeknown to the young Cameron, he had a false arm, and one afternoon was so caught in the passion of his speech to the class that he tore the arm from its moorings, brandished it above his head like an axe, and then brought it crashing down on Cameron's desk. The future war correspondent nearly fainted.

He grew up quickly, however, since both parents became, in their different ways, increasingly like a pair of dependant children. His mother developed acute anaemia and a reliance on the drugs she was prescribed; his father, meanwhile, suffered from asthma and was much given to drink. Thus, by the time Cameron entered his teens they were both a bit of a worry, and by the age of 16, Cameron had seen his mother become first bedridden and then die, and his father's writing make such limited profits that it could no longer support the boy at school. So it was that Cameron headed to Manchester, and the offices of the *Weekly News*, where he was employed, at £3 a month, as a filler of paste pots, sharpener of pencils and runner of errands. After a year or so, he was transferred to Dundee in Scotland – not the most uplifting of locations at the best of times, and the early 1930s were assuredly not those. One of the few businesses not struggling and laying off staff was the one he worked for: D.C. Thomson, publisher of newspapers, comics, weekly serial papers, and, for generations, a by-word for backward and conservative employment policies. Its head, David Couper Thomson, would not knowingly allow Roman Catholics on the premises, and his resistance to trade unions so infected his firm that long after his death in 1954 his successors refused to even recognise their existence. It is entirely consistent with their attitudes that the firm would not permit news to replace advertisements on the front page of its flagship paper, the *Dundee Courier*, until 1992, one of the very last in the Western world to make this change.

Among Thomson's titles, apart from newspapers, were children's comics; weeklies like *The People's Friend*, which peddled stories so sentimental they would even make a *Reader's Digest* editor gag; and cheap papers that relied for much of their content on a bizarre combination of cute animals and sordid crime. Cameron worked on one of the latter, *Red Star Weekly*, and in his autobiography, *Point of Departure*, he described its editorial policy:

> The most frightful things were encouraged to happen: stranglings, knifings, shootings, disembowellings, burials alive, hauntings, drownings, suffocations, torments of a rich and varied nature abounded, and each instalment was obliged to end in a suspenseful promise of worse to come, but in no circumstances and at no point was permitted even the hint of sexual impropriety.

Armed with this manifesto, Cameron had to sift through the week's stories for an episode so eye-catchingly grotesque that it would make the basis for that issue's cover illustration. One week, his eye fell upon the story of a serial killer cutting a wide swathe through a city's nubile young women. It was called 'The Man With the Glaring Eyes', and Cameron, naturally, chose the messiest of its murders to send to the artist. Back it duly came, and Cameron was most gratified by the result. It portrayed, he later wrote,

> a deeply sinister back-alley by night, lit only by the baleful gleam of an eerie street lamp, whose sickly beam threw into prominence a foreground of damp and lowering paving stones, on which lay the true purpose of the composition: the body of a young woman, her throat most palpably cut from ear to ear.

Preening himself on his selection, Cameron took it along to Mr David Donald, editor.

> When he saw it he blenched. He tore it from my hand and studied it aghast, and in speechless outrage. Finally he said: 'You must be mad!' Accepting that I might possibly on this occasion have overdone it, I murmured: 'It is a bit strong, maybe.' 'Strong, strong!' cried Mr Donald, 'It's no' a question of strong; it's no a bad scene. But for God's sake, boy – look at the lassie's skirt; it awa' above her knee.' I took the drawing back and had the hemline lowered a modest inch or two and in the cover went, slit windpipe and all.

Satisfaction must generally have been given, however, for by the age of 24, Cameron had been transferred to Glasgow and the *Sunday Post*. This was, by any standards, an extraordinary paper. Its pithy news, crimes stories in the Scottish vernacular and sentimental features gave it such a rapport with its audience that it was read by four out of every five adults in Scotland. Its non-union policy meant that Cameron had an against-the-deadline crash course in almost every branch of journalism. He might, for instance, in the course of a Saturday, go off to do a light report on a rugby match, or meeting of the Church of Scotland, return to the office, copyedit the article, draw a sketch to illustrate it (he was a talented caricaturist), write its headline and picture caption, proofread the piece, and then go down to the composing room and oversee its make-up on the 'stone' (the metal bench upon which pages of metal type were assembled in the days before computerisation). Then he would spend the rest of the night on the general subbing desk.

Most of his week, however, was spent writing the cloying first-person confession features of which the *Post*'s readership was so fond.

> I would assume [he later wrote] the character of 'A Feckless Wife', 'A Henpecked Husband', 'Wee Wully', 'Always a Wallflower', or 'A Bairn Without A Name'. Everything had to be written in paragraphs one sentence long and, as far as possible in the homely idiom of the Scottish working class.

On other occasions, he might be required to ghost-write the life story of a prominent boxer or royal servant, take on animal form and write as 'Percy the Poodle' or 'An Unloved Alley Cat', or even pen the memoirs of Scotland's more entertaining criminals or their relatives. It was, more than once, left to Cameron to compose the words that would appear underneath the headline 'Why My Son Should Not Hang'. His writing didn't end there. His father's drinking and bronchial condition had now brought him so low that he could no longer write the stories that provided his meagre income. So Cameron wrote them for him, congratulating himself on the fact that the subterfuge remain undetected (it had not, it was just that the publishers had too much grace to say so).

By now he had moved to the Scottish edition of the *Daily Express* as a down-table sub and was married, with a young wife in the advanced stages of pregnancy. Then came May 1940, a month that was to cast a shadow over Cameron for the rest of his life. First his father died, and then, a week or so later his wife, Elma, went into labour. He was just finishing his Saturday shift at the paper when the call came for him to go to the hospital. He arrived moments after his wife died in childbirth. At the age of 28 he was a widower with a baby daughter, and, a short while later, was spurned for military service on the grounds of a hitherto unknown heart defect. It is not hard to see why he accepted the offer of a transfer to the London office of the *Express*, placed his daughter in the temporary care of his in-laws, and hurried south as fast as the wartime railway service would allow.

He very soon became deputy chief sub at the *Express*, a promotion that he always ascribed to a wartime shortage of alternative candidates. With paper rationing reducing the paper to four or six pages, the job of copyediting was to distil every story so the maximum amount of information could be shoe-horned into the severely restricted space. Night after night, Cameron deconstructed stories and reassembled them in their pithiest form. It was a priceless apprenticeship in news journalism, but he loathed it. He badgered his editor repeatedly for a chance to write, until, finally – either because other options were away in uniform, or someone had the wit to recognise his talent – he got his chance. He excelled, and, in a very short while, the man who not a few years before was wringing the last vestiges of emotion from some mawkish tale of Scottish domestic tragedy was a foreign correspondent for his country's leading paper.

One of his first tasks was to go to India to report on the moves towards independence, and he had barely got to grips with that when, in the summer of 1946, word came through that he had been selected to be one of the three British observers at American atom bomb tests on Bikini Atoll. Here, on this coral outcrop in the Pacific, the Americans had two diabolical experiments to perform. In the first, a B-29 nicknamed 'Dave's Dream' dropped a bomb christened 'Gilda' on 87 defunct ships of the US Navy. In the second, a nuclear bomb would be exploded underneath the sea. Although the noise of the first was impressive ('... thudding into all the corners of the morning like a great door slammed in the deepest hollows of the sea...'), Cameron found the effects of the second infinitely more terrifying, writing, on 30 June:

> Now we have seen it. Down below the surface of the Bikini Lagoon this morning the first atomic bomb ever to be detonated under the sea has just gone off with what must be the most startling and extraordinary explosion ever contrived by the curiosity of man.
>
> ... Precisely at zero hour the bowstring line, where the sea met the sky, trembled and swelled in a vast gleaming dome of sheerest white. Through binoculars – I am rather less than ten miles away and the morning is crystal clear – it looked for the minutest fraction of a second like a grotesque bubble, then forces inside it strained and burst through in the most enormous fountain ever manufactured.
>
> At the very least a million tons of the Pacific Ocean leaped vertically in a sheer column more than half a mile wide, reaching up, it seemed, indefinitely into the clouds. It climbed lazily up till in about a minute it was nearly two miles high, then it hesitated, and dropped like a mountainous snowman into the seething boiling cauldron that is Bikini Lagoon...

These experiences horrified Cameron. He became, as he put it, 'the first atom bomb bore' and was later a founder of the Campaign for Nuclear Disarmament.

For now, though, in the late 1940s, the only association he was a member of was that most privileged of journalistic sets: the foreign correspondent in the age of intercontinental air travel but before the heyday of television. It was the final flourish, as Cameron put it, of 'show-off journalism, where nowhere was too remote nor too expensive'. And nor, at that time, were there any greater bunch of spendthrifts than the foreign desk of the *Daily Express*. It wasn't so much that expense was, to them, no object; it was simply of no concern. In just a few years, Cameron was despatched to South Asia, South America, Germany, Thailand, France, Burma, Indonesia, the Caribbean, Patagonia, South Africa, Afghanistan, Tibet, Australia – in some cases, not once but several times, and not always to any great purpose. As Cameron said:

It gave Charles [Foley, the *Express*'s foreign editor] great pleasure to devise for me abrupt and intricate changes of location all over the world involving logistical problems of great complexity and expense, and it gave me pleasure to accomplish them, as often as not to no greater end than our mutual gratification at the solution of a problem.

Where there were crises or the *Express* could not think of a reason for him to immediately turn round and head elsewhere, Cameron stayed and reported. From the Berlin Airlift on 22 July 1948, he filed:

Once again this evening as we stumble blindly home by candlelight, with aircraft rumbling incessantly overhead, it is all too like the days gone by.

... Berlin continues its grotesque representation of rational life – shabby, dowdy, wan, ridden by day-to-day problems, flogging this and fiddling that, trying to turn a baffling confusion of currency into the odd pfennig's worth of profit to themselves...

And from Peron's Argentina in March 1949:

For years past, Argentina has been a political madhouse, but until Peron it was at least rich.

... How can you impoverish a country of such unlimited agricultural wealth – a country with twelve feet of solid alluvial topsoil where no fertiliser is ever used or needed, where cattle roam over endless prairies without shelter or need of it, fattening on alfalfa all the year round, a country the size of Europe supporting a population less than twice the size of London?

How would you ruin such a place? Well Peron and his Government have nearly managed it.

With his wry, commenty style, the wonder was that a paper as right wing as the *Express* tolerated Cameron's bolshie, anti-Imperialist views for as long as it did. But then, as he explained:

My relationship with the newspaper could only be likened to that of a very remote and insignificant curate to the Holy See: I accepted their authority and paid no attention at all to their doctrine.

Not that he was perennially uppity. From Malta, whose collective courage during the war was recognised by the whole island being awarded Britain's top civilian award for gallantry, the George Cross, he once filed a piece charting the hardship its people were undergoing. It was entitled 'You Can't Eat The George Cross', and shortly after it was published he was summoned to the London flat of Lord Beaverbrook, the *Express*'s Conservative proprietor. The subject of Malta came up, and Beaverbrook proceeded to read out Cameron's recent article to him, apparently unaware that the work was that of the young man seated opposite. The piece concluded, he then added:

> That is the kind of work I wish to see in my newspapers. You are a young correspondent... Let me tell you that if you can learn to write articles in that manner there will be a future for you with my newspaper. Take it with you and study it. Goodbye to you.

Cited sometimes as an example of Beaverbrook's eccentricity, more likely it shows how awkward he found it to praise someone to their face.

Sooner or later, however, either the ownership was going to tread too heavily on its highly principled reporter's toes, or he on its; and the inevitable came in the spring of 1950. The *Express*'s sister paper, the *Evening Standard*, did what many papers do on a slow news day: it constructed a follow-up to a recent major story by finding an as-yet unexplored, political angle. And the reason this particular angle was virgin territory was that no other paper had thought of being so deceitful. The bare bones were these: Klaus Fuchs, the Communist atom physicist, had just been convicted of spying for the Russians, and this coincided with the appointment as War Minister of John Strachey, a socialist intellectual who had once written sympathetically of Soviet communism. Conflating these facts, together with total disregard for the fact that Strachey had several times repudiated his old views, gave the *Standard*, on 2 March, the following headline: 'Fuchs and Strachey: A Great

New Crisis. War Minister has Never Disavowed Communism'. There, cited in the article, were a couple of quotes from Strachey's old books, plus, of course, that tell-tale sign of the confected row story, ritual calls for an inquiry from whichever predictable rent-a-mouths could be found in the time available. The *News Chronicle*, *Observer* and *Guardian* led the protests at this sly trick, Cameron agreed with them, and, when his own paper rallied to the *Standard*'s cause, he called a family meeting, resigned from the *Express*, and wrote a letter to *The Times* explaining why:

> We have now set the precedent for the purge-by-Press, which could end at last only in a race of people talking behind their hands, knowing that the words they said yesterday, in a very different world mood, are the words they may swing for tomorrow.

Cameron was soon hired by *Picture Post*, a weekly that, like *Life* in the States, mixed high-grade photography and articles with a certain amount of whimsy. In late summer of 1950, editor Tom Hopkinson sent him and photographer Bert Hardy off to cover the Korean War. On 15 September, Cameron was part of the Inchon Landings, General MacArthur's vast version of Normandy 1944 that was aimed at slicing the North Korean forces in two. Cameron and Hardy went ashore on day one, and from there he filed:

> In the middle of it all, if you can conceive of such a thing, there was a wandering boat, marked in great letters PRESS, full of agitated and contending correspondents, all trying to appear insistently determined to land in Wave One, while contriving desperately to be found in Wave Fifty.
>
> ... The North Koreans lost their beach-head, they lost their town, they lost their lives in numbers, and with them the lives of many simple people who shared the common misfortune of many simple people before them, who had the ill-luck to live in places which people in War Rooms decided to smash... Sitting here, one is glad to be alive – a bit ashamed maybe, but glad.

What also horrified him was that the South Koreans (the Americans' allies in the crusade against communism) rather compromised their side's avowed cause of freedom by detaining, abusing and killing large numbers of what it described as political prisoners. Cameron discovered that these 'dissidents' were largely nothing of the kind: mostly people caught in the wrong place, and some of them, as he wrote, 'as much as 12 years old':

> They have been in jail now for indeterminate periods – long enough to have reduced their frames to skeletons, their sinews to string, their faces to a translucent terrible grey, their spirit to that of cringing dogs. They are roped and manacled. They are compelled to crouch in the classic Oriental attitude of subjection in pools of garbage. They clamber, the lowest common denominator of personal degradation, into trucks with the numb air of men going to their death. Many of them are.

He didn't file this immediately, but researched until he had exhausted all avenues, and presented his evidence to the United Nations (under whose auspices the anti-Communist forces were fighting). It was only when he got the brush-off from them that he and Hardy returned home and, with the aid of *Picture Post* editor Tom Hopkinson, constructed what Cameron called 'a journalistic essay of elaborate moderation'. The article, headed 'An Appeal to the United Nations' was actually on the presses when the paper's proprietor Edward G. Hulton ordered them stopped. He would not, he insisted, have his magazine used to besmirch the West's allies with 'communist propaganda'. There was a flurry of comings, goings and meetings, but the upshot was that Hopkinson was fired, Cameron in due course resigned, and *Picture Post* was never the same again. Its sales, which were 1,380,000 copies a week when Cameron left, fell to 935,000 within eighteen months, and, with content shorn of all seriousness, were scraping along at 600,000 when it finally closed in 1957.

The controversial article was a rare instance of Cameron providing a scoop. He was not, as a rule, a story-getter, or even a writer of conventional news stories, but a reporter of situations and a finder of ironies and horrors within them. He had an elegiac turn of phrase (evident even in his earliest traceable pieces from the 1930s), and this, coupled with his shrewd judgement of situations, gave him considerable leeway in what he wrote. Cameron never had much time for objectivity, his explanation being:

> It has always seemed to me that a reporter involved, however fortuitously, in a situation concerning genuine ethical values will find this famous 'objectivity' not only virtually impossible, but even maybe undesirable.

It is a point of view rather more convincingly put by someone of Cameron's experience than by greener hands inclined to use it as an alibi for not doing the required researching and thinking.

After *Picture Post*, Cameron moved on to the liberal *News Chronicle*. He said this was his happiest relationship with any paper, and it is not difficult to see why. He was surrounded by like-minded colleagues (i.e. they were intelligent, left-leaning and slightly raffish), and the paper underwrote the costs of him reporting from more or less anywhere he wanted to go. This was invariably the big crisis, calamity or conflict – what he called 'lowering situations' – of which there was no great shortage for the next two decades. He covered the Indo-China War; Franco's Spain; the Mau-Mau in Kenya; the Hungarian Uprising; the Algerian War; the flight into exile of the Dalai Lama; the trials of Jomo Kenyatta, Adolf Eichmann, and Nelson Mandela; the Suez Crisis; party political conferences, presidential conventions, peace talks, war talks; and the fall of the French Fourth Republic. And, inevitably, when there was an atom bomb to be tested, there Cameron would be, even if it meant a bit of a wait. His preview piece on Britain's weapon, from Woomera, Australia in 1953, began:

Time continues to limp along; it has been a long way to come for something that is alleged to last one threehundred-thousandth part of a second.

Light moments were, after all, hard to come by, and even when some softer interlude had been arranged, it might not always go according to plan. In 1958, for instance, by way of a change from bloodshed and apocalypse, he was assigned to interview Liz Taylor, then at the peak of her fame and marriageability. Off he went to one of London's posher hotels, and the vision from Hollywood greeted him in her negligee and with champagne at the ready. She gushed, leant forward a few times lest the magnetism of her personality be insufficient, and Cameron was so charmed that it was some while before he popped the first real question. How, he asked, are the economics of Hollywood affecting you? Miss Taylor's reply shook him. 'Well fuck that! What about your proposals for a new contract?' She had mistaken him for a fancy movie agent, the interview was over before it started, and Cameron, as he later wrote, 'found himself out on the landing in no time'.

With similar abruptness the staff of the *News Chronicle* were informed one day in October 1960 that the edition they were working on would be the last. Its sales were still an impressive million, but its owners, the wealthy Cadbury family, decided its losses were too great to recoup, and closed it. To British journalists of a certain age, it thus became a kind of newspaper version of Buddy Holly, cut down before its time and all the more subsequently legendary for that. Cameron put it more succinctly. 'The basic cause of death', he later wrote, 'was a simple thrombosis, defined as when an active circulation is impeded by clots.'

He vowed he would never attach himself to the staff of any newspaper again, and he never did, working instead for the *Daily Mail*, *Evening Standard*, *Daily Herald*, the *Atlantic*, *New Statesman*, *Harper's Bazaar*, *Sunday Telegraph*, the *Observer* and the *Guardian*. The result was less international ambulance-chasing, and more variety. He interviewed Ho Chi Minh, and Fidel Castro (the great leader, having reneged on several appointments suddenly appeared one night, plus bodyguards, in Cameron's hotel room, sat on his bed and began talking); covered the erection of the Berlin Wall; successive Middle East crises and conflicts; the Peasant Leagues of Brazil; Luther King's 'I have a dream...' speech; the Harlem Riots of 1964; India's tribulations; colonial struggles from Africa to Cyprus; and Vietnam from both sides. He wrote on early space shots:

> The apocalyptic picture of Lieut.-Colonel John Glenn that haunted every front page yesterday should be (and probably will be) preserved as a symbol of man's endurance, desperation, courage, arrogance, and blind dedication to the awful rigours of international oneupmanship. (29 January 1962)

He covered the aftermath of John F. Kennedy's assassination in 1963, making it from his London home to Dallas in nine hours, and then, still half-catching his breath, wrote this from the 26 November funeral:

> Today in the coffin of John Fitzgerald Kennedy they buried the New Frontier and the reign of youth, the hopes unfulfilled and a life untimely quenched.
>
> Three brief days ago he was a young and zealous man with breath in his body and life in his heart, perhaps the most powerful of politicians. Today he was something to be carried through the streets to the thud of muffled drums, in such immense state and circumstance as no dead man as ever had before.
>
> ... Thus is gone President John Kennedy, who should have died hereafter, for he had much to do that may not now be done. He was killed by hate and folly, but today he was buried with love.

During the Vietnam War, he became the first Western reporter to be admitted to Hanoi, determined to see for himself if the North was, as the Americans said, full of demons; or, as the Communists maintained, populated solely by heroes:

> When the sirens go these days there is a difference: the shelters are made of earth and seem built for children, the loudspeakers

chatter their warnings and exhortations in Vietnamese, so I am
unable to distinguish whether I am being urged to run like hell or
merely improve my production.

... There is practically no private civilian motor traffic in
the North, but what exists is like all military transport, heavily
camouflaged under piles of branches, palm fronds, banana leaves.
Even in the towns this phenomenon continues, cars and lorries
buried in greenery; Birnam Wood forever coming to Dunsinane.

The people, too – every citizen goes for his military exercises
with a cape of vegetation hanging about his shoulders. It is,
perhaps, taken slightly to excess: the cult of camouflage has
become in a way modish... The buses have rationalised the whole
thing by being spray-painted in a formal pattern of foliage, like
Oriental wallpaper.

And he was there for the Six-Day War and its pitiful
aftermath:

... Yesterday I went on the first survey of the whole peninsula,
perhaps one of the biggest single battlefields ever known, the place
where the Egyptian Army died. In a lifetime not too unfamiliar with
such things I have never seen anything like this... An Egyptian force
of five infantry and two armoured divisions abruptly eliminated;
an army of some ninety thousand or more men disintegrated,
with some tens of thousands killed or captured, or left, ignored,
to wander and struggle somehow or other in the general direction
of anywhere. Several million pounds worth of extremely expensive
and sophisticated military ironmongery now reduced to booty or
to crushed and blackened scrap. The tanks and vehicles litter the
desert like the nursery floor of an angry child.

Israel was one of the two places for whom he had feelings
that verged on the paternal. He was in at the country's birth
in the late 1940s, as he was with that of his other great love,
India. Although he was not naturally a schmoozer of the great
and occasionally good, he formed warm relationships with
leading figures in both countries. In Israel it was Moshe Dayan,
the general who was the architect of Israel's victory in the Six-
Day War; and in India it was Nehru and, later, his daughter,
Indira, also prime minister. India, especially, drew him back

repeatedly, as if he was some constantly migrating bird and this was his best-loved winter feeding ground. It was here, in 1971, that he had the serious car crash that nearly killed him, and here that he found his third and final wife. The two events were linked by his honeymoon, a holiday interrupted by news of hostilities breaking out between Pakistan and India. Cameron, on the grounds that it was 'against the rules for any conflict to start without me', said goodbye to his wife of a few days, went north to Bengal, and his car was hit by a truck. He was the sole survivor of the crash, but the legacy was heart trouble that led to a by-pass operation.

As time wore on, he became more than ever a writer of 'situationers', articles that examined some overseas circumstance rather than reported its blow-by-blow development. It was a natural progression from these to television documentaries, and he made a number for the BBC, always looking so much the sure-footed foreign correspondent that he could have been supplied by Central Casting. As a tracking shot closed in on a crowded Delhi street or chaotic souk, there would be Cameron, wandering quizzically along in a safari suit or similar dusty casual wear, bearing the sharp-featured face of a man not easily fooled, and languidly delivering to camera sardonic lines in a voice that, as he groped for the right word, sometimes gave the impression that he had borrowed another man's teeth.

In 1974, he began writing a column for the *Guardian*, dispensing wisdom in that self-deprecatory way of his. Sometimes, as he edged towards his seventies, the columns were filed not from his west London home but from a hospital bed. Decades of whisky and cigarette consumption, and lack of sleep and snatched meals, and that car crash had taken their toll, and he died on 27 January 1985, aged 73. His final column, about the cancer that killed him, was printed the day after, having been written three months before. Ever the reporter seeking to explain, he remains the yardstick against which all British reporters are measured.

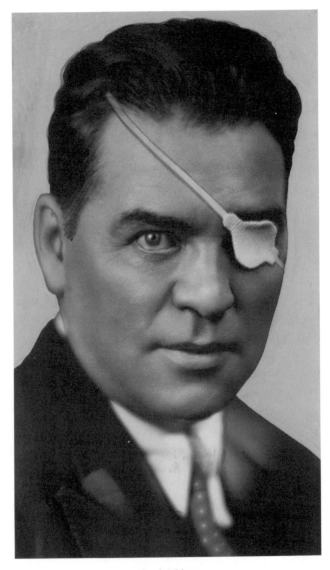

Floyd Gibbons

9

Floyd Gibbons
1887–1939

THE SUPREME EXAMPLE OF A REPORTER IN
PURSUIT OF AN ASSIGNMENT

If you had to nominate one reporter to save your skin by getting into a seemingly impossible situation and bringing out the story, then the person to send would be Raphael Floyd Phillips Gibbons, war correspondent, honorary member of the Marine Corps, and perhaps the supreme example of the amoral journalist in pursuit of an assignment. To say that he never once showed scruple, shame or a sense of fear is probably putting it a bit strong, but then, on the other hand, searching his life for these, the non-newspaper world's idea of virtues, is a fairly fruitless task. To get his story out first (or impede a rival – in Gibbons's eyes they amounted to two sides of the same task), he had no second's thought about breaking the law, damaging public property, defying a city fire brigade, putting terrorist threats to the test, booking himself on to a ship because it was likely to be torpedoed, out-bluffing the leadership of the Soviet Union, and sporting medals from dog shows to impersonate a war hero. He survived nine wars, two air crashes, a major shipwreck, being shot at by seven different armies, being bombed by four air forces, and encounters with less formal threats such as Pancho Villa and his desperados and the Japanese secret service. And all this, for the most part, equipped with only one eye, the other one being sacrificed when he was 31 in pursuit of yet another exclusive. Yes, Gibbons would definitely be the man to send.

Despatching him would also have the ancillary, but by no means insignificant, advantage of getting him out of the office. Like most extraordinary adventurers, Gibbons was not exactly what sports people call a team player, and his ego required considerably more house-room than the average newsroom had to offer. Easy-going he was not, and neither did he appear to have whatever gene it is that causes people to be domesticated. He failed to make a go of marriage, preferring a series of undemanding companions, the last of whom was an opera singer, and he was as truly nomadic as a twentieth-century male American could be, living in a succession of hotels all his adult life and only acquiring his own home when he was in his late forties.

All that may make him sound like a Hollywood script-writer's idea of the hard-bitten reporter, but it's not the whole story, and beneath that almost metallic exterior there actually was a heart of intelligent sentiment. His story of the little boy's wartime Christmas in France in 1917 is a sensitive classic worthy of even the most discerning seasonal anthology, and you would have to have the soul of a Soviet bureaucrat not to be moved by his reports of Russian peasants trying to survive the Great Famine of 1921. He was also devoted to his family, and they to him; and when he finally did buy his own home after living out of a suitcase for 30 years, some secret impulse made him install in it the very bed that he had been born in.

The time and place for that event was 1887 in a house in Washington, DC almost within sight of the White House. Neither of his parents were literary people. His father ran a butter and egg company, and, in at least one respect, did so with the chutzpah his son would later deploy around the world.

In an attempt to convince Washington matrons that their dairy needs were being served by a firm prosperous enough to run a whole fleet of vehicles, his van was marked 'No. 1' on one side and 'No. 2' on the other. This commercial *nous* later enabled him to be a successful pioneer in the trading stamp business, but young Floyd showed no inclination to join his father in these ventures. Almost from childhood he had been determined to be a newspaper reporter, and when he went to Georgetown University was so keen to start behaving like one – drinking and playing craps in the college grounds – that he got himself swiftly expelled. Academia thus having been dealt with, in 1907 Gibbons signed on at the *Minneapolis Daily News* as a police reporter at $7 a week. Gibbons Snr was not happy – so much so that he marched down to the paper's offices, buttonholed editor William G. Sheppard and asked him to give his son the sack. Sheppard heard him out, thought for a moment and replied: 'No, Mr Gibbons. I won't fire your son. He seems to have a natural nose for news.'

Indeed he did. By 1909 he was on the *Minneapolis Tribune*, his third paper in as many years, and, as the main man covering crime, had the pick of the city's murders, fires, brawls and head-breakings. He spent his days and nights hanging around police stations and courts, periodically scuttling off to the scene of the more colourful crimes. These, invariably, were committed in the city's slums, a teeming wellhead of stories that rapidly gave Gibbons the kind of education in the rawer side of human nature that no college can provide. The young Washingtonian, for instance, once found himself in a filthy room on the fifth floor of a tenement building, delivering a baby. There was also the times he spent with his room-mate and mentor, Jack Jensen, 25 years his senior and a two-bottles-of-whisky-a-day man. Jensen plied Gibbons not with booze but with books, and did so with all the insistence of a bootlegger trying to turn a weekend drinker into a dipsomaniac. It worked, Gibbons forever after paying tribute to the man who taught him to 'write by reading'.

In 1910 came his first major break – a story about a rumpus in Wisconsin called The Battle of Cameron Dam. The setting was a town called Winter near where the eccentric and ornery John Dietz, his wife, three sons and two daughters had their property. It was lumber country and the Dietz property contained the Thornapple River and its Cameron Dam, through which the Chippewa Lumber Boom Co. floated its logs. This was the cause of the trouble. Soon after Dietz bought the property in 1904 he asked the firm for $8,000 as a toll on logs driven downstream. It refused, Dietz blocked the dam; the company got an injunction, Dietz ignored it, sheriff and deputies rolled up at the dam, threats were made, rifles produced, and shots fired. And so, with increasing tension did the stand-off continue for the next four years, until, on 6 September 1910, Dietz and son Clarence went into town to vote. An argument with the head of the local school board ensued, a man called Horel intervened, fists flew, Dietz drew his gun and Horel fell, shot in the shoulder.

Dietz withdrew to his cabin, the town clamoured for revenge, the story caught the national eye, and Gibbons was duly despatched on his first big assignment. He arrived to find Winter seething, and Sheriff Madden swearing in as deputies most of its adult males, able-bodied or otherwise. Gibbons hurried off to interview Dietz in his cabin, and it was while he was collecting material for his first story that Dietz son number two, Leslie, burst in hotfoot and breathless. He, sister Myra, and Clarence had been taking the family wagon to town when they were ambushed by the sheriff and his men. Leslie managed to escape, but Clarence was arrested and Myra – shot in the back as she shielded her younger brother from the lawmen's gunfire – had been taken to a hotel. Gibbons took it all down and scuttled back to town to file his scoop.

For the next few days, his daily routine was to ride out the ten miles to the Dietz property, tell the family what was going on back in town, record their reactions and return to file from Winter's only telephone line. It was a chancy business. There were 25 other reporters, and any tardiness meant a lowly place in the queue for the phone. So Gibbons hired the town's sole car, plus chauffeur, to make sure he got to the phone first. He then discovered that his main competitor, 'Red' Schwartz of the *Minneapolis Journal*, was about to pull an even faster trick. Knowing that the state attorney-general was about to go up to the Dietz cabin and try and persuade old John to give himself up, Schwartz paid a lumberjack to sit in the general store monopolising the town phone by pretending to read, very slowly, the contents of a local newspaper to someone at the other end. Gibbons knew instinctively what to do. Before heading out to the Dietz place to see the lawman make his plea and Dietz refuse it, he hid a hatchet at the foot of the telephone pole.

As the newsmen began the race back with the news, Gibbons made Schwartz the unexpectedly generous offer of a ride back to town. Smug in the knowledge of his hired hand ponderously telephoning the columns of the local rag, Schwartz accepted; and when Gibbons's car pulled up outside the store, his rival shouted to his man to get through to Minneapolis. No sooner were the words out of his mouth than Gibbons leapt from the car, grabbed his concealed hatchet, shinned up the pole, hacked through the telephone wire, slid down, sped off in his car to the railway station telegraph, and filed the news that Dietz had refused to surrender. He beat all 24 rivals by four hours, a period about which we can be precise, since that was the length of time it took to repair the phone line.

At 2pm the triumphant Gibbons was arrested, handcuffed and put in a car for Haywood jail some 40 miles away. The journey, thanks to repeated breakdowns, took until dawn the following day, and there was just time for him to file from jail, lodge a successful bail application and speed back to Cameron Dam to see Sheriff Madden and 60 deputies lay siege to the Dietz cabin. It took more than 1,000 rounds fired at the homestead to convince old John that only his surrender could save the remains of his family. Just after a deputy fell dead from return fire from the cabin, he gave himself up. A year later he was tried for manslaughter by a jury that included four employees of the logging company, was duly sentenced to life, and served ten years before campaigners on his behalf persuaded a Wisconsin governor to free him.

Gibbons's brush with the law went more smoothly. The court said that if the *Tribune* would pay $500 for the time the phone was out of use, the criminal damage charge would be dropped. The paper, grateful for the enormous boost Gibbons's scoops had given it, was happy to cough up. It even gave him a bonus.

If ever a reporter was taught how risk-taking can pay dividends, then it was Gibbons at Cameron Dam, and he never forgot it. Indeed, within three months, he was at it again, although this time not in a way that actually involved breaking the law. Two weeks before Christmas, a Minneapolis hotel caught fire and rubber-necking crowds watched as 200 guests fled in their night attire down fire escapes, or were borne by firefighters' shoulders down flimsy ladders. It was a spectacle by any standards, made all the more entertaining for the gawpers by the fact that this was not just any hotel – it was the Brunswick, favoured trysting place for the city's swells and their ladies, not all of which relationships were sanctified by marriage. Gibbons was quickly at the scene, and, realising the journalistic possibilities in the hotel's clientele, dashed through the smoke and falling debris into the lobby, up to the reception counter, and grabbed the register with its precious and incriminating details. The guest list was published in full with his story and the paper sold out.

With antics and scoops like these, a move to a bigger city was only a matter of time, and in the spring of 1912 Gibbons took himself off to Chicago. It was not his best piece of timing, since the city was then in the grip of a newspaper strike. For a week he slept on a park bench, until he got hired by the one paper not stopped by the strike: a socialist one. Like most such publications it was also spectacularly unprofitable, and, a few months later, the inevitable happened and the editor gathered the staff together to tell them that not only was the paper closing, but there was nothing left in the pot to pay their last two weeks' wages. 'However,' he added, 'that saloon across the street owes us about $200 for advertising and if you fellows want to try to get anything out of the owner, it's alright by me.' Gibbons and 15 colleagues hit the joint, and, a few hours later, had emptied it of everything but the mahogany bar and the mirror that hung behind it.

The proceeds from the raid did not last long, and when, two weeks later, Gibbons turned up at the *Chicago Tribune* looking for work, he was a sorry sight: unshaven and dressed in an unpressed and greasy suit. Yet aided perhaps by his old socialist editor now installed at the *Tribune* as head of the copy desk, he got the job and immediately asked for a salary advance to get himself cleaned up and properly suited. The results of his shopping spree were, according to the testimony of astonished *Tribune* staffer Burton Rascoe, firmly in the tradition of journalistic fashion sense:

> Gibbons emerged with the god-awfullest suit I ever saw on a human being outside of a burlesque house... His suit was a grey one with... the largest checks you can imagine. They were about the size of window panes. The trousers... fitted him so tight that they looked as though they had been pasted on.

Clown he may have looked, but there was nothing slapstick about his reporting. The assignments were small at first, and so he set about creating an impact by carrying out investigations. Quack medicine sellers and therapists offered an obviously newsworthy target, and so thoroughly did he skewer Chicago's hokum-peddlers that his exposés of them made him the new star of the newsroom. So when, in December 1914, war looked likely with Mexico, Gibbons was the man sent south. He was soon filing sharp stories on the poor equipment of the US forces (saddles so rotted and shoddy that they might as well have been made of paper), seeing his first battle, and, in Juarez, meeting the brother of Pancho Villa, at that stage the successful rebel leader. Villa had been angered by stories written by some American correspondents and had sworn he would kill the first US newspaperman he set eyes on. This, to Gibbons, was as good as an invitation in gold lettering. When Villa's brother offered to arrange a meeting with the great man somewhere in the wilds of Mexico, Gibbons jumped at the chance and set off with a rebel escort. Three days of hard riding and an ambush by government forces later, the representative of the *Chicago Tribune* came face to face with Villa. As Gibbons had calculated, he got, not a bullet, but an interview. So effectively did Gibbons insinuate himself into the Villa camp that he was allowed to stay with the rebels and was with them when they captured Chihuahua. The city had large factories for railway rolling stock, and Villa was by this time so enamoured of Gibbons that he ordered a private carriage made for him and coupled to his own train. Thus, in a car marked in Spanish 'The Chicago Tribune – Special Correspondent' and staffed with two Chinese cooks and an interpreter, did Gibbons trail in the rebel leader's wake for four months filing copy that the rest of the American press could only read and envy.

From then on, Gibbons was the *Tribune*'s main man, covering Mayor Thompson's cross-country tour, interviewing evangelist Billy Sunday, profiling senators, investigating rumoured Japanese naval incursions off the California coast (which he did by signing on as one of the crew of a fishing boat), reporting on President Wilson's marriage and honeymoon, and, in 1916, the US expedition to try and capture Pancho Villa.

In 1917 the paper told him he was going to London to cover the Great War. It was then still a European conflict. America was yet a novice world power, and had strong pro-German and isolationist lobbies. But that mood of 'wait-and-see' was about to change, and Gibbons was to play no small part in it. He had received his new assignment in February, a month that had begun with a German threat that any ship entering the Atlantic approaches to the British Isles and France was liable to be sunk without warning. His paper therefore booked him a berth on the SS *Frederick VIII*, which was taking home the discredited German ambassador to the United States, Count von Bernstorff. Gibbons was having none of this namby-pamby nonsense. He found out which would be the first boat out of New York to defy the German ultimatum and, in the hope of a sensational scoop, booked himself on it. The ship was the Cunard liner *Laconia* and when, on 17 February, it left New York, there in stateroom B-19 was Gibbons, perhaps the only man ever to sail the Atlantic hoping that his ship would be sunk.

Eight days later he got his wish. Two hundred miles off the Irish coast, the *Laconia* was torpedoed by a German U-boat and sank within the hour. Gibbons and most of the passengers and crew took to the lifeboats, were picked up by a British minesweeper, and, less than two days later, were deposited safely at Queenstown, Northern Ireland. It was from there that Gibbons filed a report that began:

> The Cunard liner *Laconia*, 18,000 tons burden, carrying seventy-three passengers – men, women, and children – of whom six were American citizens – manned by a mixed crew of two hundred and sixteen, bound from New York to Liverpool, and loaded with foodstuffs, cotton, and war material, was torpedoed without warning by a German submarine last night off the Irish coast. The vessel sank in about forty minutes.

He then told the narrative of that night: the hit as he sat chatting in the smoking room ('the ship gave a sudden lurch sideways and forward. There was a muffled noise like the slamming of some large door at a good distance away...'); the 60-foot drop into the sea from the deck; the un-*Titanic*-like orderly evacuation of the ship; the behaviour of the passengers ('only one appeared hysterical – little Miss Titsie Siklosi, a French–Polish actress...'); the lurching at a 45-degree angle of Gibbons's lifeboat as it was lowered; a shout from above ('... A man was jumping... he passed beyond us and plunged into the water three feet from the edge of the boat...'); the old fishing boat captain who took charge of the lifeboat; the hitting of a second torpedo half an hour after the first; the ship's final minutes ('... the tiers of lights dimmed slowly from white to yellow, then to red... there remained only the dim outline of a blacker hulk standing out above the water like a jagged headland, silhouetted against the overcast sky...'); its end ('... The ship sank rapidly at the stern until its nose stood straight in the air. Then it slid silently down and out of sight like a piece of disappearing scenery in a spectacle...'); the submarine pulling alongside lifeboat No. 3 and a German voice asking in thickly accented English what ship they had just sunk; how the lifeboats spread out for fear of crashing into one another; the hours of pulling on oars, the seasickness; and the cold, until, after six hours, a light was seen in the distance. It was a British minesweeper, and soon they were alongside.

> A score of hands reached out, and we were suspended in the husky, tattooed arms of those doughty British jack tars, looking up into the weather-beaten, youthful faces, mumbling thanks and thankfulness, and reading in the gold lettering on their pancake hats the legend 'H.M.S. Laburnum.'

His report – including an account by Able Seaman Walley of how two American women were swept to their deaths by a wave – was printed in dailies across America, and read from the floor of both houses of Congress. Five weeks later, America declared war and, on 8 June, the leader of its advance guard, General Pershing, sailed into Liverpool – an innocent enough fact, except the British censors would not allow reporters to say where he was landing. Gibbons rose to the challenge, cabling his paper: 'Major General John J Pershing landed at a British port today and was greeted by the Lord Mayor of Liverpool.' The censors passed it.

By mid-June, Gibbons was in France, one of 18 American war correspondents attached to the US expeditionary force. He was soon chaffing at the restrictions, the reporters being chaperoned to selected parts of the front by officers and interpreters, and having about as much freedom to roam as toddlers on a kindergarten outing. So, being Gibbons, he disappeared. His colleagues, who included Damon Runyon of the *New York American*, had not the slightest idea where he was. For six weeks they speculated what had become of him as they waited to be taken to the story they all hankered after: the firing of America's opening shot of the war. Eventually, word came through that it would be the artillery. So, with their guides, minders, interpreters and censors in tow, the reporters began the journey to the front line where the great event would happen. As they jolted along, they exchanged the odd tut-tutting regret that Gibbons – wherever he was – would miss the story. Some of them may even have meant it. Then, within five miles of the front, a French sentry stepped out, halted their convoy and refused to let it pass. They pulled off the road, lit their cigarettes and watched as, moments later, a US artillery company droned past. Runyon looked up, and thought he saw, sitting beside a field gun, a familiar figure. 'Well I'll be damned,' he shouted. 'There's Gibbons! How the hell did he get there?'

How indeed. Well, six weeks before, Gibbons had headed south and attached himself so effectively to the Sixth Field Artillery that soon he was a member of Battery 'A' gun crew. And, in a typically Gibbonsonian piece of luck and prescience, it was this crew, along with Batteries 'B', 'C' and 'D', who were rumbling down this road towards their date with history. So, when Battery 'C' fired America's opening salvo, Gibbons was on hand to see it, record the time (6.05am and 10 seconds on 23 October 1917), the place (one kilometre east of Bathelemont) and the names of the crew. He even retrieved the shell case. Once again Gibbons had the front page to himself.

Such good fortune was bound to run out at some stage, and in June 1918 it finally did. Gibbons had been warned that to go on patrol with the Fifth Marines in woods near Lucy-le-Bocage, 40 miles north of Paris, would be too risky, but he was undeterred. Sure enough, as Major Benjamin S. Berry and his men, accompanied by Gibbons, crossed a wheatfield they came under heavy machinegun fire. Every man flattened himself on the ground, but Berry was hit in the hand, and Gibbons began to crawl towards him. He had not gone more than a yard or two when he was hit, first in the left arm, then in his left shoulder, and, finally, for the third and most devastating time, when a bullet ricocheted off a rock, took out his left eye, fractured his skull and exited, ripping a three-inch hole in the right side of his helmet.

The time was 6pm and for the next three hours Gibbons lay there, losing blood but fully conscious, until light artillery knocked out the German machinegunners and he could be helped from the scene. He was taken from the first aid station, to a clearing station ten miles away, and thence, in the back of an ammunition truck, to Military Base Hospital No. 1 at Neuilly-sur-Seine where he was operated upon. Meanwhile the story he had filed before going on patrol had been widely published back home. It had begun: 'I am at the front and entering Belleau Wood with the US Marines…', and, despite its revelation of both a precise unit and its location, the censors passed it because they thought Gibbons was dying, and it would be churlish to stop his 'final' despatch. The Third Army, fighting alongside the Marines in defence of Paris, wished they had done. Gibbons's story, and the excitement and speculation it generated, did much to create the impression that the Marines single-handedly saved the French capital, and it, perhaps more than any other piece of journalism, gave birth to the idea that the corps were the twentieth-century equivalent of the Seventh Cavalry.

Gibbons recovered quickly, and, sporting the white eye patch that was to be part of his own mythology, was back at the front by mid-July. A month later, the French awarded him the Croix de Guerre, and he was chosen to make a lecture tour of the US. He arrived back in New York to find he was the war's latest celebrity. A Marine guard of honour and jostling newsmen greeted him, as, eventually, did President Wilson, and a full house at Carnegie Hall. So it was with an extra strut in his walk that he returned to Paris in December to run the *Chicago Tribune*'s army edition and European service from an office next to Harry's Bar.

He was damned, however, if his new job, and the lack of an eye, was going to stop him reporting. He went to Ireland to cover the suppression of Sinn Fein (and cheat the British censors once more by defying their ban on interviewing jailed republicans), and in 1920 set off for Warsaw for the Polish–Russian War. To get there, he hired a pilot and his bone-shaking Sopwith plane. They took off from Paris with Gibbons carrying a spare tank of fuel between his legs, muddled their compass bearings and somehow ended up in the foothills of the Alps, where they crash-landed. Gibbons started the journey back to Paris, sent word for another plane to meet him, only for this to crash as it came into land at the rendezvous. So Gibbons, undeterred, drove all the way to the Polish border, where, having pinned all his medals on his old uniform (plus some impressive-looking medallions from dog shows), bluffed his way past guards, marched into the presence of the Polish Army's chief of staff and imperiously demanded a military escort. He got it, and for 47 days was the only Western correspondent at the front.

In 1921 came his greatest triumph of all: the Russian Famine. Some time that summer, word began to leak out of the new Soviet state that people in their millions were starving in the Volga region. Checking these rumours was easier said than done. The Bolshevik government allowed no Western journalists to be based in Moscow, and coverage of the country was in the hands of reporters who hung around Riga's restaurants talking to émigrés, White Russians and other unreliable witnesses. But as sketchy reports of a fearful famine gained momentum, so did interest in the story back home, and in mid-August Gibbons received this cable from Chicago: 'Concentrate all available corrs on Russia. It is the greatest story in the world today. We must have first exclusive eye-witness report from corr on the spot.' He sent two reporters, who soon joined all the other correspondents milling about Latvia waiting for permission to enter Russia. The Soviets were not letting them in; they wanted US food aid, but were afraid the full extent of the tragedy would be revealed. After the *Tribune*'s men kicked their heels for a week, Chicago cabled Gibbons to go to Riga himself. Two days later he arrived – and was promptly arrested for landing without a visa. A bribe took care of that, and, once in town, he took the advice of colleague George Seldes and hatched a plan that might just get him into Russia. The rest of the press had dutifully filled out an application form for entry. Not Gibbons. Instead he told his German pilot to keep his plane primed for take-off, and let it be known around the bars that he was thinking of making an illicit flight into Russia. Sure enough, informants picked up the story, and next day Gibbons was summoned to see Litvinov, the Soviet ambassador.

The meeting pitted the two wiliest brains in Riga against each other. Litvinov said he knew about Gibbons's plane, and warned him that if he tried to fly across the border he would be shot down. Gibbons countered by pointing out that the Russian border ran from the Baltic to the Black Sea, and anti-aircraft guns covered a mere fraction of it. Litvinov then threatened to have Gibbons arrested, to which the reporter replied that the Soviets had just released all their US prisoners in order to secure food aid and were not likely to start incarcerating Americans again. Checkmate. That night, while the rest of the press fumed in Riga, Gibbons boarded a train for Moscow with Litvinov, and, after a few days in the capital, was on another train bound for the Volga. The ride took 40 hours, but the scene that greeted him in Samara was of such medieval degradation, it might as well have been a journey back through the centuries. So awful was the stench of death as he stepped from his carriage, and so high the risk of cholera and typhus, that he did his reporting with a towel soaked in disinfectant held to his face. The report he wrote contains one of the enduring images of disaster reporting:

> A boy of 12 with a face of sixty was carrying a six-month-old infant wrapped in a filthy bundle of furs. He deposited the baby under a freight car, crawled after him and drew from his pocket some dried fish-heads, which he chewed ravenously and then, bringing the baby's lips to his, transferred the sticky white paste of half-masticated fish-scales and bones to the infant's mouth as a mother bird feeds her young.

Writing it was one thing; getting the story out was quite another, for when Gibbons got to the local telegraph station he saw that the keyboard used to transmit messages had, naturally enough, only Cyrillic letters. He had to write out his report again, changing each Latin letter to its nearest local equivalent. So, in this hybrid language, was his report transmitted to Moscow where Seldes, by now arrived, translated it and despatched it Chicagowards. It was the world's first account of the famine from a non-Soviet source.

In February 1923 came an altogether different kind of mission impossible, the kind normally guaranteed to offend the war and disaster reporter's idea of his or her own high seriousness. It was a stunt, and, worse, it involved Hollywood. The cable from Chicago to Gibbons read:

ORGANISE AND EQUIP CAMEL CARAVAN CROSS SAHARA
DESERT OBTAIN TRUE PICTURE SHEIKS AND THEIR
APPEAL ANGLO-SAXON AND AMERICAN WOMEN. MRS
HULLS BOOK THE SHEIK CREATING WIDE INTEREST
HERE AMONG WOMEN-FOLK WELL AS RUDOLPH
VALENTINO'S CHARACTERISATION IN MOVIES. CABLE
WHEN CAN LEAVE.

It is not something that today's frontline reporters would
be asked to do, but these were different times, and this was
Gibbons. He threw himself into the project, planning to cross
2,000 miles of the Sahara in half the usual time for the journey,
and by the end of March was setting out from Columb Bechar,
Algeria in his sheik's costume with a fully equipped caravan
in tow. It was, as background features to the movie of the
moment go, no picnic: sandstorms, local brigands, temperatures
reaching 145 degrees, weeks without contact with the outside
world, getting lost for three days while trying to find the only
well for 500 miles, and his cook's toe so infected that Gibbons
had to amputate it. On 1 July, three months and five days after
he set out, Gibbons and party arrived in Timbuktu. It was a
triumphant personal achievement, but, for his editors back
home, a let-down. He had, after all, failed to find any swarthy
Valentino types throwing wide-eyed blondes over the camels
and galloping off into the desert night.

For an encore, Gibbons poled 800 miles up the Niger River,
explored the entire west African coast down to Cape Town,
returned to Paris via London, thence to Rome and the election
of a US cardinal, back to the US for the first time in five years,
whereupon, after just three weeks, he was sent to Australia to
write about its Labor government, interviewed Dame Nellie
Melba, and rounded off the tour by reporting from New
Zealand, New Guinea, Singapore, China and Siberia. Then,
after a mere two weeks in Paris, it was off to cover the war
in Morocco. It was after he returned to the States from this
conflict that he started appearing on radio, and, within a short

while, was doing regular talks as 'Your Headline Hunter', a soubriquet that presumably sounded less toe-curling then than it does now. Being Gibbons he could not just broadcast as other folk. His trademark was an ability to speak faster than any other radio voice, and he was once recorded at a scarcely believable 217 words a minute. Somehow enough listeners understood the barrage for him to soon be receiving a thousand fan letters a day.

By 1930 he had acrimoniously parted company from the *Tribune*. So when war loomed between China and Japan, it was for the International News Service that Gibbons headed to Manchuria via Tokyo. Here he met high-ranking Japanese army officers who presented him with an inscribed vase and, as was their habit, asked him to sign a receipt for it. Gibbons, as was his own habit, automatically refused to do what officialdom requested, took it to the US embassy, where a translator told him that the 'receipt' was, in fact, an agreement to spy for the Japanese. Thus uncompromised, Gibbons flew off to cover the war from first one side then the other, the highlight of which for the seasoned old campaigner was watching Japanese planes bomb Shanghai from the roof of his hotel. He returned to the States for an incessant round of broadcasts, speaking tours and covering major stories like political conventions for both radio and the INS.

Not even a heart attack could stop him. He suffered one while on holiday in January 1934, but a year later accepted an offer from INS to cover the Italian campaign in Ethiopia. Gibbons, predictably, was the first correspondent to arrive at the front, and for several months he reported from his base at an altitude of 8,000 ft where the temperature reached 135 degrees by day and slumped to 50 at night. It was no place for a 48-year-old with a heart condition, and he duly collapsed during a broadcast and had to be airlifted out to Khartoum. His convalescence was spent in Cairo, after five days of which he began to get itchy for news, removed himself to Jerusalem and reported for two weeks on the developing acrimony between Arabs and Jews. On his way home he dropped off in Rome and interviewed Mussolini. Six months later he sailed to Spain for the Civil War, his ninth conflict as a reporter. He covered it from both sides, a project not without risk. But then, in the Spain of that time, almost any form of questioning and free expression was potentially lethal, as Gibbons discovered when he walked into a studio to broadcast and found it occupied by 12 Loyalist soldiers armed not only with fixed bayonets but also orders to shoot him if he said anything against the Spanish republic. His tension was not eased by the fact that they spoke not one word of English.

He survived that, sailed for home, and began at last to spend some of the considerable fortune he had accumulated, buying two farms and a yacht. And it was at home, just over two years later, in the very bed that he had been born in, that Floyd Gibbons died of a heart attack at the age of 52.

Thus ended the life of this most supreme of story-getters. Outwardly flinty, trusting almost no one, and with a rat-like nose for his own advantage, he seems a man easier to admire at a distance than to know close-up. And yet there was another Gibbons that the relentless pursuit of stories never entirely extinguished. It emerges most strongly in the story he wrote from the village of Saint-Thiebault at Christmas 1917. Here, 70 French children faced the season with their fathers, brothers and uncles dead or away at war. They would, as per the local custom, place their boots and shoes on their hearths, but the grown-ups knew there was little hope that Papa Noël would fill them with goodies. Until, that is, the US regiment stationed in the town decided to plan a secret Christmas. A whip-round raised 1,300 francs, gifts were bought, Red Powers, 'the shortest, fattest, and squattiest man in the battalion' was rigged up as Papa Noël, Hindenburg, 'the most docile mule in the wagon-train' slotted between the shafts of the sleigh, the regimental band struck up, and the whole parade set off, drawing excited children from their homes and down to the village church. Here, in a ceremony made poignant by the absent men it could not include, the children were called by name to step forward and receive their gifts.

All, that is, except one – little Pierre Lafite, who, in an attempt to improve his hearthside chances with Papa Noël, had earlier borrowed a hip boot from Moriarty, the tallest man in the regiment. Every other child's name had been called, not once but four, even five times, and the pile of packages on the table shrunk smaller and smaller. Still the fatherless child sat, empty-booted. Then at last, Pierre's name was called and he dragged the big rubber boot up the aisle...

... All the elders in the church were watching his progress.

'For Pierre Lafite,' repeated M. Lecompte, holding up the enormous boot, 'a pair of real leather shoes to fit in the foot of the boot.' He placed them there.

'And a pair of stilts to fit in the leg of the boot.' He so placed them.

'And a set of soldiers, twenty-four in number, with a general commanding, to go beside the stilts.' He poured them into the boot.

'And a pair of gloves and a stocking cap to go on top of the soldiers.

'And a baseball and a bat to go on top of the gloves.

'And all the chinks to be filled with nuts, figs and sweets. Voilà, Pierre.'

And with these words he had poured the sweetmeats in overflowing measure into the biggest hip boot in the regiment.

Amid the cheers of the men, led by Big Moriarty, Pierre started towards his seat, struggling with the seven-league boot and the wholesale booty, and satisfied with the realisation that in one haul he had obtained more than his companions in five.

Company B quartet sang 'Down in A Coal Hole' and then, as the band struck up outside the church, all moved to the street. The sun had gone down; the early winter night had set in, and the sky was almost dark.

It is a sentimental story, all the better for being told without any artificial tugs at the heartstrings or adding of journalistic violins in the background. But Gibbons would still find it strange, that of all the thousands of stories he wrote – of crimes, battles, starvations and bombings, of great events, and reports that changed the mood of his times – the one most likely to be anthologised should be the tale of little Pierre Lafite and his borrowed rubber boot.

10
Hugh McIlvanney
1934–

THE BEST WRITER EVER TO APPLY WORDS TO NEWSPRINT

It is a sobering thought that, for a brief period in my late twenties and early thirties, I worked directly with one of the newspaper trade's true phenomena and never realised it. I knew at the time that the man was good, the best by far on one side of the Atlantic, but it wasn't until I came to study what others have hailed as the greats, and immersed myself in the reading required for this book, that I appreciated just how good. Hugh McIlvanney is, I realise now, very probably the best writer ever to apply words to newsprint.

As might be expected from such an operator, he was not low-maintenance, either in salary, space or the editorial anxiety expended in wondering whether he would file on time, or even, on occasions, the precise location of his whereabouts. But when he came through with his piece, which he always did with the timing and element of gratifying surprise associated with the Seventh Cavalry, he was worth it. He could ad-lib down the phone a 2,000-word account of a major event that was, when you received it, as inventive, lucid and considered as if it had been written with a goose-quill pen over three weeks. His features were researched to the point of definitiveness, and

Hugh McIlvanney

every sentence, as he always insisted, 'carried freight'. There was plenty of humour, but he was never the kind of writer to, as he put it, 'run up a side street just to shove a joke in your letterbox'. But, more than any of this, what made him so special was an ability with language that was at its most striking when defining a subject in one line. For those unfamiliar with his work, here, in a small sample, is McIlvanney on:

- The late January weather on Ayr racecourse: 'It was the kind of wind that seemed to peel the flesh off your bones and come back for the marrow'.
- The notoriously taciturn Liverpool manager Kenny Dalglish: 'The day he becomes a gusher of controversial quotes, stones will be queuing up to give blood transfusions'.
- His native Scotland as it exited yet another major football championship: 'Doomed forever to be nothing more than a kilted cabaret at the World Cup finals'.
- Jockey Bill Williamson: 'who sometimes looks as cheerful as a man trying to get a cyanide capsule out from behind his teeth'.
- The skinny build of snooker champion Stephen Hendry: 'Never has a wearer of dinner suits been so urgently in need of dinners'.
- The punch with which George Foreman beat a sub-standard opponent: 'The blow that flattened Terry Anderson was in transit so long that it could have been done in oils before it landed'.
- Boxer Joe Bugner: 'the physique of a Greek statue but fewer moves'.
- A last-minute goal that defeated Scotland in a rugby international: 'If an entire nation can be kicked in the crotch, the last swing of Jon Callard's boot had that effect at Murrayfield'.

- A deliberate mismatch in boxing: 'an occasion that is meant to be about as competitive as a ticker-tape parade'.
- The outcome of the fight when it actually took place: 'McNeeley's impersonation of a dervish with a death-wish had lasted only 89 seconds when it was terminated by the illegal intervention of a manager who found he had less nerve at ringside than he had shown when signing the contract'.
- And on any fan who might complain afterwards: 'like someone bemoaning the lack of true love in a whorehouse'.
- A depressingly poor football match between England and Ireland: 'Our football made its entrance to the World Cup like someone arriving at a symphony concert on a skateboard with a ghetto-blaster turned up to full volume'.
- Real Madrid and its collection of star players: 'Amid the dressing-room egos, managerial authority seems to have the survival prospects of a leg of mutton in a piranha pool'.

Those who know McIlvanney will be aware that such phrases were the part of writing that came easiest to him, for they were not some voice affected for the page, but how the man talked. Using language in that way was not something he was trained to do, it was with him from his earliest days. He had been born in Kilmarnock, Scotland in 1934, and raised in what Britons call a council house, and Americans a housing project. Some might find it a curiosity that a man who can write with such skill (as can his brother, novelist William, for that matter) emerged from the home of a miner and a woman who left school so early the teachers barely had time to learn her name. But successful writers and artists are rather more liable to spring from the wrong side of the tracks than the insides of Pullman carriages, especially if, as with McIlvanney, that home's lack of a galleried library is more than compensated for by a mother who set great store by books and the intelligent reading of them. And, for all the harshness of life in the west of Scotland at that time, it was a working-class culture where learning was not sneered at. McIlvanney explained in an interview with the *Observer*'s Kevin Mitchell for the paper's archive in 2002:

> People pay attention to the hard guys in those quite rough working areas, but they're much, much more impressed by someone who's talking sense... I was brought up with people who really understood that language was part of the furniture of the realities of life.

He left school at 16, began work for the *Kilmarnock Standard*, and then moved on to his country's premier paper, the *Scotsman*. He wrote news and features until, in 1960, his editor Alistair Dunnett asked him to start covering sport and took the canny precaution of giving his promising young writer a copy of *The Sweet Science*, a collection of A.J. Liebling's boxing pieces. McIlvanney's initial reluctance evaporated, he became the man entrusted with coverage of big events. The first he was despatched to was the European Cup Final played in Glasgow between Real Madrid and Eintracht Frankfurt. Real won 7–3, a busy score-line that might have troubled a writer for a monthly magazine, let alone one like McIvanney who was doing 'a runner', a piece composed – and filed – in chunks as the action happens (e.g. 400 words at half-time, 350 at three-quarter-time and a 'top', and – if you're lucky – tail of 250). He began:

> Almost 130,000 Scottish football enthusiasts were privileged last night to see Real Madrid display the unmatchable talents that have made them the greatest club side in the history of world football.
>
> The fact they were engaged in winning the European Cup for the fifth successive year seemed equally inevitable and incidental, in the midst of some of the most magnificent sporting artistry Hampden Park has ever seen.

Fittingly, the great Glasgow stadium responded with the loudest and most sustained ovation it has given to non-Scottish athletes. The strange emotionalism that overcame the huge crowd as the triumphant Madrid team circled the field at the end, carrying the trophy they have monopolised since its inception, showed that they had not simply been entertained. They had been moved by the experience of seeing a sport played to its ultimate standards.

McIlvanney was 26. His report showed not only what was to become his trademark fluency and conjuring of the memorable phrase ('... to list the Real team is to chronicle greatness...'), but also his rare ability to calibrate the quality of what he was seeing. His judgement, made on the fly, that the game had attained greatness, was inch perfect. Even today, nearly 50 years on, coaches still show film of it to impressionable young players in the hope that some of its attacking verve might rub off.

After two years he decided he wanted to try to come to London. As he told Mitchell in that 2002 interview:

I'd listened to too many of my fellow toilers in Scotland telling how it wasn't such a hard job to crack the London newspapers scene and it was just that they didn't fancy the place. I didn't want to be talking that way 10 or 15 years on, so I wrote a few letters.

The most encouraging of the replies came from the *Observer*, Britain's oldest Sunday newspaper, and down McIlvanney came to London for an interview. 'The first question I put to the *Observer* was "Where do I get a shave?"' He'd forgotten to bring a razor, not the last time that a certain disregard for the minor practicalities of life would intrude, but the paper was sufficiently unfazed, and impressed with his cuttings, to offer him a job.

The post was not a writing one, but assistant to sports editor Clifford Makins, a man whose background was unusual, even by the Bohemian standards of the *Observer*. He was a former stage manager who went on to write a comic strip biography of Sir Winston Churchill, edit the *Eagle*, a pioneering comic for boys, and such books as *The Girl Annual for 1962*. Once installed as the *Observer*'s sports editor, he presided over bibulous lunch sessions in famous Fleet Street bar El Vino, and was, courtesy of colleague Christopher Wordsworth's pen, the original 'legend in his own lunchtime'. Added to all this, Makins was, in the ways of newspaper production, a relative novice. He had, however, an unerring eye for writing talent. So when, after a week or so, young McIlvanney began to tire of getting to grips with the complexities of Sunday newspaper make-up, Makins did not stop him writing his first piece for the paper. In November 1962, another followed. It was about a boxer called Phonse LaSaga who had been brought over from Newfoundland to provide cannon fodder for a rising British heavyweight called Billy Walker. McIlvanney went along to the bout, and in a subsequent report described how LaSaga 'vaulted the ropes and lay down soon afterwards'. Makins and other wise heads asked themselves why the Scotsman was not writing more for the paper, and, within a short while, McIlvanney was permanently liberated from desk duties.

The world of national newspaper sports reporting that McIlvanney entered was different from the one experienced by US counterparts (the best of whom he fervently admires). He had to write with authority on a far wider range of activities: soccer, horse racing, golf, rugby union, rugby league, cricket, boxing, track and field, baseball, American football, snooker, and any one of a number of other sports, like rowing, at which a Briton might suddenly win an Olympic gold. A phobic fear of crossing salt water was not an option, as it was for counterparts in Boston and New York. Where, however, McIlvanney's experience in the 1960s and 1970s was similar to the American one, and differed from what Britons find now, lay in the remarkable access to the leading performers enjoyed by writers for top papers. Quality time with them was not only possible, but for a reporter as keen as McIlvanney to do the job in person rather than on the phone or via record books, routine. He spent many hours in their close company, and the result, in the case of footballers such as George Best, Paddy Crerand and Charlie Cooke, and managers like Bill Shankly and Matt Busby, was that he actually knew the men rather than merely lobbed questions at them from the floor of a press conference. A few examples, the first of which involves the May night in 1967 when Celtic, managed by Jock Stein, became the first British football club to win the European Cup. After setting the scene ('Today Lisbon is almost, but not quite, back in Portuguese hands at the end of the most hysterically exuberant occupation any city has ever known...'), he describes the match, ending with this:

> ... It was hard work appearing so relaxed and the effort eventually took its toll of Stein when he made a dive for the dressing rooms a minute before the end of the game, unable to stand any more. When we reached him there, he kept muttering: 'What a performance. What a performance.' It was left to Bill Shankly, the Scottish manager of Liverpool (and the only English club manager present), to supply the summing up quote. 'John,' Shankly said with the solemnity of a man to whom football is a religion, 'you're immortal.'

The entré to dressing rooms did not always generate such warm memories. One of the scenes that McIlvanney regards as the saddest he ever saw in sport was the one played out after Henry Cooper's 1970 defeat of Jack Bodell, a boxer from rural Derbyshire whose agricultural gaucheness was emphasised, rather than diminished, the nearer he got to the bright lights:

> Half an hour afterwards, as Cooper and the rest of us were preparing to leave the other dressing-room along the corridor, Bodell suddenly appeared in his overcoat and plonked himself down in a chair just inside the door of the small ugly room. He had two bottles of beer and was obviously in a mood to be sociable. It was impossible not to feel a warmth for this large, simple-natured, likeable man. In that strange moment the mindless mocking of him seemed to amount to real cruelty. All of us hesitated, sensing he

should have company, but Cooper had a party to host and with a last mumble of inadequate pleasantries we filed out, leaving the loser sitting alone in the winner's dressing-room.

Some who enjoyed such proximity to the performers became little more than itinerant, unpaid publicists, taking on the onerous role of drinks buyer and ego massager. That, for all his fondness for standing a round, was never going to be McIlvanney's style, and several sporting legends found that his taste for having the last word was not confined to articles published on Sundays. One was Sir Alf Ramsey, who managed England to its World Cup victory in 1966. He objected to a piece McIlvanney had written, and, after telling him so, concluded with what he hoped would be a clinching 'How many caps [the cloth mementos awarded for international appearances] have you got?' McIlvanney replied: 'Alf, I've got no caps and never was within light years of a cap. Nobody has more respect for experience than I have, but experience is only relevant in relation to the intelligence that is exposed to that experience. If you send a turnip round the world, it still comes back a turnip, not an expert on geography.' Ramsey: 'Words, words, words.' McIlvanney: 'Alf, they're very handy if you want to say something.'

There was no shortage in the 1960s and early 1970s of extraordinary people and events at which McIlvanney could deploy his prodigious vocabulary. Apart from England's World Cup win, there were remarkable talents like footballer George Best ('feet as sensitive as a pick-pocket's hands'), boxers like Muhammad Ali ('compared with him, the most vivid of his predecessors are blurred figures dancing behind frosted glass'), and jockeys like Lester Piggott ('a volcano trapped in an iceberg'). As chief sports writer for the *Observer* his year was timetabled by the major sporting occasions of the Western world – not just British ones such as Cheltenham National Hunt Festival, the Grand National, FA Cup Final, Football League championship, rugby internationals, The Derby and

Open golf championship, but international ones such as big title fights, the Masters, one or more of American racing's Triple Crown, grands prix and the Olympics. It was not long before the quality of his writing had made him one of the very few British writers to be commissioned by *Sports Illustrated* when it was in its pomp.

McIlvanney's output was divided for many years between a feature, profile, interview or preview of around 1,500–2,000 words delivered for the inside pages, and then a live report from racecourse or football ground on a Saturday afternoon. These, given that his paper's deadline was 5pm for events that only ended at 4.50pm, were filed as running reports, which he would write in long hand up to a certain point and then ad-lib the rest, invariably while standing up. Ronald Atkin, who often went with him to Cup Finals and the like to write a colour or interview sidebar, says:

> He would watch the first half, making notes, and then pick up the phone and dictate from his notes a beautifully coherent account. When the second half started he would still be dictating, so I was deputed to write down what had happened. First three minutes was all Liverpool pressure, mainly from the right etc. He would then translate my prosaic stuff into his words of genius.

The extreme time pressures never prevented him from coming up with an intro to set the blood racing, as with this, filed from the Grand National in 1977:

> There were enough sentimental tears to make an extra water jump at Aintree yesterday as Red Rum, the most popular horse British racing has ever known, galloped inexorably away from his shattered pursuers to become the first steeplechaser in history to win three Grand Nationals.

McIlvanney loved this time at the *Observer*. 'You went to the office with a spring in your step,' he said. But for all the intellectual companionship, professional freedom and liberal politics the paper represented, it was full of, and certainly ruled by, people who were born into considerably more comfortable circumstances than McIlvanney. The result was that salaries were regarded less as a form of remuneration the paper gave to its staff than, in their paucity, a subsidy they were expected to give it. So, in 1972, he was lured to the *Daily Express*, then some way into its lengthy decline, but still a believer that its best journalists should live high on the hog with wages to match. He reported from the Far East on the aftermath of the Vietnam War, from Africa (where he interviewed Ugandan despot Idi Amin), from the Middle East, and from the US, where he covered the 1972 Democratic Convention. But his experience as a roving reporter for the *Express* was ultimately less satisfying than he had hoped. Some friends say he found the restricted length of pieces too limiting, and more than one tells the story that, for an early assignment at a race meeting, McIlvanney rang the office for his allotted length. '800 words! 800 words!' he is said to have exclaimed. 'Jesus Christ, my intro's longer than that.' Yet McIlvanney says the association was only terminated because he was being asked to 'throttle down, rather than up', as he had been at the *Observer*. Before contacting agent Bagenal Harvey to negotiate a speedy return to his old paper (he was one of the very few British reporters even to have an agent), he had, however, contributed this pithy put-down of Ascot, the venue for high-society race meetings:

> Ascot, for all the magnificence of the racing, often suffers the disadvantages of an open-air cocktail party. It is coiffured, decorated and deodorised, its stuffiness jealously protected by an army of belligerent gatemen and petty officials. Those men, who give the impression of having nearly made sergeant-major, seem to divide their time between touching forelocks to the privileged and feeling the collar of anyone who looks as if he has less than 50 grand in the biscuit tin.

His first piece back at the *Observer*, in November 1973, was at a different kind of race course, Ludlow in a misty, autumnal Shropshire, beside whose 'stand with the pillared and fretted façade of a Victorian railway station', he saw a lady owner 'scattering kisses like moistened buckshot', and watched as a horse called Overall, owned by friends, won a novice hurdle worth £204 in such style that 'it would have taken the Jodrell Bank telescope to find the rest of the field'. Within a year, he was witnessing a different kind of triumph, that of Muhammad Ali over the formidable George Foreman. He called it 'undoubtedly the most enthralling sports event this reporter has ever experienced'. Foreman went to that fight as a world heavyweight champion who, in McIlvanney's words 'quarters the ring with a deadly sense of geometry, employing a perfectly timed side-step that cuts off escape routes as emphatically as a road block'. But, when it came to the fight, Ali, gaining the title for the second time, was at his matchless peak. McIlvanney's report began:

> We should have known that Muhammad Ali would not settle for any ordinary old resurrection. His had to have an additional flourish. So, having rolled away the rock, he hit George Foreman on the head with it.

The piece was informed by time spent with one other journalist at Ali's rented house in the hours after the fight, and a visit later that day to Foreman in his Kinshasa hotel room. McIlvanney's verdict was this:

> The most vivid recollection will not be the inspiration of Ali's tactics or the brilliance of his technique, spellbinding though they were. It will be the glittering, flawless diamond of his nerve... his decision to invite Foreman to crowd in on him must be seen as an astonishing act of calculated bravery. His ability to function at maximum efficiency, without the slightest impairment of concentration, while the bombs were flying round his head in the early minutes, testifies to a fearlessness that even the prize-ring has rarely produced... The man could pick flowers in a minefield and never miss a bloom.

His pen was dipped in a different kind of liquid four years later when he was in Argentina to see a Scotland football team whose manager Ally MacLeod had assured a nation of supporters never lacking in fanciful expectation that his squad would assuredly bring back the World Cup. Even without hindsight it was a preposterous claim, and McIlvanney had to watch as the project disintegrated on impact with the first available opposition: Iran. After defeat to Peru, McIlvanney wrote, 'MacLeod... had the appearance of someone stumbling away from a plane crash,' and his next piece began: 'If there is ever a World Cup for self-destructiveness, few nations will have the nerve to challenge the Scots.' Twelve years later, after Scotland's failure to beat Costa Rica at the 1990 World Cup, he was having to describe a performance that was 'a monument to ponderous inadequacy', complete with 'trundling attempts to break from midfield, moving at a pace that might have been bettered by a woman pushing a pram'.

To quote such barbs might lead a reader unfamiliar with his work to conclude that the sharpness of his phrasing sometimes overcame the subtleties of a situation. In fact, McIlvanney was addicted to precision. He said in his interview for the *Observer* archive:

> If you're trying to analyse a performance or get some understanding of the nature of a performer, then I don't think the sweeping brush strokes help you very much. I think you've got to get down to the detail and make sure before you put anything down on paper there is a clarity in your own head about it. What you deliver may not be worth very much, or enlighten very much, or excite people very much, but before it leaves you, you have to be sure, be precise about the emotions and physical happenings. I think there is an absolute duty to keep working on it. I just hate letting it go if it's not as true as I can make it.

If that sounds like hard work, it was. Donald Trelford, who edited the *Observer* for 17 of McIlvanney's 30 years at the paper, said: 'Part of the reason he was so good was that he worked harder at it than anyone else. He always did a phenomenal amount of research for each piece.' He would consult widely with fellow writers and performers in whatever field he was tackling that week, and Ronald Atkin was not alone in reporting that a piece of information or anecdote passed on would be subjected to a road test of checks with several other witnesses before McIlvanney accepted it as authentic. Alan Hubbard, who, like Atkin, knew McIlvanney both as a sports editor and writing colleague, tells of the time when they were in Barcelona for the 1992 Olympics: 'Hugh was writing, late at night as usual, and wanted to check one fact about the German team. He rang me and got me out of bed. Then he did the same to a German colleague, and finally he rang the German embassy at 1am. He got the fact checked.' And if he was writing a running report, then he would be improving, polishing and, in the words of Hubbard, 'seeking perfection all the time. He would go to a football match, in Liverpool, Manchester, or Sheffield, travel back by train, and come bustling into the office at about 10.15pm asking for the proofs so he could go through them.' If the paper's London office was not reachable, then he was known, in the days before mobile phones, to get off his train and catch a later one to make what other writers would regard as a trivial change. He once, for instance, rang his sports editor at 2am to ask if he could change 'late spring' to 'early summer'.

I was once deputy sports editor of the *Observer*, and, as such, one of the two executives nominally in charge of Hugh McIlvanney. This is a bit like saying you were Beethoven's boss because you helped manage the concert hall where he premiered his works. In reality, you just provided the space – and worried if he was going to show up on time. With McIlvanney, this was no frivolous concern. In his younger days, his fondness for a drink meant, occasionally, several days of a week might be lost in a black hole of sociability; he could make his coats, glasses, wallets, cash, briefcases and hirings from Moss Bros disappear with the efficiency of the Bermuda Triangle; and he had a track record of roistering disputes that could end in fisticuffs. He once, at a New York party, answered an unprovoked head-butt from Norman Mailer by flooring the novelist with a right hander, and the following, from fellow-writer Peter Batt's autobiography, while not characteristic of his passage through the world's airports, contains part of the essence of the younger McIlvanney:

> After a day-long wake on schnapps in Deutschland, Hugh McIlvanney and I arrived home at London airport, according to *Private Eye* magazine 'tired and emotional'. We had a rumpus with some of the porters at the baggage collection point and I landed flat on my back on the luggage carousel, pinned there by a posse of porters while one of their number, a beefy guy answering to the name of Fred, slung numerous ponderous punches at me to the accompaniment of McIlvanney's voice loudly laying the odds on the outcome of the fracas and inviting bets from the crowd of people who had gathered to watch this unseemly spectacle.

Neither was McIlvanney known for arriving at football matches many minutes before the kick-off, and that interval, on a Saturday afternoon, was sometimes occupied with filing the second part of a feature he should have delivered 24 hours before. When he did come on with a match report, the process was, according to *Observer* copytaker John Hawkins, 'often like giving birth to a baby. But the result was always brilliant and he never forgot, at the end of the call, to apologise and thank us.' The labours of writing match reports were, however, as nothing compared to features. McIlvanney, according to sports editor, writer and friend Peter Corrigan, 'likened writing to "the tunnel". If we were on a job together, he would ring me and say "Are you out of the tunnel yet?" Writing to him was like pulling teeth. He suffered for the process more than any one I know.' As McIlvanney himself once wrote: 'If you think reading the stuff can be an ordeal, you should try writing it.'

Once the piece was to his satisfaction, he would fight like a cornered wildcat to preserve every word from depredations that sports editors or lawyers might want to visit on it. In the early 1970s he once detained his friend and fellow reporter

Colin Hart in his room at the Algonquin Hotel, New York for an entire lunchtime while he spent all that time on an expensive Transatlantic phone call arguing with the *Observer*'s lawyers, editor and sports editor over their desire to cut one line referring to the Mafia connections of a character called 'Honest' Bill Daley. Hart says: 'I sat there for two and a half hours while Hugh argued, until, finally, the line was allowed in. He put the phone down, satisfied. We never did get lunch.' And if, when published, there was the slightest error or literal in it, he was suicidal. One Saturday evening in the early 1990s, for instance, he covered a fight at Alexandra Palace, London. The fight was late, so was McIlvanney, and a wire report had to be hastily rewritten to fill the space before McIlvanney's story came through to make the final editions. The following morning sports editor Alan Hubbard was in bed with the papers at 8am when the phone rang. It was McIlvanney. 'What a disaster!' he said. 'Last night. Complete disaster.' Hubbard thought he was referring to the lateness of his story, but he wasn't. The 'complete disaster' was a literal that meant the referee's name had been misspelled.

By 1980, McIlvanney had been working as a sports reporter for 20 years, and having witnessed the prime of such performers as Muhammad Ali and footballer George Best he now found himself having to write the chapters that closed their legends. In 1978, against Leon Spinks, Muhammad Ali had taken the world heavyweight title for an unprecedented third time, but two years later he came up against Larry Holmes in Las Vegas. McIlvanny began his preview of the fight: 'For nearly 20 years Muhammad Ali has been imposing an extravagant fantasy upon his life but somewhere, surely, reality is crouching in ambush, waiting to take revenge.' It was, and a week later, McIlvanney wrote: 'The ring activities of Muhammad Ali now have all the grace and sporting appeal of Russian roulette played with a pump-action shotgun.' A year later, came the final indignity for Ali, with defeat by Trevor Berbick. 'To see him lose to such a moderate fighter in such a grubby context,' wrote McIlvanney, 'was like watching a king ride into permanent exile on the back of a garbage truck'.

Soon he found himself writing real obituaries, as well as mere sporting ones. None were more heartfelt than those he wrote about three of Britain's greatest football managers: Liverpool's Bill Shankly, Manchester United's Matt Busby, and Celtic's Jock Stein, all of whom came from the same west of Scotland mining communities that McIlvanney sprang from. Here he is in 1981 on Shankly, the man who transformed Liverpool Football Club into the best in Britain by, among other astute devices, refusing to acknowledge his team was bested, even when it had, occasionally, been beaten:

> Opponents of Liverpool Football Club would be rash to assume they have done with Bill Shankly. Once Bill's ashes have been scattered on the pitch at Anfield any visiting forward who is setting himself to score an important goal is liable to find suddenly that he has something in his eye.
>
> … With his drill-sergeant's hair-style, his boxer's stance and his staccato, hard-man's delivery he did not fit everybody's idea of a romantic. But that's what he was, an out-and-out, 22-carat example of the species. His secret was that he sensed deep down that the only practical approach to sport is the romantic one. How else could a manager persuade grown men that they could find glory in a boy's game? Shankly did that and more.
>
> … 'Me havin' no education,' I once heard him say, 'I had to use my brains.' He used his heart, too. It was as big as a town.

Four years later, Jock Stein, the man who assembled a side consisting of men born within a 30-mile radius of Glasgow and built it into the best in Europe, collapsed on the touch-line of the Wales *v* Scotland game. When, minutes later, news reached the press box that he had died, it was, McIlvanney wrote, 'as if our spirits, our very lives, had been burglarised'. Then, in 1994, came the death of the final member of this triumvirate, Sir Matt Busby. As was often the case with McIlvanney, the

piece he wrote, for the *Sunday Times* contained truths that had
relevance far beyond the mere playing of ball games:

> In the language of the sports pages, greatness is plentiful. The
> reality of sport, like that of every other area of life, shows that
> it is desperately rare. Greatness does not gad about, reaching for
> people in handfuls. It settles deliberately on a blessed few, and
> Matt Busby was one of them.
>
> If Busby had stood dressed for the pit, and somebody alongside
> him in the room had worn ermine, there would have been no
> difficulty about deciding who was special. Granting him a
> knighthood did not elevate him. It raised, however briefly, the
> whole dubious phenomenon of the honours system.
>
> Busby emanated presence, substance, the quality of strength
> without arrogance. No man in my experience ever exemplified
> better the ability to treat you as an equal while leaving you with
> the sure knowledge that you were less than he was. Such men do
> not have to be appointed leaders. Some democracy of the instincts
> and the blood elects them to be in charge.
>
> That innate distinction was the source of his effect on footballers.
> He never had to bully. One glance from under the eloquent
> eyebrows was worth 10 bellows from more limited natures.

Towards the end of that tribute, McIlvanney observed that
Shankly, Stein and Busby came from an area covered by a small
coalfield which once spread across part of Lanarkshire and
southern Ayrshire. 'Plainly,' he noted, 'there were more than
coal seams running through that bleak landscape in the west
of Scotland. There were seams of rich humanity, of working-
class pride and wit and energy and character.' Three years
later, he turned the idea that the men's shared origins were no
coincidence into a television documentary called 'The Football
Men'. All three, said McIlvanney in his commentary, worked in
the pits. 'They understood the true dynamics of camaraderie.
They were brought up among people whose lives could depend
on teamwork.'

Sport is never liable to run out of telling contrasts, and
in the same year that Busby died, McIlvanney reported on
the ending of a career that was, finally, as tawdry as Busby's

was noble. Diego Maradona had, in the mid-1980s, been a footballing talent that threatened to be the equal of Pele as the best the game had ever seen. From the 1986 World Cup in Mexico, which was eventually won by Maradona's Argentina, McIlvanney began a piece:

> If there is an effective way of killing off the threat of Diego Maradona by marking him, it probably involves putting a white cross over his heart and tethering him to a stake in front of a firing squad. Even then there would be the fear that he might suddenly dip his shoulder and cause the riflemen to start shooting one another.

But, eight years later, the player failed a drugs test at the World Cup, the latest in a line of trouble that involved cocaine, prostitutes and an excessive capacity for self-destruction. McIlvanney began his piece from Texas:

> It was the grubby tumult of an unscheduled press conference in Dallas on Thursday evening that most effectively conveyed the sadness seeping through the squalor of Diego Maradona's expulsion from the World Cup. As a mass of hands holding microphones closed around him like a carnivorous plant, the drawn, slightly hunted look on his Spanish-Indian face said more about the nature and origins of his predicament than the predictable words of denial and complaint that came from his mouth.

It was by no means the first time McIlvanney had found himself having to cover a breaking news story, for his territory occasionally threw up such convulsions, and anyway he regarded himself as first and last a reporter whose beat just happened to be sports. He had covered the lethal disturbances at the Mexico Olympics, the shooting of Israeli athletes at the Munich Games, and his news sense was as developed as any war correspondent's, as I learnt on the afternoon of 16 April 1989. It was a fairly standard press day for the *Observer*, which happened to coincide with the semi-finals of the FA Cup, one of which McIlvanney was attending in Sheffield. About 20 minutes after what should have been the kick-off, the Press

Association wire reported delays to the start of the Sheffield game because of crowd disturbances. Worth a paragraph or two on the front, I thought, as I sat in the middle of the newsroom. Then my phone rang. 'David, it's Hugh. This is a bad one. There are bodies on the edge of the pitch, and the guys giving them the kiss of life are just reeling away with their heads in their hands.' It was, I recall, not for another 30 minutes that the Press Association reported any deaths, and by that time the editor and I had, despite protests from some of the more fastidious brethren, started clearing the front page. The *Observer* was the only quality paper that led on the story in its first edition, an advantage that was due entirely to the alert from McIlvanney and his subsequent report. Within hours the death toll had reached 94.

Three years later he found himself a court reporter, and, in a report on boxer Mike Tyson's trial that is a definitive answer to those who think of sports reporters as the boys at the back of the bus, he began:

> After waiting nearly two weeks to have his say in a trial that threatens him with 60 years in jail, Mike Tyson took the witness stand to pour out lurid endorsement of a defensive strategy apparently aimed at proving he is an aggressive, foul-mouthed sexual predator but not a rapist. In the high, slightly lisping voice that is forever at odds with the menacing hulk of a former heavyweight champion of the world, Tyson spent 75 minutes late on Friday afternoon enlightening a jury of eight men and four women in the Marion County Superior Court about the blitzkrieg of ghetto directness that is his favoured way of wooing.

In 1993, the *Observer* was sold to the *Guardian*, the only other quality title that shared its leftward values and lacked a seventh-day paper. But those of us who actively campaigned for this purchase (the alternative was a sale to the *Independent*, and absorption into its Sunday paper) had reckoned without the new owners, as McIlvanney put it, 'coming in like an occupying army'. It was less a victory for the righteous than the self-righteous, and several of us, after tasting the new life for a brief while, sought terms on which to surrender our *Observer* passports and move on. McIlvanney was soon in negotiation with the *Sunday Times*, a bigger, brasher rival to the *Observer*, and which, unlike the latter, was profitable. They made him an offer nearly 50 per cent larger than his not inconsiderable salary, and, at the age of 59, he quite understandably went. He continues, in his seventies, to write a column, add to the list of awards that has made him one of the most decorated journalists ever, and to do occasional reporting.

If it ever came to choosing just one piece that represents the quality of McIlvanney, his colleagues and editors are in no doubt which it should be. It was written in September 1980 just a few hours after the Welsh boxer Johnny Owen had been knocked out and carried insensible from the ring to hospital. The following is a brutal truncation of the 1,800-word original, but some inkling of its power, especially the last paragraph, remains:

> It can be no consolation to those in South Wales and in Los Angeles who are red-eyed with anxiety about Johnny Owen to know that the extreme depth of his own courage did as much as anything else to take him to the edge of death.
>
> ... In the street, in a hotel lounge or even in his family's home on a Merthyr Tydfil housing estate, he is so reticent as to be almost unreachable, so desperately shy that he has turned 24 without ever having had a genuine date with a girl. But in the ring he has always been transformed, possessed by a furious aggression that has driven his alarmingly thin and unmuscular body through the heaviest fire.
>
> ... It was in the fourth round that Pintor's right hand first struck with a hint of the force that was to be so overwhelming subsequently,... By the 10th, there was unmistakable evidence that the strength had drained out of every part of Owen's body except his heart... There were just 40 seconds of the 12th round left when the horror story started to take shape. Owen was... dropped on his knees by a short right. After rising at three and taking another mandatory count... a ferocious right hook threw him on to his

back. He was unconscious before he hit the canvas and his relaxed
neck muscles allowed his head to thud against the boards. Dai
Gardiner [Owen's trainer] and the boxer's father were in the ring
long before the count could be completed and they were quickly
joined by Dr Schwartz, who called for oxygen.

… Boxing gave Johnny Owen his one positive means of self-
expression. Outside the ring he was an inaudible and almost
invisible personality. Inside, he became astonishingly positive and
self-assured. He seemed to be more at home there than anywhere
else. It is his tragedy that he found himself articulate in such a
dangerous language.

Two months later and without ever regaining consciousness,
Johnny Owen died at the age of 24. As McIlvanney has said:
'The truths in sport may not be momentous, but neither are
they negligible.' It is a comment that could be applied, with
some modification, to almost everything the man ever filed.
He never wrote a negligible paragraph, and some of his pieces
were truly momentous.

11
Ernie Pyle
1900–1945

THE REPORTER WHO NEVER FORGOT WHO HE
WAS WRITING FOR

To non-Americans of the postwar era, it takes a little time to get around to the work of Ernie Pyle. Whether it was because he had a name that makes him sound like a bit-part character in *It's A Wonderful Life*, or whether because his war reporting was the basis for *The Story of G.I. Joe*, you are likely to assume at first hearing that he was a piece of folksy, localised culture that would travel about as far from American shores as a Hudson riverboat. The journalistic equivalent, if you like, of frat houses, church bake-outs and afternoons at a ballgame – very American, very tribal, and not something the outsider was likely to get a full handle on.

It's a view that doesn't long survive a reading of a few of Pyle's war reports. Read these, and about his life, and you become aware that what he achieved, and, more importantly, how he achieved it, makes him not only a very special reporter, but one whose lessons are universal. In the Second World War he developed, via the printed page, something like the relationship with a mass audience only ever achieved by a few others via networked radio or television. His reports from the side of American servicemen as they fought in North Africa,

Ernie Pyle

Italy, Normandy and the Pacific were more like letters home than conventional stories, and they were read in an estimated 14 million homes, through syndication to 400 dailies and 300 weeklies. Such was the affection in which Pyle was held, and so constant the danger he faced, that *Time* magazine called him 'the most prayed for man in America'. And when he died, cut down by a machinegunner on Ie Shima just weeks from the war's end, he was mourned publicly by the president, high-ups and generals, but, mostly, privately by the G.I. Joes and their waiting families for whom his despatches had become the almost daily link with their loved one.

But if he was remembered then as an American institution, it is as a journalistic one he should be treasured now, for what made Pyle a great reporter was that he was unerringly attuned, like some human radio telescope, to both his subjects and his audience. It wasn't a trick, and it wasn't an accident. Nor was Pyle some kind of hick 'sensitive', born with a gift for empathy he neither recognised nor understood. What he was, in fact, was something much more simple than that: a reporter who spent years roaming America, and meeting more readers in more states than probably any journalist before or since. And having met all these potential readers, he listened to them; and, when he was far away, writing about their sons and brothers and husbands and cousins in uniform, he had the manners and good sense to never forget who he was writing for. It's a knack that journalists both sides of the Atlantic, sealed off from the ordinary run of readers by car travel, high aspirations, remote control news gathering via phone and Internet, and political agendas, may one day lose.

Ernest Taylor Pyle was born on 3 August 1900, the only son of a couple who farmed, in a modest way, near Dana in Vermillion County, Indiana. His childhood in this land of creeks and fields and woods, with friends like Thud Hooker and the Saxton boys, had all the ingredients for a Huckleberry Finn sort of existence, except one: his character. Ernest, for that was what his family always called him, was on the shy side and fidgety, traits that were to remain with him for the rest of his life. He didn't want to finish high school, hankering instead to join the navy, but his parents made him stay. They could not, however, keep him down on the farm. At 18 he went off to the University of Indiana to study journalism, partly because he had a small fancy for the roving life, but mainly because he'd been told the subject was 'a breeze'. He wrote for, and then edited the *Daily Student*, but, true to form, didn't stay the whole college course. He left a few months before graduating to be a reporter on the *La Porte Herald-Argus*, where he hung around for a few months and then headed east, for the *Washington News*, a one-cent tabloid only 18 months old and still sufficiently unsure of itself to have, shortly before his arrival, gone through three city editors in a single day.

He joined the paper in 1923 as a reporter, but editors soon found he had a talent for headline writing, and on a tabloid that was too precious an asset to waste on scuttling about the city in search of stories. He was switched to the copy desk, and, for perhaps the first time in his life, discovered a job and an atmosphere that didn't make him feel he was merely passing through. He kept regular hours, played cards with the guys, fell in love with a young lady, a civil servant called Jerry Siebold, and, in as much as he ever did, settled. Three years of headline writing and copy-polishing was, however, enough, and in 1926 he and Jerry threw up their jobs, bought a Ford roadster for $650 and took off to drive around the edge of the United States. Ten weeks and 9,000 miles later, they reached New York, limping up Fifth Avenue, as Pyle later wrote, 'in a down-pouring rain, on two cylinders, with knots as big as teakettles on all four tires, and had to sell the precious thing for a mere $150 to get something to eat'. After only two days of job-hunting he found a place on the graveyard shift, midnight to 8am, on the copy desk of *New York World*. Soon he was on the move again, transferring to the *New York Post*, and, within the year, back to Washington as editor in charge of wire stories. He'd hardly got his feet under that desk before he asked if he could write an aviation column on the side, plugging into one of his own interests, and the enthusiasm stirred by Lindbergh's 1927 trans-Atlantic flight.

So, for the next few years, he would begin each morning by calling every local airport for news of which planes were landing or departing, finish editing around two in the afternoon, and then head off to the old Washington-Hoover Airport, Anacostia Naval Air Station, small airports such as College Park, Maryland, or the Army's Bolling Field. Soon he was so well known to the fliers and airport staff that, it was said, if a pilot baled out, Pyle would get a call before the man hit the ground. The column was such a success it became a full-time task, but, in 1932, this congenial work came to an end. To Pyle's horror, the paper asked him to be managing editor. He felt he couldn't refuse, and so, after a touching little ceremony at Washington airport, when Amelia Earhart presented him with a watch on behalf of the fliers and their crews, he slid reluctantly into the editor's chair at the under-resourced paper. He had no office and no secretary, but all the headaches of getting a competent paper out with too few staff. It was not a challenge he relished. 'It is hard and fatiguing work,' he wrote to his friend Gene Uebelhardt, 'and I get no chance to do any writing.' His life, he wrote, was 'routine and deadening', and three years of it took its toll on his patience and his health. In 1934, after a severe bout of flu, his doctor advised him to get some prolonged sun on his back. Once again, he and Jerry took off in their car, this time to Arizona and California. It was to prove one of the most productive convalescences in newspaper history, creating the role that made Pyle, first, widely read, and, then, a legend. He and Jerry were away for a couple of months and when they returned, Pyle wrote a series of columns about the trip. They proved popular, and Pyle, seizing the chance to be rid of life as an executive, managed to talk George 'Deac' Parker, his editor-in-chief, into appointing him roving correspondent for the Scripps Howard news agency. His job would be to roam America, writing six columns a week about the people and places he met. 'I've had a stroke of luck,' he wrote to Gene Uebelhardt. 'I will go where I please and write what I please. It's the kind of job I've always wanted.'

He and his wife left Washington on the day before his 35th birthday. For the next five years, he and Jerry wore out three cars as they clocked up hundreds of thousands of miles. They criss-crossed America 35 times, and went north to Canada and Alaska, travelled 1,000 miles down the Yukon, over to Hawaii and down to South America, which he then toured by plane. Each week he would file 6,000 words – six 1,000-word columns – back to Washington, where they would be syndicated to a growing number of Scripps Howard papers. A few columns were on the big story of the day – his first, for instance, on 8 August 1935, was from the New Jersey home of Bruno Hauptmann, the Lindbergh baby kidnapper. Some columns were straight reporting, such as the first session of the Supreme Court in its new building ('I defied both tradition and good taste and wore my white and brown checkered racetrack coat, with the green sweater and the gray pants'). And when he passed through Hollywood, he interviewed, among other stars, Ginger Rogers, Shirley Temple, Joan Crawford, Clark Gable and Olivia De Havilland ('So beautiful I couldn't do anything but stand and stare at her').

But Pyle wasn't really interested in conventional news, and certainly not in celebrity features. He once told a friend he'd gone three weeks without reading a paper or listening to the radio. What he loved most to write about were the people and places he met on the road: Rudy Hale, the professional rattlesnake collector from Yuma, California; Gutzon Borglum who was carving the profiles of four presidents into the rock of Mount Rushmore, South Dakota; Josie Pearl, a gold prospector from Winnemucca, Nevada; Ike Proebstal from Tacna, Arizona, who found missing men in the desert; Conrad, the chef at La Fonda, Sante Fe, who cooked turkey so tender 'you could cut it with a glance'; the ruckus in Ontario when the famous Dionne quintuplets were put on view for tourists; the old farmer from Hiawatha, Kansas who spent all his money erecting life-sized effigies of himself and his late wife (11 so far); Sim Webb from Memphis, who was Casey Jones's fireman; William Andrew Johnson, the last surviving slave owned by a president; Fred Hisey, an old *Washington News* friend, now serving a murder sentence in Lorton Penitentiary, Virginia; the retired couple who lived in Death Valley, 80 miles from the nearest store; Cannon Ball Baker, automotive record breaker from Indianapolis, Indiana who'd crossed America 118 times; Ad and Plinky Topperwein of San Antonio, Texas, the best husband and wife sharp-shooting team in the West; and thousands of less extraordinary Americans.

These scenes and characters were described in what read, not like news stories, but letters home from a travelling friend. Here, for instance, he is on the dry dirt of Montana and the Dakotas in the drought.

> A drought is not a spectacular thing ... Crops are gone. Farmers are broke. The heat is terrific. The whole thing is awful. And yet feel sure that a city-bred man, who had heard about the drought and who came out to see the devastation, would be disappointed.
>
> People don't gasp for water. Houses don't catch fire. Cattle aren't dead on the road. Trucks aren't moving panicky-eyed families out before sunset. Farmers don't strike a pose and hang their heads in despair ... We think of farmers standing around in groups, making desperate decisions. A drought isn't like that. A drought never definitely passes a crisis. A farmer never knows just what day or even in what week he was ruined...

On interviewing female stars in Hollywood:

> I am sick unto death of trying to write about the great women stars of the movies. It is true that those I have finally been permitted to see have been very nice. But the rigmarole you have to go through,

the stalling around and waiting, the few little precious minutes they finally give you, their apparent inability to break down and talk plain talk, all gives me a pain...

And on Ervin Robertson, whose diet had once been so bad he lost all his teeth to scurvy, and so, living in isolated Eagle, Alaska, made his own dentures:

> For the four front ones he used mountain-sheep teeth. He said they were almost like human teeth, except longer; so he just filed them down. Back of these, four on each side, he used caribou teeth. And for those grinding molars, bear's teeth... He made his plate of aluminium, drilled out holes for the teeth, set them in, and then worked the warm aluminium over to hold them tight. It took him a month. He made both uppers and lowers. And he wore them for nearly twenty-five years. He told me he ate a lot of bear meat with them, but not the bear the teeth came from.

It was a truly nomadic existence. 'I have no home,' he wrote. 'My home is where my extra luggage is, and where the car is stopped, and where I happen to be getting mail this time. My home is America.' It is an uncharacteristically grand statement for a man who was always modest about himself (he feared people would not like him), and modest in his needs. His day-book entry for 3 August 1935 is typical:

Room for night	$2.00
2 Breakfasts	$0.75
Gas (Andover, N. J.)	$1.06
Fruit	$0.94
2 Dinners (Perona Farms)	$2.20
	$6.95

He was often invited by people to stay at their home, but always made an excuse and stayed, instead, at the local motel. 'You meet 'em, you talk with 'em, you figure what's interesting, you write about it, you move on,' he wrote.

Behind that B-movie one-liner lay a lot of technique. Like a lot of good writers who had once worked as a copyeditor, he found the experience sharpened his eye for a story, his ear for a memorable quote and his ability to fashion a phrase that might make a headline. And added to this was a relentless work-rate. He carried on the back seat of his car a considerable library of books, plus a state-by-state card index of story tips and ideas. And each place he stopped, he would visit the town newspaper, the drugstore, gas station, diners, bars, motels, post offices and anywhere else he felt might harbour some nugget or lively character for a column. And, when he had gathered enough for several pieces, he would go back to his hotel room, take about half a day fretting and fussing over each column, marking change after change in pencil, before finally, and reluctantly, handing each to his wife Jerry who typed a clean copy and sent it off. She, 'That Girl who rides with me', as she was known in the column, seemed a perfect companion. Her suggestions for pieces were often good ones, she knew how to handle his moods, and, when Pyle was driving, she didn't talk much, which was fine with him. But at some point on their travels, the silence that was consideration for a mind concentrating half on the road and half on the next column slipped into a brooding lack of communication that was a sign of serious depression. She developed a dependence on drink, sedatives and finally Benzedrine that cast a shadow over her and Pyle for the rest of their lives.

So the travelling and writing life went on, until, in late 1940, Pyle casually suggested to his bosses at Scripps Howard that he should go to London to report the war. He was astonished when they readily agreed. And so, on 16 November, he sailed on the liner *Exeter* for England. He arrived in London on 9 December, and twenty days later this ex-copyeditor from Indiana filed perhaps the best piece written on the Blitz:

> Some day when peace has returned to this odd world I want to come to London again and stand on a certain balcony on a moonlit night and look down upon the peaceful silver curve of the Thames with its dark bridges. And standing there, I want to tell somebody

who has never seen it how London looked on a certain night in the holiday season of the year 1940...

It was a night when London was ringed and stabbed with fire... Shortly after the sirens wailed I could hear the Germans grinding overhead. In my room, with its black curtains drawn across the windows, you could feel the shake from the guns. You could hear the boom, crump, crump, crump of heavy bombs at their work of tearing buildings apart...

I gathered a couple of friends and went to a high, darkened balcony that gave us a view of one-third of the entire circle of London.

... The closest fires were near enough for us to hear the crackling flames and the yells of firemen. Little fires grew into big ones even as we watched. Big ones died down under the firemen's valor, only to break out again later... Into the dark, shadowed spaces below us whole batches of incendiary bombs fell. We saw two dozen go off in two seconds... These white pinpoints would go out one by one as the unseen heroes of the moment smothered them with sand. But also, as we watched, other pinpoints would burn on, and pretty soon a yellow flame would leap up from the white center. They had done their work – another building was on fire.

The greatest of all the fires was directly in front of us. Flames seemed to whip hundreds of feet into the air. Pinkish-white smoke ballooned upward in a great cloud, and out of this cloud there gradually took shape – so faintly at first that we weren't sure we saw correctly – the gigantic dome and spires of St. Paul's Cathedral surrounded by fire.

... Below us the Thames grew lighter, and all around were the dark shadows of buildings and bridges that formed the base of this dreadful masterpiece.

... The thing I shall always remember above all the other things in my life is the monstrous loveliness of that one single view of London – stabbed with great fires, shaken by explosions, its dark regions along the Thames sparkling with the pinpoints of white-hot bombs, all of it roofed over with a ceiling of pink that held bursting shells, balloons, flares, and the grind of vicious engines.

Most of all, that dreadful season of bombing, he wrote about the people – those in the shelters, the anti-aircraft gun pits, the air raid warden posts, and the clerks and stockbrokers fire-watching from the roofs of their offices. His bosses were thrilled.

Roy Howard cabled him: 'Your stuff not only greatest your career but most illuminating human and appealing descriptive matter printed America since outbreak Battle Britain.' Pyle was not altogether convinced. 'I seem to be suffering more than ever from timidity and an inferiority complex,' he wrote to his wife. 'It's just a horror for me to go out and talk to people. I feel like I'm conspicuous and ignorant and have reached forty years old with so little knowledge I can't even hold a conversation with twenty year olds.'

He overcame these little demons of doubt, but his wife could no longer deal with the larger ones inside her head. When he flew home after four months, he found her in the grip of 'a triple personality', as he called it in a letter to a friend. 'One side of utter charm and captivation for people she cares nothing about; one side of cruelty and dishonesty toward the few people she does care about; and another side of almost insane melancholy and futility and cynicism when she is alone.' So bad did the moods and the drinking become that, at her suggestion, and with the agreement of her doctors, nurse and mother, a radical therapy was decided: a divorce, 'on the gamble', wrote Pyle, 'that it might shock her into a realization that she had to face life like other people... If she can regain herself within a year or so, we'll be remarried.' He left home the same night, leaving her a note which began 'My Darling, My heart is breaking, too...' and ended: 'As long as there is the slightest hope, there is no other woman in the world for me...'

By now America was in the war, and in June 1942, Pyle flew to report on the first wave of US troops training in Ireland and Britain. By November, he was on a troop ship bound for North Africa, landing in Algeria two weeks after the invasion had begun. His first notable files, which caused a minor, if fleeting, sensation back home, were two reports on how pro-Nazi French officials were being allowed to remain in post and organise sabotage. Soon, however, and especially after

January, when he moved to the US bomber base at Biskra, he was back in his favoured routine of writing about ordinary Joes like himself who found themselves transported to places of peril by a war they couldn't entirely understand. Here he is on the scene at the air base as men scanned the skies, hoping against hope, that the missing Thunderbird, reported hit by ground fire, would make it home:

> And then an electric thing happened... we saw the plane – just a tiny black speck. It seemed almost on the ground, it was so low, and in the first glance we could sense that it was barely moving, barely staying in the air. Crippled and alone, two hours behind all the rest, it was dragging itself home... a far dark speck struggling toward us with such pathetic slowness.
>
> All of us stood tense, hardly remembering anyone else was there. With our nervous systems we seemed to pull the plane toward us. I suspect a photograph would have shown us all leaning slightly to the left. Not one of us thought the plane would ever make the field, but on it came – so slowly that it was cruel to watch. It reached the far end of the airdrome, still holding its pathetic little altitude. It skimmed over the tops of parked planes, and kept on... The wheels touched softly. And, as the plane rolled down the runway, the thousands of men around that vast field suddenly realized that they were weak and that they could hear their hearts pounding...

And here he is on the return of men from the front lines in Tunisia in May 1943:

> ... A narrow path comes like a ribbon over a hill miles away, down a long slope, across a creek, up a slope and over another hill.
>
> All along the length of this ribbon there is now a thin line of men. For four days and nights they have fought hard, eaten little, washed none, and slept hardly at all. Their nights have been violent with attack, fright, butchery, and their days sleepless and miserable with the crash of artillery.
>
> The men are walking. They are fifty feet apart, for dispersal. Their walk is slow, for they are dead weary, as you can tell even when looking at them from behind. Every line and sag of their bodies speaks their inhuman exhaustion. On their shoulders and backs they carry heavy steel tripods, machine-gun barrels, leaden

boxes of ammunition. Their feet seem to sink into the ground from the overload they are bearing.

They don't slouch. It is the terrible deliberation of each step that spells out their appalling tiredness. Their faces are black and unshaven. They are young men, but the grime and whiskers and exhaustion make them look middle-aged. In their eyes as they pass is not hatred, not excitement, not despair, not the tonic of their victory – there is just the simple expression of being here as though they had been here doing this forever, and nothing else.

The line moves on, but it never ends. All afternoon men keep coming round the hill and vanishing eventually over the horizon. It is one long tired line of ant-like men…

Pyle was now 42, a wiry, even frail, little man (he stood 5ft 8 inches and weighed only 110 lb) worried more about the state of his wife back home than the prospect of being killed himself. In that he was probably not unlike many of the men he now found himself alongside. He was with them as they cowered in trenches when bombers came, understood when they lapsed into silence at the news that the platoon wise-cracker had been killed, and joined in when they bitched about all the little indignities of service life. As his Algerian room-mate A.J. Liebling said, Pyle did not, unlike many correspondents, treat the war as a crusade, a chance for glory, a big boys' adventure or a vacation from the tedium of the sports desk, but as 'an unalleviated misfortune'. This, for all that it was necessary and justified, was probably how most of the men mixed up in it, and their families back home, saw it. And because of this, and because, from his constant touring of America he knew the national readership probably better than any reporter before or since, his writing struck a chord. At the start of the war his column was printed in some 30 dailies; that soon increased to 45, then 60, and, by 1944, it was more than 100. By the war's end, his words were in 300 newspapers.

There was a further benefit of those years on the road. When he wrote about soldiers, they were not nameless numbers, 'an Arkansas infantryman', or even 'Sgt Bill "Skeets" Millar'.

When Pyle wrote about the American soldier it was 'Corporal Martin Clayton, Jr., of 3400 Princeton St., Dallas, Texas', 'Warrant Officer Ernest Pike of Savoy, Texas', or 'Pfc. William Gross of 322 North Foster Street, Lansing, Michigan'. This was more than a sense of the importance of place to Americans, it was making plain, in almost every column he ever wrote from the field, that the vast numbers in the services were not just units, brigades and divisions, but made up of real men from real places. Many a correspondent must have disdained such touches as parochial, but not Pyle. And no reporter better described the life of troops in the field, shorn, as it was, of any comfort:

> You can scarcely credit the fact that human beings could adjust themselves so acceptingly to a type of living that is only slightly above the caveman stage…
>
> They have not slept in a bed for months. They've lived through this vicious winter sleeping outdoors on the ground. They haven't been paid in three months…
>
> They never take off their clothes at night, except their shoes. They don't get a bath oftener than once a month… Very few of the front-line troops have ever had any leave… Nurses tell me that when the more seriously wounded reach the hospital they are often so exhausted they fall asleep without drugs, despite their pain…
>
> The discomfort is perpetual. You're always cold and almost always dirty… You don't have chairs, lights, floors, or tables. You don't have any place to set anything, or any store to buy things from. There are no newspapers, milk, beds, sheets, radiators, beer, ice cream, or hot water. You just sort of exist, either standing up working or lying down asleep. There is no pleasant in-between. The velvet is all gone from living.

Newsweek said that 'covering the war in North Africa are many score correspondents – and Ernie Pyle'; *Time* called him 'America's most widely read war correspondent'; and papers like the *New York World-Telegram* ran his stuff on page one. Readers clipped his column, and mailed it to their boys, and service paper *Stars and Stripes* began running it. The result was that the troops saw him not just as a good, accurate read, but their voice. This was no idle accolade. In a column from Italy in early 1944, he proposed that soldiers be given a bonus for battle, in the way that airmen got extra pay for flying missions. Within five months Congress awarded soldiers a 50 per cent raise when they were in combat. It was known as the Ernie Pyle Bill.

Pyle wrote through the North Africa campaign, through Sicily, and in between all this missed Jerry so much that he arranged to remarry her by proxy. In September 1943, he flew home, and realised for the first time the impact of his columns. The *World-Telegram* wanted to interview him, so did *Editor and Publisher*, army intelligence, the British ambassador, Secretary of War Stimpson, the Pentagon and the radio networks – one so badly that it offered him $1,500 for a single broadcast. He turned it down, as he did the offer of a lecture tour with a $25,000 guarantee. The Office of War Information wanted him to broadcast, as did the WAC recruiting office and War Bond campaign. Friends, old soldiers, families of men he had been with all besieged his New York hotel with calls, autograph hunters followed him, companies asked him to endorse their goods, and Hollywood wanted to talk about a movie based on his columns. Despite escaping to see Jerry in Albuquerque, and his father in Dana, he knew now that however much he might have preferred to stay at home, he had created by his writing an obligation to so many people that he couldn't shirk. He had to return to the front. 'I dread it and I'm afraid of it,' he wrote. 'But what can a guy do? I know millions of others who are reluctant too, and they can't even get home. So here we go.'

Italy was where he went, and such was his standing that the *Boston Globe* published his first report under an eight-column headline on the front page: 'Ernie Pyle Writes Again'. To his usual fretting over the column was now added the knowledge that millions were now hanging on his words. It didn't make writing any easier. AP correspondent Don Whitehead found him working in his room one night. Pyle looked up. 'This stuff stinks,' he said. 'I just can't seem to get going again.' By way of proof he tossed over three columns. Whitehead picked one up. It was the story of Captain Waskow, one of the most affecting pieces of war reporting in history:

> Frontlines in Italy—In this war I have known a lot of officers who were loved and respected by the soldiers under them. But never have I crossed the trail of any man as beloved as Captain Henry T. Waskow, of Belton, Texas.
>
> ... I was at the foot of the mule trail the night they brought Captain Waskow's body down. The moon was nearly full at the time, and you could see far up the trail, and even part way across the valley below. Soldiers made shadows in the moonlight as they walked.
>
> Dead men had been coming down the mountain all evening, lashed onto the backs of mules. They came lying belly-down across the wooden pack-saddles, their heads hanging down on the left side of the mule, their stiffened legs sticking out awkwardly from the other side, bobbing up and down as the mule walked.
>
> ... The soldiers who led them stood there waiting. 'This one is Captain Waskow,' one of them said quietly. Two men unlashed his body from the mule and lifted it off and laid it in the shadow beside the low stone wall. Other men took the other bodies off. Finally there were five, lying end to end in a long row, alongside the road.
>
> ... The unburdened mules moved off to their olive orchard. The men in the road seemed reluctant to leave. They stood around, and gradually one by one I could sense them moving close to Captain Waskow's body. Not so much to look, I think, as to say something in finality to him, and to themselves. I stood close by and I could hear.
>
> One soldier came and looked down, and he said out loud, 'God damn it.' That's all he said, and then he walked away... Then a soldier came and stood beside the officer, and bent over, and he too spoke to his dead captain, not in a whisper but awfully tenderly, and he said:
>
> 'I sure am sorry, sir.'
>
> Then the first man squatted down, and he reached down and took the dead hand, and he sat there for five full minutes, holding

the dead hand in his own and looked intently into the dead face, and he never uttered a sound all the time he sat there.

And then finally he put the hand down, and then reached up and gently straightened the points of the captain's shirt collar, and then he sort of rearranged the tattered edges of his uniform around the wound. And then he got up and walked away down the road in the moonlight, all alone...

Grove Patterson, editor of the *Toledo Blade*, spoke for many when he described this as 'the most beautifully written newspaper story I have ever read'. In January 1944 it was published on front pages across America, and one paper, the *Washington Daily News* put the entire text of it on the front with not even a headline. The paper sold out. By now the column was in more than 200 daily papers, a Pulitzer Prize duly arrived, and, what with the syndication rights and sales of book collections of his pieces, Pyle was rich.

By mid-April 1944, he was back in London, reporting on preparations for the Normandy landings, and by 3 June he was in LST 353 heading for Omaha Beach. He had been offered a comfortable berth aboard General Omar Bradley's command ship *Augusta*, but declined. He landed on D-Day plus one:

It was a lovely day for strolling along the seashore. Men were sleeping on the sand, some of them sleeping forever. Men were floating in the water, but they didn't know they were in the water, for they were dead. The water was full of squishy little jellyfish about the size of your hand. Millions of them. In the center each of them had a green design exactly like a four-leaf clover. The good-luck emblem. Sure, Hell, yes.

And then, on 17 June, he followed a column about the military hardware wrecked on the beach with this:

But there is another and more human litter. It extends in a thin little line, just like a high-water mark, for miles along the beach. This is the strewn personal gear, gear that will never be needed again, of those who fought and died to give us our entrance into Europe.

Here in a jumbled row for mile on mile are soldiers' packs. Here are socks and shoe polish, sewing kits, diaries, Bibles and hand grenades... Here are toothbrushes and razors, and snapshots of families back home staring up at you from the sand. Here are pocketbooks, metal mirrors, extra trousers, and bloody, abandoned shoes... Here are torn pistol belts and canvas water buckets, first-aid kits and jumbled heaps of lifebelts. I picked up a pocket Bible with a soldier's name in it, and put it in my jacket. I carried it half a mile or so and then put it back down on the beach. I don't know why I picked it up, or why I put it back down.

Soldiers carry strange things ashore with them. In every invasion you'll find at least one soldier hitting the beach at H-hour with a banjo slung over his shoulder. The most ironic piece of equipment marking our beach – this beach of first despair, then victory – is a tennis racket that some soldier had brought along. It lies lonesomely on the sand, clamped in its rack, not a string broken.

On 25 August, he was with General LeClerc's division when it entered Paris, and found himself, in the thick of the celebrations, kissing babies like a politician and declaring: 'Anyone who doesn't sleep with a woman tonight is just an exhibitionist.' The euphoria didn't last long. He had been overseas 29 months, written more than 700,000 words, and seen more men die than most had ever done. 'It seemed to me that if I heard one more shot or saw one more dead man, I would go off my nut,' he wrote, and telling his readers 'I don't think I could go on and keep sane,' he sailed home – utterly exhausted but convinced also that he was running out on his comrades. He returned to the by-now usual round of offers from radio stations and lecture circuits, interviews, invitations (some of which, like tea at the White House with Eleanor Roosevelt, could not be refused). 'Tell me,' one partygoer asked him, 'just exactly what is it you don't like about war?' Pyle wrote later: 'I think I must have turned a little white, and all I could do was look at him in shock and say, "Good God, if you don't know, then I could never tell you."' He dropped into Hollywood, too, to catch up with the movie being made of his columns: *The Story of G.I. Joe*. Starring Burgess Meredith as

Pyle, and Robert Mitchum in a part that was, in effect, Captain Waskow, it finally premiered in July 1945.

And then there was Jerry. There were two suicide attempts that spring, and, when the time came to consider returning to war, Pyle was torn between conflicting duties: staying by the side of his increasingly unstable wife, or reporting on how the American soldier was faring on the one front he had not yet visited: the Pacific islands. His column won. 'I'm going simply because there's a war on and I'm part of it,' he wrote. '... I'm going simply because I've got to – and I hate it.' In January 1945, in a demonstration of the expectation that now travelled with him, he was seen off from San Francisco by an army brass band and 1,000 cheering men. He promised Jerry (and himself) it would be his last tour.

Pyle sailed first for Guam, then Saipan, the base from which B-29 bombers were taking off for the 14-hour missions to Japan, and he was part of the landings on Okinawa. With every action, he felt his luck could not last much longer, writing to a colleague: 'I wouldn't give you two cents for the likelihood of me being alive a year from now.' But when the opportunity arose to be part of the 77th Infantry's seizure of Ie Shima, an island a mere ten miles square, Pyle was there. The day after the initial landings, and with no more than a strip of coast secured, Pyle went ashore on Red Beach No. 2. Next morning, he was in a jeep driven by Colonel Joseph B. Coolidge, of Helena, Arkansas when, as they approached a road junction, a Japanese machinegunner on a ridge above them started firing. Coolidge braked, and he, Pyle and two others dived into a ditch. In a break between the bursts of fire, Pyle stuck his head up and asked Coolidge: 'Are you all right?' Another rattle of fire came in. Coolidge ducked. When it stopped, he turned to Pyle. The reporter was lying face up, hit in the left temple. He was dead.

He was buried, with the speedy ceremony of war, in a makeshift cemetery on that little island, with an engineer one side of him and an infantry private on the other. GIs had made a coffin of sorts from planks, and they insisted Pyle wore his helmet. 'They felt,' the chaplain later wrote, 'he looked more natural that way.' And over the newly dug ground the men erected this sign:

> At This Spot
> The 77th Infantry Division
> Lost a Buddy
> ERNIE PYLE
> 18 April 1945

Jerry, with now nothing to live for, lasted little more than another seven months. She died in Albuquerque on 23 November 1945, but not before insisting that Pyle's body should have no high-profile homecoming but rest always among those of others who had fallen in the Pacific campaign. It lies today in the National Memorial Cemetery of the Pacific in Punchbowl Crater, near Honolulu.

The news of Pyle's death was a major story from coast to coast. *Time* carried a full-page tribute, headlined simply 'Ernie', and tributes poured forth, from President Truman, the Secretaries of War and the Navy, and generals from Eisenhower to Mark W. Clark. The silence of others was even more eloquent. When General Omar Bradley was told, he put head in hands and could say nothing for some time. But perhaps the most poignant tribute of all, the one a reporter would want, was the preservation of his work, not in archives, museums, books and websites, but in homes across America. Cuttings of his column, yellowing now but folded with obvious care, are still preserved in keepsake drawers, veterans' tin boxes, in frames on old men's study walls, in scrapbooks, or fall fluttering to the floor as an old book is opened.

His knowledge of average Americans from all those prewar trips meant he knew better than any other journalist how to pitch the language and the subject matter of his articles. But it also meant something else, something that sealed the special relationship with his readers. He didn't bullshit them. Never once did he pretend he knew more than he did, echo back some news editor's armchair view of what he was reporting, give events a political spin, drown out the truth with ra-ra patriotism or plunge into sentiment. When he died, a final, incomplete column was found in his pocket. It was on the end of the war in Europe, and, after writing how sad he was that he couldn't be with his friends in that theatre at their moment of victory, he added this:

> In the joyousness of high spirits it is easy for us to forget the dead. Those who are gone would not wish themselves to be a millstone of gloom around our necks. But there are many of the living who have had burned into their brains forever the unnatural sight of cold dead men scattered over the hillsides and in the ditches along the high rows of hedge throughout the world.
>
> Dead men by mass production – in one country after another – month after month and year after year. Dead men in winter and dead men in summer. Dead men in such familiar promiscuity that they become monotonous. Dead men in such monstrous infinity that you come almost to hate them.
>
> These are the things that you at home need not even try to understand. To you at home they are columns of figures, or he is a near one who went away and just didn't come back. You didn't see him lying so grotesque and pasty beside the gravel road in France.
>
> We saw him, saw him by the multiple thousands.

Those who think that each generation's journalism is better than the last need only reflect on those words, and then compare them with coverage of fresher conflicts, in the Gulf and Iraq. Which is more honest, and which serves its country better? Ernie Pyle may have been an American, and an American at war, but he reserved his true patriotism for the truth.

Ann Leslie

12
Ann Leslie
1941–

THE MOST VERSATILE REPORTER EVER

In the late summer of 1989, in the aftermath of the Tiananmen Square massacre, a middle-aged British woman moved among surviving dissidents, interviewing them in secret through her interpreter. Two months later, she rode in a sputtering little East German car through what, just 24 hours before, had been the impenetrable barrier of Checkpoint Charlie in Berlin. The following year, she was outside a South African jail when Nelson Mandela walked to freedom. The year after that, she abandoned her vacation to fly to Moscow and see the coup against Gorbachev disintegrate in vodka-fuelled farce. She was there in Iraq in 1991 watching US troops halt on the road to Basra and weep as they saw Iraqi families trying vainly to flee Saddam's slaughter squads. She was on a New Mexico airstrip when a campaigning Bill Clinton fixed her with his magnetic gaze, and then released it when he saw she was not a voter. She was nearby when Sarajevo market-place was shelled, and a lot closer when the Serbs said it was all a Muslim trick to fool the West. And she was there when Hong Kong was handed over to the Chinese, when the body of Princess Diana was borne to her grave on a sea of English emotion, when a jury made America gasp as it found O.J. Simpson not guilty, when Putin was elected, in the aftermath of 9/11, and there when, once again, war came to Iraq. Wherever the eyes of the late twentieth and early twenty-first centuries were, Ann Leslie was there.

And she was there when no one in authority wanted her to be there. Undercover, in China, interviewing dissidents again. In Hungary, as the withdrawing Red Army smashed everything they could find and poisoned the ground with oil. In New England poking around in the strange world of the Kennedys. In El Salvador, where insurgents rang her hotel room and clicked the safety catches of their guns on and off to remind her to go away. On Death Row in Virginia, asking the condemned what it feels like when sentence of execution is passed. In Cuba, finding and interviewing Castro's illegitimate daughter. On the North Korean border, illicitly talking to victims of that distant and terrible famine. In a Moscow room, asking Russia's most feared 'businessman' about a contract killing. And, in Tehran, disguised in the all-enveloping uniform of the Islamic woman, meeting dissidents in the dead of night. Ann Leslie was there.

And there, too, for those other stories: a Rolling Stones concert; sumo wrestling; Princess Diana's sex life; a national disco dancing contest; Cherie Blair's quirky fashion sense; teenage eating disorders; Miss Worlds; suburban hedge wars, and Imelda Marcos's shoes. She has interviewed Mikhail Gorbachev and Julio Iglesias; Indira Gandhi and Swedish tennis players; Margaret Thatcher and Shirley Maclaine; two American presidents, one world heavyweight boxing champion, Europe's top male model, three people on Death Row, Arab princesses, chat-show hosts, umpteen terrorists, assorted megalomaniacs, half a dozen demogogues, and Andrew Lloyd Webber. Her cuttings files run the gamut of late twentieth-century notoriety from Idi Amin to Pia Zadora. No journalist has ever been there like Ann Leslie. In more than four decades she has reported from more than 70 countries, and on an unparalleled range of subjects.

It is, perhaps, not all that surprising that a woman who would spend so much of her life insinuating herself into the planet's least pleasant places, exploring its least wholesome habits, should turn out to be a descendant of the world's first female sanitary engineer – Mary Martin, a pioneer who plied her trade in the East End of London but who spent much of her life in China where she was known as 'Granny Ming'. Leslie's immediate antecedents were only marginally less exotic, being born the daughter of a prosperous oilman, in what is now Pakistan, in 1941. Her unusual childhood circumstances were compounded by having as a mother a woman cursed, as Leslie later put it, 'by an almost incredible beauty', and who seemed at that time to be ambivalent about her daughter's very existence. In the invariable absence of this unmaternal socialite, the young Leslie's main source of affection and caring was instead her father's servant, Yah Mohammed. It was to him that she would always run when she wanted soothing, and she loved this illiterate Muslim with 'an almost unbearable intensity'. The feelings were reciprocated. He once dealt calmly with a deadly snake that invaded her bedroom, and during the Great Calcutta Killing of 1946, as Hindus and Muslims butchered each other in the streets into which his little charge had wandered, Yah Mohammed risked his life to scour alleys and back streets, until he had found her and carried her to safety on his back.

His bravery was impressive. He had been far more at risk from the sectarian violence than she was, a fact she recalled almost 50 years later in describing a journey with her mother in 1947:

> The long Indian train clattered and screeched to a halt somewhere in the middle of nowhere. A sudden silence. And then the screams. My mother clutched me to her, covered my eyes, told me not to

be scared, there was nothing to worry about. And there wasn't: not for us, at least... in the shabby first-class compartment of what was to become one of the 'killing trains'... In an orgy of sectarian bloodletting, up to a million people died and at least 14 million became refugees... Why weren't my mother and I killed that dreadful summer afternoon? Because we, the so-called 'colonial oppressors', simply didn't matter any more... we were not the targets of the Sikh jathas – armed bands – who'd ambushed the train. Their targets were Moslems. Many years later... my mother told me how, when the train moved again, it was full of blood and bodies, men, women and children, with their throats slit. Further bodies lay strewn in the bloody dust alongside the track.

The future foreign correspondent was just six years old.

Sanctuary from the city's religious passions, and from the summer heat, was sought by colonialists in the hill stations. The Leslie family's hot-season retreat was Ootacamund, a chintzy re-creation of Edwardian Surrey, complete with gabled villas named 'Iris Cottage' and 'Sunnyside', and, for young Ann, a boarding school called St Hilda's. But the colonial habit was, when children reached 10 or 11, to send them back 'home' to be educated, and so, in time, she was packed off – sans parents, sans Yah Mohammed – thousands of miles away to school in England. Long holidays were spent with her parents at their current base (by 20, she had added Pakistan, Afghanistan and Iraq to the list of places she called 'home'), and in due course she won a scholarship to study English at Lady Margaret Hall, Oxford. In three years, she wrote not a line of student journalism, but, when graduation came, the job of reporter seemed the least unappealing of available options while she decided what she really wanted to do with her life, and she submitted herself for interview with the *Daily Express*. Ushered, in due course, into the presence of the editor in London, she was asked a few desultory questions by a moody-looking individual who never once looked up, and was then informed, in a way which suggested that refusal was not an option, that she started in Manchester on the Monday. Without having shown much in the way of aptitude or enthusiasm, she suddenly found herself a national newspaper journalist at the age of 21.

Any attendant glamour was soon dispelled by the realities of life in a northern English city. 'Manchester was horrendous,' she told the *Independent on Sunday*'s Johann Hari in a 2004 interview.

> From the moment I walked into the office, the news editor hated me. I was everything he didn't like – a woman, with a la-di-da accent, who came from the south, who'd been Oxbridge-educated... I had been reading *Cosmopolitan* – or whatever its equivalent was – about how career women should dress, so I had bought a very cheap Chanel suit. One of the men in the office jeered, 'You're not in the bloody Savoy now, missy.' This monstrous news editor said on my first day that I was 'keeping a good man out of a job'. In fact, if he hadn't hated me so much, and I hadn't hated him, I would probably have left journalism at this point, but the iron entered my soul and I decided I would leave the job on my terms.

These charmers, determined to prove that the University of Life was a superior academe to Oxford, despatched her to provincial trade fairs to produce eight-page special editions single-handedly, sent her to make police calls in the knowledge that any promising tit-bits from the blotter would be reserved for the crime correspondent, and kept from her the *Express* Style Book, without which no journalist on the staff could hope to be aware of the many clichés and eccentricities the paper then insisted upon (all roast dinners were, for instance, 'succulent', any task involving bodies automatically had to become 'grim', and holiday crowds, unless there was actually snow on the ground, were always 'shirt-sleeved'). She responded with gritted teeth or tears, whichever she thought would work better, and seemed to be making but little progress until she was sent to Oldham to interview a dwarf who claimed to have been at school with Cary Grant. Leslie was offered, and enjoyed, copious amounts of her subject's illicit drink supply, and was then discovered by the little man's wife, in what might be called journalistic *flagrante*. ('She took one look at her drunk dwarf husband, cross-eyed with drink and this strange young woman,' Leslie told Hari, 'and chased me out of Oldham.') Back at the office, she wrote up the interview, including the reason for its early termination, and the night editor was so taken with the result he ran the story with a boxed by-line, then the *Express*'s typographical equivalent of a roll of drums. Despite the news desk's churlish response (she was despatched the following day to cover a custody dispute between two Stockport neighbours over a budgerigar – 'Make a clever story out of that, missy!'), she had made a breakthrough of sorts.

She also had as a rival for a while an older female reporter called Peggy Robinson who deemed it necessary to wear combat fatigues to cover the Pennines, a rural area in the north of England, which has a bleak beauty but, if truth be told, few snipers. From this gung-ho character, she learned some of the skills then thought essential to the practice of tabloid journalism in Britain: an extensive repertoire of profanities, the knack of removing the diaphragms from public phones so your rivals couldn't use them, and how to disable their cars to give you a head start.

It was now the early 1960s, and the youth culture that actually began several years before finally seeped into the clichéd consciousness of the men who ran the *Express*. To their great surprise, they found that the world, as well as being populated by shirt-sleeved holiday crowds eating succulent roast beef dinners while reading about mercy dashes and starlets in love triangles, also included human beings under the age of 25 who were not necessarily 'tots' or 'school kids'. A 'youth page' was decreed, and, in casting around the newsroom for someone to fill it, the gaze of the eyeshade-and-braces wearers fell upon the person they had hitherto thought of as their over-educated bluestocking, now instantly transformed in their eyes into 'pert, blonde, Ann Leslie, 21'. She found herself removed from police calls and, instead, interviewing pop groups from northern cities, such as the then almost unknown Beatles. The result was some mildly zany copy, thought to be sufficiently 'with it' to secure a swift summons to London, where editor Robert Edwards cleared space on the leader page and gave her a column headed 'A provocative new name – and she's only 22!'

As well as her youth, Leslie soon found herself making use of her looks. While lacking the legendary beauty of her mother (which caused, among other palpitations, film director David Lean to fall at her feet and future Poet Laureate John Betjeman to rhapsodise), she was quite prepared to doll herself up to get a story. In May 1966, for example, Muhammad Ali flew into Britain, bringing with him his entourage and his well-known eye for 'little foxes', as young women sporting mini-skirts and startling amounts of make-up were known. In expectation of a few hammed-up moments from the great man, half of Fleet Street decamped to Heathrow and swilled around the arrivals lounge. Standing apart from them, wearing a bright-coloured sleeveless mini-dress, and with spectacles perched on her powdered nose, was Leslie, doing her best to look as if she was nothing to do with the press pack. This – plus a quiet word with a show-business agent who was hanging around and had Ali contacts – worked. As the world's most famous sportsman swept through the airport, she was spotted, asked if she wanted a meeting with 'the Champ', and led to his waiting Rolls-Royce. As the car bearing Ali and what appeared to be a mysterious new young companion drove off leaving the almost quoteless reporters behind, Leslie could not resist winding down the window and shouting: 'Actually, I'm Ann Leslie of the *Daily Express* and I've scooped you all!'

With the Ali piece, she had made her reputation as an interviewer all too successfully, and in the next few years Leslie, still typecast as representative of pert youth, was packed off to elicit mildly interesting quotes from that then-staple subject: wives of famous men. This was not what she wanted, especially when she was sent to interview the England cricket captain's wife for the third time. What she did want was to report news, preferably overseas. This was what the paper's foreign editor, David English, wanted, too. He sent her on some assignments, especially in the States, and put her up to run the New York office, but was told: 'You can't have a female running a bureau.' So she left to go freelance, writing from such locations as Australia, the Bahamas and Fiji for upscale magazines like *Queen* and the long-defunct *Nova*, and covering, among other stories, the Manson trial in Los Angeles. She even had a spell as European picture editor of *Playboy*, although her skills in the dark-room were never deployed on the photo-spreads that were its main selling point. David English, meanwhile, had become editor, first, of the *Daily Sketch*, and then, of the *Daily Mail*, which he forged into the most formidable paper in British journalism. His secret was, first, to reflect perfectly the concerns of 'Middle England' (a tactic that rivals tried to emulate but none pulled off with the same verve); and, second, to invest serious money in reporting (a policy that was not widely copied). And it was the idea of working for English again, plus the knowledge that he had the money to send her on far-flung stories, that lured Leslie to the *Mail*.

So began more than 30 years of applying her ferocious curiosity to the world, sometimes to the war or crisis of the day, at others to a situation or theme that had caught her eye or English's. In doing so, she developed what was to be one of her trademarks: the multi-part report. In 1975, for instance, there was the 'Women of the Arab States' series, in which she penetrated the harems (not, she pointed out, 'the domesticated brothels of male fantasy', but populated by the wives of men who ruled the newly oil-rich Gulf states; one of which, Abu Dhabi, had the honesty to carry engravings of oil derricks on its coins). Or it might be what was then called Rhodesia, whose white minority may have been fighting against insurgents to preserve its domination but in whose capital, she reported, the Mercia Hetherington Dancing Academy was putting on a jolly production of 'Here's Entertainment' in aid of the Border Patrol Welfare Fund. Then, in 1979, came the five-part 'China Exposed' series, in which she spent an illicit evening with Xianni and Gladys Yang, jailed for four years for a crime never specified, interviewed a judge and learnt of Chinese muggers' favourite ploy of following victims into a public lavatory and, while they perched over a ditch full of flowing water, literally catching them with their trousers down; met a pair of Model Sweethearts, who worked as lathe operators (the girl, when asked what attracted her to her beau, told Leslie 'I was very grateful to Yang for advice in helping me to improve my lathe-operating techniques'); and reported on communist 'saints', like Shih Chuan-hsiang, the Model Sewer-Man; Ch'en Tai-shan, the Model Car Worker, and Lei Feng, the Model Soldier:

> Lei Feng exhibitions toured China, displaying 'authentic' photographs of 'Lei Feng helping an old woman across the road', 'Lei Feng giving his lunch to a comrade who forgot his lunch-box', and 'Lei Feng secretly doing his comrade's washing'. How very fortunate it was that whenever the Model Soldier decided to do some very secret good deed with lunch-boxes, old ladies, or other squaddies' smalls, there just happened to be an official photographer present.

When not engaged on a series, her range of subjects was remarkable: one week the violence of Zimbabwe, the next a colour piece on the Mini Miss UK contest; one month the Atlanta child murders, then David Niven's funeral; crime in Singapore, a royal tour, an election campaign, or a night at London's casinos to try and find the allure that caused the Duchess of Bedford's daughter-in-law to fritter away £3 million in less than three years. She interviewed firebrand left-wing politicians, feminist Germaine Greer, Prince Charles, Roger Vadim, and, in one of the final audiences granted before her downfall, Imelda Marcos. Not long afterwards, the Philippines spendthrift had to flee the country with her husband, leaving behind 1,200 dresses, 200 girdles, 500 bras, 1,000 panties and 6,000 shoes. She was, Leslie later wrote, 'the vainest woman I ever met', a considerable accolade considering that Leslie's personal collection of Lady Macbeths also took in Elena Ceaucescu of Romania, and Mira Milosevic of Serbia, the size of whose wigs, Leslie once noted, were an invariable sign of the totteriness of their husband's regimes. The remark was typical. What Leslie gave *Mail* readers was reporting with attitude, lots of it – as in August 1987 writing on Jim and Tammy Bakker, the soon-to-be disgraced US television evangelists who prayed with, and upon, their trusting followers:

> Jim and Tammy told them God wanted his born-again children to get rich, same as godless folks did. 'If you pray for a camper,' Jim roguishly urged his flock, 'be sure to tell God what colour!' He made God sound like a celestial mail order magnate – but instead of sending your savings or your welfare cheques to heaven, you mailed them to Jim and Tammy Bakker. And if the fridge never came, the Winnebago camper remained an impossible dream (not least because you'd been sending money to the Bakkers) – well, that wasn't Jim and Tammy's fault. It was yours; you hadn't believed strongly enough.

Or, in April 1987, on Japan's Hell Camp, a bleak place with a freezing exercise yard, steel stairways, uniforms, floodlights, no recreation periods, TV or visits, and a 16-hour day:

> … I saw grown men sobbing like babies, laughing maniacally, collapsing to the floor in despair, enduring endless humiliations at the hands of their 'warders'. Why? What crimes had these inmates committed? None. These… are decent law-abiding, respectable 'Salarymen', Japan's equivalent of that nice Mr Tomkins in Sales, or cheerful Mr Pendle, the high-flyer of Forward Planning… This is not a prisoner-of-war camp, but a Japanese management training course.
> … Two hours after rising, the hapless Salarymen have still not had breakfast. In one dormitory, an instructor is dragging sheets and bedding out of cupboards and screaming at the inmates. These captains of Japanese industry have not folded their bedding

properly; they must do it again – at the double. In another room a dozen men, squatting on the floor, are bent over pieces of paper. They are writing their daily 'letter home' to their bosses, describing their progress. The letters are read by the instructors – and marked according to how well they conform to a prescribed format.

Most of Leslie's stories were not plump fruit hanging from official trees waiting to be leisurely picked by anyone who could read a handout (never, probably, has a reporter written so much and used the word 'spokesman' so infrequently). They had to be mined, sometimes under cover, and sometimes by presenting herself as the world's least likely-looking foreign correspondent, such as on her first ever major foreign trip, in the 1960s to follow the drugs trails in Mexico. While walking in a remote hill district she was alarmed to be ambushed by armed men who leapt suddenly from their cover in the cactus scrub. They, however, were possibly even more taken aback; for they saw coming towards them Leslie, dressed, as if for Ascot, in a white and yellow print dress, white gloves and matching handbag. They duly lowered their rifles. She also discovered the benefit of playing what she called 'the bird-brain female', especially in the kinds of macho cultures that breed wars and insurgencies. In a contribution to a book called *Secrets of the Press*, she wrote:

> Even the most stunted, scrofulous and crotch-scratching example of local manhood believes, in his heart of hearts, that he is – compared to a mere woman – a Master of the Universe. The woman who conforms to his birdbrain stereotype is therefore no threat to him at all... Your job is not to educate them in gender-equality politics: your job is to get them to help you.

And if that meant looking like a tourist, an escapee from a church outing or wearing a fox fur coat on the front in Bosnia, then that is what Leslie would do. Similarly, if she lacked relevant paperwork at a border, she would root through the seemingly endless contents of a capacious handbag until a goon's impatience reached the point where he would wave

her past. Besides, she preferred this to the tactics once urged
on her by mentor and friend Anne Sharpley: upon arrival in
a strange place, sleep first with the Reuters man so you can
read his copy before it's filed, then with the local police chief.
Leslie preferred putting on the ditz to lying back and thinking
of her by-line.

What this (or, occasionally, when she found it necessary,
a boom-voiced daughter of the Raj persona) disguised, of
course, was a canny resourcefulness that didn't conform to
any stereotype, female or otherwise. In El Salvador in 1984,
while travelling a road on which a Dutch TV crew had been
recently shot by insurgents, she and a companion realised their
vehicle lacked a white flag. Leslie's white petticoat was pressed
into service. In Tokyo in 1990 for Emperor Hirohito's funeral
and faced with security that was intent on keeping the press in
a tent half a mile away, her solution was to march imperiously
through the various checkpoints in her fur coat, haughtily
ignoring all requests to produce her credentials, until she found
herself standing in the same row as President George Bush. It
gave her, and her alone, the story of the day, for she was close
enough to observe that Prince Philip did not, unlike Presidents
Mitterand, Bush and Aquino, bow to the remains of a man
whose armies were once a by-word for cruelty. 'Never,' wrote
Leslie, 'have I seen such eloquent body language.'

And her performances disguised something else: she was a
very fly, and early, adopter of new technology. Long before
some of her more hairy-chested colleagues had even heard
of e-mail and laptops, and years before some of them finally
overcame their phobic fear of them, she was writing, in 1984,
pieces extolling the wonders of both. After all, she could recall
the days when making a call from, say, Leningrad, meant, not
picking up a mobile or sat phone, but booking it four days
in advance and hoping for the best. Such techno-savvy came
in handy in covering the mayhem in Zaire in 1993. She had
been refused a visa, and so was stranded the wrong side of

the Congo River while the action was all in Kinshasa on the opposite bank. Neither sat phones nor local landlines were working, but Leslie knew what to do. She found a man called Mr Massamba who was allowed to cross the river, asked him to acquire a Kinshasa mobile and some numbers, and, by using them, got the story of the chaos caused by 7,000 per cent inflation in a land ruled – and robbed blind – by Mobutu, a president worth £6 billion who built, among the poverty, a residence twice the size, and triple the luxury, of Buckingham Palace.

In giving credit to Mr Massamba, Leslie was, among foreign correspondents, highly unusual; for it is a conceit of many in the trade not to acknowledge the role of fixers, the local sidekicks of overseas reporters who translate, drive, have contacts and know whom to bribe. Leslie never pretended that the getting of the story was all her own work, and she looked upon fixers as friends, staying in touch with them and their families long after she'd moved on to the next case. In the momentous news years of 1989–91, her fixers repaid such loyalty handsomely. There was 'Mr Zhou' in China for the student protests that became the Tiananmen massacre; Igor Kuzmin in Moscow, who, when Leslie flew straight from her holiday in the Swiss Alps to cover the attempted 1991 coup against Gorbachev, had sufficient pull with his old KGB colleagues to arrange her admission to Russia despite the lack of a visa; and, perhaps most crucially of all, the woman who worked with her on the biggest story of 1989: the fall of the Berlin Wall. It had stood for 28 years, a 28 mile-long concrete barrier that kept Easterners penned up in their claustrophobic state. Families were cut off from each other, and over the years many had died trying to make it past the heavily guarded border posts and across the mined no-man's-land. But, by the late 1980s, the pressure for change building up inside Eastern Europe was ready to blow. Something somewhere had to give; and that somewhere was Hungary, still, officially, in the Soviet bloc but never one of its most enthusiastic members. In September 1989, the Budapest government decided to open its borders with Austria, and thousands of East Germans packed up their little state-produced cars, motored down to Hungary for a vacation, passed through it and into the West.

Less than a month later Gorbachev told the stolid East German leadership it was time for 'fundamental reform'. In the days that followed, vast pro-reform demonstrations clogged East German cities, and hard-line East German leader Erich Honecker resigned. The rallies, however, continued: half a million people marched in Leipzig, and, on Saturday 4 November, more than a million in East Berlin. The next day, Leslie flew to Berlin and crossed, illegally, into the East. There she met her fixer, Wiebke Reed, a remarkable woman who had been the second wife of an even more remarkable man – Dean Reed, an American known as the Red Elvis. (After some modest home chart success in the early 1960s, Reed went to Latin America where his gigs would mix hits like 'Tutti Fruiti' with calls to the workers to rise up. Expelled from Argentina and Chile, he made spaghetti westerns in Italy, and then met Wiebke, moved to East Germany, and became a major star there and in Russia. He was planning a US comeback when, in 1986, he was found dead in a lake in mysterious circumstances.)

Events in East Berlin now had an inexorable momentum. On the Monday were the biggest demonstrations yet. That night the Politburo resigned; next day, the entire government fell. Then, early on Thursday evening, Leslie went to a press conference given by East Berlin Party boss Gunter Schabowski. For nearly an hour he bored on through a long list of Party business; and then, almost casually, announced that East Germans could now travel freely to the West. 'When?', asked journalists. 'As far as I know, immediately,' came the reply. Uproar. (When Leslie interviewed him ten years later, he admitted he'd made a terrible mistake. The Party had intended to impose stiff restrictions on travel, but Schabowski hadn't read his briefing properly.) He realised his error too late. The presser was broadcast live, half of East Berlin knew within minutes, and there was no putting that pent-up cat back in the bag. Leslie went immediately to Checkpoint Charlie. It looked, she later wrote, as it had always done:

> floodlights, concrete blocks, heavily armed border-guards muffled up in greatcoats blowing on their fingers, their breath hanging like steam in the freezing night air: a clichéd scene from endless spy movies... Apart from the guards, I was the only person there.

The guards didn't know what was happening, so she went to another crossing at Friederichstrasse. Same story.

A few young people arrived, and began queuing. Then a few more came. And soon the trickle became a flood. As she recalled:

> In the next few hours a tidal wave of excited, ecstatic people began pouring through the checkpoints... East Berlin – a shabby, ill-lit city, stinking of cheap petrol and lignite-coal fumes, which usually closed its eyes early – became electric with excitement throughout that delirious night.

East Germans began to head for the crossings in their Trabants and Wartburgs, and Leslie realised that to be part of this joyful exodus would make her story. If ever a good relationship with a good fixer paid off, it was now. For, thanks to Wiebke Reed, in the early hours of the next morning, Leslie was able to pass into the West as East Germans were now doing it – in a coughing little Wartburg car. It was, she said, 'the most emotional night of my life':

> ... A massive roar erupts from the West German crowd as we approach that sign which, adorned with British, American and French flags, tells us and all the hundreds of little coughing Wartburgs and Trabants behind us 'You are now entering the Allied Zone'.
>
> 'I cannot believe this!' sobs Wiebke. 'Here I am, Wiebke Reed, driving freely across Checkpoint Charlie. All our lives we have

dreamed of this. All our lives we have waited for this and suddenly now, at last, it is happening...'

... Small children, in their high trebles, like chattering starlings, flock around us chirruping excitedly, 'Welcome, Welcome!' and throw chocolates, sweets and pocket-money coins into the car. 'These West Berliners love us, they actually seem to love us' cries Wiebke wonderingly. 'We are not enemies any more.'

Her reports that weekend filled page after page of the *Mail*, and the effort of that, plus the almost total lack of sleep, prompted her to complain to editor David English that she was exhausted. 'Don't complain to me, woman,' he replied. 'I shouldn't be paying you. You should be paying me.' As Leslie said: 'He was right.'

Two months later, another historic drama was played out, this time in Cape Town. On 3 February 1990 Leslie began a news story: 'It was 11.30am South African time when President de Klerk took Afrikanerdom by the sunburnt neck and shook it free at last of its lunatic delusions of perpetual white supremacy.' He had removed the ban on the African National Congress, and, in so doing, had set the stage for the release of Nelson Mandela. Eight days later Leslie stood among a milling crowd outside Victor Verster Prison, watching for Mandela to emerge after 27 years of imprisonment. As he walked towards them in a grey suit, he gave a clenched fist salute, the crowd pitched forward and Leslie was knocked to the ground. Two days later, in Soweto to see Mandela's homecoming at a sports stadium, she made sure of a better, although no safer, vantage point. On her way, she saw a large JCB being driven along, its giant scoop crammed with 'comrades'. She stopped her car, ran to the back-hoe and clambered aboard. Once up there, she asked where they'd got the machine. 'Hijacked,' she was told.

My question, however, somewhat offended one skinny comrade with broken teeth who looked about 14, and whose tight dusty curls were crammed into a black beret, a popular 'struggle wear' fashion item in these parts ... 'Hey man, you with the struggle?' he demanded.

'Amandla!' (power) I shouted firmly, anxious that there should be no potentially lethal misunderstanding and for a moment wishing that, like half the self-preserving media here, I'd invested in a few struggle wear items myself. 'Awethu!' (is ours) the Comrades on the JCB shouted joyously back.

Thus deemed to be one of the gang, she progressed to the stadium.

But for all her experience and research, sometimes it was luck that got her the story; as in December 1990, when, covering a Bush–Gorbachev summit held on a Russian ship moored off Malta, she went in search of an elusive cup of coffee, finally located one in a remote room – and found herself face to face with Mikhail and Raisa Gorbachev, into whose quarters she had unwittingly stumbled. When she got back to a familiar part of the ship, a colleague asked where she'd been. 'Oh, having coffee with the Gorbachevs.' And then there was her encounter with the famously frosty Indira Gandhi. Soon after starting the interview, which had taken much painstaking supplications to arrange, Leslie had to rush to the bathroom, courtesy of an ill-advised curry the night before. Between violent bouts of vomiting, she heard the sound of singing. It was Mrs Gandhi, transformed into a motherly hen, cooing her a lullaby. The Indian prime minister, so cold and stiff moments before, now not only fussed over the sick Leslie, but opened up and talked as never before. Leslie wrote: 'As I eventually staggered, whey-faced, out of her office, I thought, "I've got a cracking interview here, if it isn't all a hallucination."' And luck was with Leslie, too, when she covered the brutalities of the Balkans in the early 1990s, keeping her out of the way of the seemingly random shelling and so able, in Bosnia, to practise one of her more artful stratagems. Barred by the Serbs from getting up to the front line at Gorazde, she talked endlessly to their troops about a beautiful orthodox church near town that she'd heard about. How she yearned to see it, she told them, but, of course it was too dangerous, her family would never forgive her for taking the risk, and, anyway, she was too scared. Eventually, of course, the Serb soldiers virtually frog-marched her there. She was the only journalist to reach that front line.

She was now in her fifties, and in late 1993, she went to Haiti and produced perhaps her finest piece of writing. The country's first democratically elected president, Father Jean-Bertrand Aristide, popularly known as 'Titid', had been overthrown, and, in response, an international oil and weapons embargo was imposed, backed by British, US, Canadian, French and Dutch warships. Leslie arrived, and, on 17 November, she filed a story that is not far short of the definitive foreign situationer:

> From the filigreed verandah of the decaying Oloffson Hotel (beside an area of the capital called Lower Not Very Much), I cannot actually see HMS *Active* patrolling the blue-green waters off Port-au-Prince. But I know she's there.
>
> … We're 'restoring democracy' largely by further starving seven million of the poorest people in the Western hemisphere – on an island already riddled with Aids, voodoo, drugs, hysterical gunmen and assorted political thugs, torturers and adventurers. And how's this 'restoring democracy' business going? Er, not very well. Not very well at all …
>
> They lay tied together like a scarf across the murdered man's neck: the strangled newborn kitten, the dead rat with its tiny paws and its astonished eyes gazing up at me and the blazing Haitian sun. Another dead rat peeked out of the crotch of the second man, whose arms had been tied behind his back before he'd been shot. 'The animals? Oh, for voodoo!' explained a ragged youth as he and a small, nervous crowd gathered round the men's bodies, dumped on a rubbish heap in La Saline, one of Port-au-Prince's most fetid slums.
>
> … And no one, of course, will investigate their deaths. After all, 'everyone knows' who did it. Sweet Mickey's men … Illiterate black men from the slums, these armed plain-clothes thugs fan out… and roam Haiti's streets at night in their pick-up trucks, killing their fellow illiterates for a handful of dollars from on high. And all because Sweet Mickey, his greedy military chums, and the

mulatto millionaires nibbling lobster thermidor in their mountain mansions will that it should be so.

Night after gun-punctured night, I can lie in my bed in the ghostly Oloffson... and listen, as Graham Greene once listened, to the distant staccato sounds of the poor killing the poor in the interests of the rich.

... Unlike the broken black bodies in that rubbish-dump far below the cool, mauve mountains of Kenscoff, mulatto Monique's skin gleams like honey. Monique's French is elegant, her American-accented English perfect... these teenagers are the spoiled-darling daughters of the MRE, the Morally Repugnant Elite – the name given by an exasperated U.S. Ambassador to the top layer of mulatto and Arab families whose greed and corruption have helped to reduce Haiti to one of the ten poorest nations in the world (it was once the richest country in the Caribbean).

... These three little Haitian 'princesses' are beautiful and bubbly – and bored out of their pretty little minds. Once they could flit in and out of their mountain 'paradise' to Miami, Paris, New York... But the beastly international community has put a stop to all that ... overseas assets have been frozen, Monique can't go back to her American university because her visa... has been cancelled. 'And thanks to the embargo,' said Monique, chewing crossly on a flower-stalk, 'my father's got only half a tank of gasoline left for one car!'

The MRE's Mercedes, their BMWs, their gleaming Toyota Landcruisers now lie like shoals of dead porpoises behind the huge walls of grotesquely luxurious mansions, which overlook equally grotesquely pot-holed roads. Their daughters can't even twitter for hours on the telephone to each other any more... The embargo may be causing 1,000 extra deaths a month among the poor, whose average life expectancy is already a mere 54 years – but hell, it's causing much worse than that in Kenscoff! It's causing . . . inconvenience!

... The three little Haitian princesses, curiously enough, scarcely seemed to notice 'them', the black silent tide of the poor who are rising relentlessly up the mountainsides, chopping down the trees for charcoal, skinning the mountains bare, building their shacks against the very walls of the princesses' palaces ... I could see dozens of abandoned millionaire villas which had already been squatted in by the poor, their elegant interiors looted.

... Armed intervention by outsiders, however well-meaning, has never been a success in Haiti. It is rarely a success anywhere today. In the meantime... beautiful, mad, spirit-haunted Haiti will remain, perhaps forever, a tiny black empire of the doomed. A Haitian black comedy without end.

Through that decade, and into the next, Leslie continued to deliver her 2,300-word, or longer, reports: on the Russian elections; the young wasted males of Britain's sink estates; Israel's tortured politics; Amsterdam's ending of its love affair with porn; Signor Bossi, a dotty Italian who wanted his region to secede from Rome; the O.J. Simpson trial; the death of Diana; the prostitutes of Baku; IRA punishment squads; the culling of girl babies in China, which left the country with 111 million more males than females; the Monica Lewinsky affair; King Hussein's funeral; academics who fell foul of political correctness; and an interview with George W. Bush on the 2000 campaign trail. After wangling that rare thing for a British reporter, a one-to-one with a US presidential candidate, she tried repeatedly to ignite Bush's supposedly short fuse by asking him about his reputation for being mentally 'two sandwiches short of a picnic', as she put it to the-then Texas governor. But she got back only good humour in reply, and, as she was escorted back to the press section of the plane, Bush gave her a knowing look and said: 'You know, I've been misunderestimated all my life.' Once on the ground, she rang her editor in London and told him: 'Bush is one of the wiliest people I've ever interviewed.'

She also investigated, in the spring of 1998, the famine reportedly killing millions in North Korea. Not content just to talk to aid agency, intelligence and UN sources in the comfort of London or New York, Leslie flew instead to China, travelled to its remote north-east, and, after a five-hour trip along dirt roads and through People's Liberation Army checkpoints, reached the banks of the Tumen River marking the North Korean border. There she met Lee, a teenager who watched his father die from hunger, saw his stepmother sell his brother to get food, and then, when thrown out of home to fend for himself, was unable to survive on nettles and roots and so fled across the river to China. He was 15, but looked about nine. She met Mrs Piao, a widow so poor her home's only furniture was a bed, but who was prepared to risk a huge fine to hide Lee and others from Chinese authorities. She heard of the village schools so infected with hunger that only six in a class of 30 had the strength to attend. She learnt of the city-dwellers, some of whose state-controlled food allowance was a mere 100 grammes a day, the equivalent, she pointed out, of four small digestive biscuits. And she met, Mr and Mrs Zheng, who, down a filthy lane in an industrial town in north-east China, ran a secret orphanage for children who had escaped starvation. She came away convinced of a 'massive, largely unreported famine'.

In 2001, in her sixtieth year, Leslie hit what for many people's careers would be the buffers: four months in hospital and three serious operations that left her needing to take medication for the rest of her life. One might imagine that such an experience would breed caution. Not a bit of it. By April 2002, she was in Bethlehem, where, for more than two weeks, around 200 armed Palestinians were holed up inside the Church of the Nativity, in Manger Square. Many of the media were kept outside the cordon of closed-off streets surrounding the church, forced to rely on rumour. Not Leslie. First, wearing ('wimpishly', she says) her ceramic plate flak jacket, she tried walking through the checkpoints. Repulsed at the first hurdle. Next day, she shed the jacket and all evidence that she was a journalist, and dressed, as she wrote, 'in dingbat middle-aged mum mode and touting a handbag full of harmless detritus such as old lipsticks, parking tickets and family snaps', this 60-year-old mother and recent long-term hospital case presented herself at the barricades where Israeli soldiers were prodding back journalists and TV crews at the point of several guns.

Bizarrely, as a foolish middle-aged 'non-journalist' mum, and an obvious non-Palestinian, I'm the only one allowed to pass. Perhaps I reminded these frightened young soldiers of their mothers, a bearer perhaps of some nice kosher chicken soup to see them though yet another terrifying day. I walk utterly alone through the deserted stone alleyways, pick my way around dozens of bomb-flattened and burned-out cars and fly-fizzing mounds of decaying rubbish ...

For the first ten minutes... the only human beings I see on the streets are Israeli patrols... 'Where are you going? Why were you allowed in?' barks one helmeted, heavily armed Israeli soldier angrily. 'I'm a church-worker – I've got permission to visit a priest who's trapped near Manger Square!'... I walk extremely slowly towards each patrol, a couple of times with my hands up... It's not easy to persuade these jittery soldiers of my innocence. Once convinced, they suddenly became enormously protective. I tell them I'm lost, can't find the house containing my fictitious friend, the priest. 'I don't know Bethlehem. Do you happen to have a map?' I ask them innocently.

They roll their eyes: typical-woman! ... Another patrol is rumoured to have a map: it is fetched. In 'typical woman' fashion, I hold it upside down. I then realise that even holding it the right way up, none of the baffled soldiers can make head nor tail of it. Each time I leave one patrol, its leader shouts out in Hebrew to the patrol around the corner, warning it to: 'Hold fire, she's OK!'... At one particularly dangerous point, a patrol detaches a couple of soldiers to accompany me, their guns pointed upwards towards the shuttered windows of the houses as we pass. 'Snipers ... snipers ...' And there it is: Manger Square. I am now fewer than 50 yards from the Nativity Church itself...

... Suddenly a crackle of nearby gunfire breaks out... 'You must get out now!' my previously affable Israeli chums shout. I do not hesitate to obey...

She made it back to the safety of the perimeter, and went on reporting: on Syria, from Germany on the 2002 elections, from the Gulf at the start of another Iraq War, on her eighth US election campaign, and from San Francisco on gay marriages. She filed from New York's Ground Zero, Moscow, Saudi Arabia, Washington and Tehran – where she gave her official 'minder' the slip, donned obligatory Islamic long black dress and headscarf and met dissidents secretly in the woods of a city park, in a cemetery, in windowless buildings late at night, and by smuggling herself into a hospital. Such clandestine dates were not some reporter's melodrama. Only the year before, a Canadian woman journalist who had been poking around talking to reformists was arrested and tortured to death in Tehran's Evin prison.

Some years ago, former *Observer* editor Donald Trelford, researching a piece for the *Evening Standard*, asked Leslie why, after three life-threatening operations, and at an age when most woman have retired, and with a family who would rather she confined herself to writing what she calls 'neat little essays about supermarket trolleys', she still exposed herself to high-risk reporting, such as in Jerusalem and Tehran. 'Because,' she said, 'it's the most interesting job in the world.' It's the kind of reply you would expect from a journalist whose intelligent curiosity and refusal to be thwarted has made her not only the finest reporter of her generation, but, when you consider her range, perhaps the most versatile reporter of any generation.

Meyer Berger

13

Meyer Berger
1898–1959

THE REPORTER'S REPORTER

He was a failure as a war correspondent, having to be shipped home ulcerated and homesick after just two months. He couldn't say 'no' to callers at the office, spending untold hours listening to trivia that was never going to make a line; he was shy and unassertive, his eyesight wasn't up to much, and his formal education stopped at the age of 13. Yet if I was allowed to hire only one reporter for a celestial newsroom it would be Meyer Berger; for 'Mike', as his colleagues always called him, is, more than any other operator in this book, worthy of the title: the reporter's reporter.

What makes him that are a whole cascade of qualities: his careful removal of self from his reporting (even the closest study of his stories defies an attempt to discover if he was radical or conservative, roué or prude); his ear for a telling quote; his memorable phrasing with no hint of smart-arsery; and an eye for detail and ability to catch it in a way that sticks in the reader's mind like a happy childhood memory. He also turned the much-mocked theory that everyone has a story to tell into a vividly human column that vindicated the concept on a thrice-a-week basis; and, to these sensibilities, he added the practical skills of vivid recall, superb shorthand

and a trained speed at the typewriter that could produce 1,000 words of clean copy in just 30 minutes. And besides all that, he was simply the best writer of an intro that journalism has ever produced.

Only very occasionally were these talents deployed on national stories, and even more rarely on international ones. Berger's province was the comings and goings, the doings and undoings, of his native city – the hoodlum's trial, a summer heatwave, the escaping of a circus lion, and the mourning of its war dead. He was the ultimate hometown reporter, and it was his good fortune that his town just happened to be New York, the richest mother lode of stories on earth. He spent virtually all of his reporting career at the *New York Times*, and, to keep himself supplied with raw material, had not only the paper's city desk but also entire boroughs full of priests, hot-dog vendors, nuns, street-car conductors, hobbyists, freaks, eccentrics, policemen and janitors all ready to trust him with their tales. Then, just to make sure – like some neurotic prospector turning over every rock on the hillside lest some nugget elude detection – he spent his days off, notebook in hand and camera over shoulder, walking the city's sidewalks, stopping, talking and listening, and, when he'd got round the next corner, jotting it all down.

The man who was to chronicle the lives of ordinary and extraordinary New Yorkers was born to a poor immigrant family in a Lower East Side slum on 1 September 1898. His father, originally from the Czech Republic, was an unsuccessful tailor, and his mother ran a candy store. They produced no fewer than 11 children, and so, at the age of eight, Mike was out selling newspapers to supplement the family income. By the time he reached 11 he had been found a night job, and two years later, at the advanced age of 13, his parents informed him that they could no longer afford to keep him in the luxury of mere part-time employment. After just two terms at Brooklyn's

Eastern District High, his schooling was abruptly ended and the barely teenaged Berger was set to full-time work.

By some felicitous miracle, his night job had been as a messenger at the old *New York World*, running copy between its offices in Park Row and Brooklyn at $1.50 a week. Right from the start he was enthralled by the smoky and mysterious excitements of producing a newspaper. Persuading him to trade the schoolroom for the newsroom was not, therefore, a problem. He was already hooked. 'I could stand near the long copy table in the cavernous old *World* office,' he later wrote, 'and watch the poker games. Here I absorbed all the legends of the craft, ancient and contemporary. I contracted newsprint fever in this way, by a kind of osmosis.' His unknowing tutors were long-forgotten men by the names of Big Bob McNamara, Charles McCarthy and Buck Moran, and, in between fetching them coffee and hot bean sandwiches from Dirty Smith's or cold pints from Dixon's, Berger listened, and learnt and longed to be old enough to join them.

The chance came sooner than he could have imagined. One October day, around 1911, someone called the *World* office to report a most strange going-on. A beery-looking man with a stubbled chin had approached an applecart at Fulton Ferry in Brooklyn and said to the vendor: 'Will you let me eat all the apples I can for a quarter?' Since 25 cents then bought 20 apples the stallholder figured this was a pretty good offer, and he accepted. That was mid-morning. By 2pm, when the call came in to the *World* office, the beery man was still eating, and the vendor was looking a little nervous. As Berger told it some 30 years later, the city editor looked around the newsroom, saw there were no reporters, and called the 13-year-old office boy over. 'Berger, get down to Fulton Ferry and learn what you can about some fellow eating apples. Get all the names and addresses and listen to what people say.'

Young Berger hurried off, thrilled, yet puzzled that a great newspaper should be interested in something as prosaic as the eating of apples. When he arrived at the scene, he found the beery man flushed, but still eating steadily, and a crowd of stevedores and water-front loafers encouraging him and trading bets. By 6pm, the 250th apple was demolished, a small cheer went up, and the vendor, now catastrophically out of pocket, made a move. 'I gotta go now,' he said. A collective growl from the assembled dockers told him to stay put. It was fully dark when the 257th and final apple went the way of all the others, and the crowd, as Berger put it, 'bore the bloated champion across the cobbled drayway toward a water-front saloon'. Berger scurried back to the office. 'I had it all on copy paper,' he wrote, 'the count, the names, the addresses, what the men had said. I had careful notes about the changing lights and sights on the river; enough, I recall, for a 10,000-word thesis on apple-eating.'

The city editor, Major Norris A. Clowes who had been trained by the great Joseph Pulitzer himself, was, wrote Berger, 'white-haired and very wise. "No," he said gently, "Not a column. Try to keep it to ten lines."' Berger did so, and then saw in the morning, as he tore open the first copy of the *World* he could lay his hands on, that his nine lines had been reduced to four or five. 'They seemed quite changed. But my heart tried to escape through my ribs when I found them … I had caught ink fever and I never got over it… two hundred and fifty-seven apples had shaped my career.'

Gradually the paragraphs in the *World* mounted up, and more copy-table wisdom was absorbed until, in 1917, the US entered the Great War and the 18-year-old Berger tried to enlist. The army rejected him. Poor eyesight, they said; and there his military career might have ended had he not memorised the eye chart, passed the subsequent retest, and was soon on his way to France as a sergeant in the 106th Infantry. Within a few months the weedy-looking, short-sighted 'reject' had won both the Silver Star and Purple Heart for carrying wounded men back to American lines under fire.

When he got back to New York, he was immediately taken back on by the *World* as a police reporter, and began to show a facility for writing news stories at speed and with a degree of style that few of his colleagues could match. That qualified him for a job common then, rare now, of the rewrite man: those anonymous alchemists of the newsroom who turn the clunky words of the wires or tone-deaf colleagues into what will pass for a little against-the-clock poetry. In time word got around about who was turning out the snappy prose at the *World*, and the Standard News Association hired Berger as its top rewrite man for its Brooklyn office. By 1927 the *New York Times* had its eye on him, and when the paper started a Brooklyn–Queens news section early the following year, Berger was taken on as chief rewrite man. Gradually he began to insinuate some reporting into his routine, and it didn't take him long to prove that the years as a rewrite man – taking others' stories apart and rapidly reconstructing them as something fluid and catchy – had not been wasted. A series of stories on murders of Brooklyn longshore gangsters was run prominently, and Berger soon found himself the paper's unofficial racketeering correspondent.

It was in this role that, in the early fall of 1931, he was sent to Chicago to cover the trial of Al Capone for tax evasion. This, with a sharp eye on both jury and defendant, is how he reported the opening testimony:

Chicago, Oct 12—The jury in the Alphonse Capone trial for income tax evasion – rural gentlemen of simple and rather careless habits of dress – pursed its lips in Federal Court here today as it learned from salesmen witnesses for the government what the well-dressed gangster wears, his tastes in home decoration and his preference in diamonds and motor cars.

Silk shirts at $30 each, silk underwear at $14 a set, sack suits at $135 apiece, diamond belt buckles at $275 each (bought by the dozen), ties at $5 (by the dozen) were a few samples of Mr Capone's taste in haberdashery and suitable garments for street wear.

His cars cost him $12,000 apiece, his glassware and silver came high and he was finicky about interior decoration for his home, picking the colours and fabrics himself.

Grave, sometimes lost in day dreams, Capone listened to the public revelations of his expenditures as if he were disinterested; but when one of the salesmen began to describe the texture of the glove-silk undies he blushed all over his fat face and added an embarrassed smirk to the chorus of laughter evoked by the description.

Having set the scene, Berger then described how a series of salesmen and women came to the stand to tell of Capone's fastidiously expensive tastes:

'Four shirts, $22.50 each; one for $30; three at $12 each; eighteen collars at $2 each; six collars at $1 each; twenty-four monograms for the sleeve at $17.'

A low murmur worked its way around the chamber. The two jurors who park their false teeth outside let their upper lips drop a little lower on their chins in astonishment.

Mr Arl [a salesman] recited other purchases, batches of shirts at $22 each or $24 each, more $2 collars, more monograms, all bought by Capone. Sometimes he had some of his followers with him. He picked their shirting too, and paid for it, teaching the boys what the well-dressed racketeer should wear.

As Arl testified Capone shifted a mint in his heavy jaws and stared off into space. A look of baby-like innocence was spread over his countenance.

Finally, there was Mr Oles, the underwear salesman, describing with the precision only an enthusiast can bring, the shorts – 'athletic style, you know' – which Capone regularly bought. Oles's insistence that they were made of the 'finest Italian glove silk' and were 'really just a nice suit of underwear' provoked laughter.

Mr Capone joined in it. His head turned around in a pivotal attempt to show all in the room that he was laughing with them, but the half-inch scar that seams his left cheek, from temple to the mouth corner, stood out as he blushed...

Five days later, the evidence was complete and Berger was there to describe the ending of Capone's reign. Federal Attorney G.E.Q. Johnson, closing for the prosecution, '...paused between sentences as he stripped from the shoulders of Capone the light mantle of generosity and innocence draped over them yesterday by defense counsel...'; the defendant himself, 'looking like a head barber off to meet his best girl, stood in the corridor after the jury went out. He was smiling, but the smile seemed the equivalent of the quavery music of the whistler passing the graveyard...'; and Capone's reaction as the verdict of guilty on five of the 23 counts was read out:

Capone faces a maximum of seventeen years' imprisonment and $50,000 fine. He did not seem to realise that. He kept grinning at all and sundry in the court room, his bulky figure in a screaming green suit (one of the $135 ones) drawing all eyes toward him. As soon as the verdict was entered, he got out of his seat and virtually ran from the room. He rushed on lumbering feet across the dim corridor, stepped into the elevator and as soon as it touched the rotunda floor he ran out to the street to a waiting automobile. No one interviewed him.

The stories that Berger filed from Chicago were duly nominated for a Pulitzer Prize.

For most of the next decade, Berger's principal task was to track the rise, and often explosively sudden falls, of America's celebrity hoodlums. When Brooklyn mobster Abe Reles fell (or was pushed) from an upper floor of the Half Moon Hotel on Coney Island, Berger crept out onto the relevant window sill so he could describe what Reles would have heard and seen as he teetered on the brink of eternity. He reported their shootings ('Albany, Dec. 18 1931—Jack (Legs) Diamond, human ammunition dump for the underworld, was killed in a cheap rooming house yesterday...'), and he acted as a kind of unadoring Boswell to Dutch Schultz. He interviewed him ('Syracuse, N.Y., April 14. 1935—Brief but not too intimate glimpses into his past were afforded this afternoon...'), and profiled him in bravely critical terms (Schultz once cornered the bespectacled Berger and asked him if it was true the reporter had quoted someone saying that the gangster was a 'pushover for a blonde'. Berger, visibly shaking, admitted it, prompting the man responsible for criminal mayhem across America to injuredly inquire: 'What kind of language is that to use in the *New York Times?*'). And Berger was there to obituarise Schultz when the inevitable happened in 1935:

> Arthur (Dutch Schultz) Flegenheimer, killed by gunmen in Newark, was just an unambitious, sloppy flat-burglar and package thief in the Bronx until he was caught up on the big beer wave during prohibition and lifted to great power in New York's criminal empire.

By the mid-1930s, Berger was beginning to write the kind of stories about more ordinary folk that he was eventually to make his speciality. These, normally characterised by that absurd phrase 'human interest', are often an excuse for the laziest and softest of starts followed by a stream of almost fact-free paragraphs bulked out with vacuous quotes. Not in Berger's hands. When, for instance, a blind musician fell to his death on the subway in 1936, Berger began his story:

> The sixth sense that had preserved Oscar England from harm through the thirty-four dark years of his life betrayed him yesterday. One step too many in the BMT Union Square station and he was wedged, lifeless, between a north-bound express and the concrete platform.

Such a story would normally be the cue for nothing more than a news in brief paragraph, but Berger went down to the Buskwick district of Brooklyn, where he knew blind musicians lived in a small colony, and pieced together with the aid of the dead man's neighbours not only the story of Oscar England's last journey, but of his life playing for the Capitol Dance Orchestra, and his family: wife Lelah (blind too), and his three sighted children. It was writing like this that persuaded Harold Ross to offer him a berth on the *New Yorker*, but after less than a year, Berger could stand the slow-burn of lengthy magazine pieces no more, and hurried back to the immediacy of the daily *New York Times*. He was to remain there the rest of his life.

He was now the paper's frontline colour writer, covering political conventions, presidential inaugurations, virtually every day of the city's four-month long World Fair in 1939, and even a parade of 'Gone With The Wind Stars' through the streets of Atlanta. In 1942, the paper sent him to London to cover the Blitz, but, after just two months, he was invalided home, his stomach ulcers having been unequal to the task of coping with rationed food. So, like some real-life George Bailey, he never got to travel and go to war, but instead stayed behind to cover the advent of the Zoot suit, the sale of Liberty Bonds and big domestic news stories like the circus fire that claimed 139 lives in Hartford, Connecticut in July 1944 ('One hundred and thirty-nine dead and 174 badly burned persons were pulled from the charred ruins of the main Ringling Brothers and Barnum & Bailey circus tent in Hartford this afternoon after fire swept the enclosure end to end along its entire 520-foot length' – a model of the precise, encapsulating first paragraph).

Like Bailey, Berger was popular, too – not something one could say of every talented journalist – and the portrait of him at this time painted by a fellow *New York Times* staffer is done with an affection not always evident in tributes to journalistic colleagues:

> In temperament Mr Berger was the very opposite of the prima donna. He sat by choice in the middle of the *Times*'s big city room, ceaselessly interrupted by phone calls, admiring colleagues and a stream of visitors – policemen, thieves, porters, bankers, all sorts of persons. He was constitutionally unable to dismiss anyone, no matter how busy he might be. He was sweet-tempered, shy, gentle and friendly toward everyone all the time, even when his stomach ulcers were bothering him and the deadline for the first edition loomed.

When the war ended, Berger was into the second half of his forties, but his best work was yet to come. What his own paper considered his finest story was an account of the return to American soil of the first consignment of war dead in October 1947. Even today, its clipped but sensitive prose has the power to raise the hairs on the back of even the most cynical necks:

> The first war dead from Europe came home yesterday. The harbor was steeped in Sabbath stillness as they came in on the morning tide in 6,248 coffins in the hold of the transport *Joseph V. Connolly*. One coffin, borne from the ship in a caisson, moved through the city's streets to muffled drumbeats and slow, cadenced marches, and 400,000 New Yorkers along the route and at a memorial service in Central Park paid it the tribute of reverent silence and unhidden tears.

He described the measured progress of the ship and her escorts towards the dockside berth, the wreaths flung by sailors slapping onto the water, the 21-gun salute of the USS *Missouri* from its distant station out at sea, and the assembling of the 6,000-strong procession that would accompany the lone coffin through Manhattan to the service in the park.

> ... Then came the long march up Fifth Avenue's pavement. The crowds at the curb were moved. Some let the tears run freely. Some wiped them away. Some made the sign of the cross as the caisson rolled past them. In the Metropolitan Tower, bells tolled and the pealing echoes hung over the marchers. In Fifth Avenue's canyons muted brass played 'Onward, Christian Soldiers'... Outside the park, a little street sweeper held his broom stiffly with his left hand while his right hand rose in salute as the caisson rolled past him. No one smiled. Men and women stared at the street sweeper with grave understanding, and bowed their heads to their chests in silent salute.

Then, in the park:

> ... In the dead quiet, the strains of the dirge 'Dolore', played by the Fort Jay band with muted brass – a kind of sobbing in the music – lay in the heated air. The band and the paratroop escort of honor came down a wide grassy aisle with heart-breaking slowness of

tread. Everywhere on the Meadow tears started and women stifled their weeping.

In a front seat, a woman started up. She stretched out her arms and screamed the name 'Johnny'. The dirge lifted and fell. Then in a brief space of silence the woman screamed out again: 'There's my boy, there's my boy,' and other women, beside her, put comforting arms on her shoulders. She stifled her cries, but her shoulders shook with emotion…

And, after describing the service, his final paragraph:

The coffin, still wrapped in the flag, was set gently back on the caisson. The honor guard took up position behind it. The armoured car rolled, and the caisson swayed slightly, came true, and followed. It rolled southward out of the park in the twilight with the United States Army Band sending after it the sweet melancholy of the dirge, 'The Vanished Army'.

The story contained not a line of comment, not a single instance of pressing the writer's reaction on the reader, and not a single quote, save the lone woman's cries. *Times* legend has it that when publisher Arthur Sulzberger read the story before it was printed he said he didn't want the piece to run on page one. When asked why, he said it was because it made him cry. The story duly ran the next day on page one, across four columns.

Two years later came Berger's greatest feat of reporting. On the morning of 7 September 1949, reports began to filter in of a gunman randomly shooting people in Camden, New Jersey. Berger was despatched, and by the time he reached the scene, a young army veteran called Howard B. Unruh had shot dead 12 neighbours and passers-by. For the next six hours, Berger retraced Unruh's steps as he went about his killing in the blocks around his East Camden home. Berger interviewed 50 witnesses, including prosecutors who carried out the initial interview with the arrested killer, then went back to the New York office, sat down and wrote, in just two and a half hours, a 4,000-word account for the first edition, not one word of which was changed by any editor. It began:

> Howard B. Unruh, 28 years old, a mild, soft-spoken veteran of many armored artillery battles in Italy, France, Austria, Belgium, and Germany, killed twelve persons with a war souvenir Luger pistol in his home block in East Camden this morning. He wounded four others.
>
> Unruh, a slender, hollow-cheeked six-footer paradoxically devoted to scripture reading and to constant practice with firearms, had no previous history of mental illness but specialists indicated tonight that there was no doubt that he was a psychiatric case, and that he had secretly nursed a persecution complex for two years or more.
>
> The veteran was shot in the left thigh by a local tavern keeper but he kept that fact a secret, too, while policeman and Mitchell Cohen, Camden County prosecutor, questioned him at police headquarters for more than two hours immediately after tear gas bombs had forced him out of his bedroom to surrender. The bloodstain he left on the seat he occupied during the questioning betrayed his wound. When it was discovered he was taken to Cooper Hospital in Camden, a prisoner charged with murder.
>
> He was as calm under questioning as he was during the twenty minutes that he was shooting men, women and children... He told the prosecutor that he had been building up resentment against neighbours and neighbourhood shopkeepers for a long time. 'They have been making derogatory remarks about my character,' he said. His resentment seemed most strongly concentrated against Mr. and Mrs. Maurice Cohen, who lived next door to him. They are among the dead...

The story then reconstructs, from the evening before the shootings, the killer's every move: his night at the cinema sitting through several showings of the double-feature *I Cheated The Law* and *The Lady Gambles*, the military trophies that filled his bedroom, the weapons and ammunition he packed before leaving the house, the precise trail he took on his deadly mission, the gunning down of the cobbler, the tailor's wife, the little boy in the barber's chair, the barber, toddler Tommy Hamilton whose face appeared at a window just as Unruh was glaring at it, the TV repairman in his car, and then the Cohens:

> ... Cohen had run to his upstairs apartment and had tried to warn Minnie Cohen, 63, his mother and Rose, his wife, 38, to hide. His son Charles, 14, was in the apartment, too. Mrs. Cohen shoved the boy into a clothes closet and leaped into another closet, herself. She pulled the door to. The druggist, meanwhile had leaped from the window onto a porch roof. Unruh, a gaunt figure at the window behind him, fired at the druggist's back. The druggist, still running, bounded off the roof and lay dead in Thirty-second Street.
>
> Unruh fired into the closet where Mrs. Cohen was hidden. She fell dead behind the closed door and he did not bother to open it. Mrs. Minnie Cohen tried to get to the telephone in an adjoining bedroom to call the police. Unruh fired shots into her head and body and she sprawled dead on the bed. Unruh walked down the stairs with his Luger reloaded and came out into the street again...

On went the report until the move-by-move account of the brief siege that ended in Unruh's arrest. Berger's story had pace, and the kind of detail only an experienced reporter incessantly asking witnesses 'And then what happened?' can accumulate. There is not a single quote stating the obvious, not even half a sentence of police jargonese, and the words 'shocking', 'tragic' or 'I' do not appear once. And all written on a typewriter at a rate of nearly 2,000 words an hour. The story at last brought Berger a richly deserved Pulitzer and its $1,000 prize. He gave the money to Unruh's widowed mother.

Many a reporter with the Pulitzer ribbon on their chest might have insisted on the right to cover only those stories that matched their own new-found grandeur, but Berger was content to go on as before. He covered the captures of bank robbers, the escape of a circus lion ('Jackie, a young but lassitudinous circus lion, won more than an hour of freedom by escape from his cage in Madison Square Garden basement yesterday, but frittered it away in dreamy brooding'), holiday weather, the defeats of the Dodgers, and significant trials ('Joe

Adonis, gambler and racketeer who had been brought up from the New Jersey State Prison in Trenton but still was the best-dressed man in the courtroom, went on trial in Federal Court here yesterday on a contempt charge').

In 1953 he resumed the 'About New York' column that had begun in 1939, but which was soon dropped because of wartime paper restrictions. It had been an occasional diversion then, but now it became a thrice-weekly 700 words on some oddity, or oddball, of New York life: the city's only praying mantis farm; the load-bearing experts who work out which streets are strong enough to take which vehicles in parades; the couple who keep five hives of bees on the balcony of their fourth-floor apartment; Sterling H. Parlee, sidewalk angler, who 'fishes' drains for keys, rings, small change and other things dropped down gratings; the Rev. Joseph Lynch, whose seismographs measure the impact on New York of distant earthquakes or city gas explosions; the bus company that takes gamblers to racetracks (and whose buses are cleaned by a professional gambler down on his luck); Miss Delphine Binger's hoard of 500,000 chicken, turkey and goose wishbones; and Sig Klein's Fat Men's Shop on Third Avenue (74-inch waist trousers a speciality).

It was for this column that Berger would tramp the New York streets on his days off, collecting anecdotes, gazing into intriguing shop windows, taking pictures and listening patiently to anyone who pressed their life story on him. Mostly these weekend perambulations were inspired by Berger's innate interest in his city and its people, but they must have been fed in part by the pressures of producing, three times a week, a story that was worthy of the standards he set himself – the same pressures, which, when a freshly completed column released him from them, would sometimes see this Pulitzer Prize winner in his late fifties climb onto his desk and lap the newsroom, jumping from desk to desk.

One of his best sources of stories were the city's Roman Catholics, and it was from the nuns who ran a hospital on East 71st Street, in early 1959, that Berger heard of an old, blind derelict who had just been admitted. His column of 23 January told how the man's story was gently coaxed from him. His name was Laurence Stroetz, and he said he had been a violinist in a symphony orchestra many years ago. Used to many a tall tale from graduates of the Bowery, the nuns rather doubted his word, but then one of them remembered that an old fiddle lay in Sister Francis Marie's room, and they brought it to him. Berger wrote:

> Laurence Stroetz groped for it. His long white fingers stroked it. He tuned it with some effort, and tightened the old bow. He lifted it to his chin... He played 'Sidewalks of New York' true, but quavery.
>
> The fingering was stronger in Handel's 'Largo', in 'Humoresque', and 'The Blue Danube'. Before each number the old man mumbled the composer's name and hummed opening bars to recapture the lost melody.
>
> ... An audience assembled in the tiled corridor as the strains quivered and hung in the quiet. Laurence Stroetz murmured another tune, barely heard by the nuns and the nurses. Then he played it, clear and steady. It was Gounod's 'Ave Maria'.
>
> Black-clad and white-clad nuns moved lips in silent prayer. They choked up. The long years on the Bowery had not stolen Laurence Stroetz's touch... The music died and the audience pattered applause. The old violinist bowed...

And then Berger added, as an afterthought:

> If someone would offer a violin that he could call his own again, he would know ecstasy.

Three days later Berger reported:

> Eight violins were offered the other day to Laurence Stroetz, the 82-year-old, cataract-blinded violinist who was taken to St. Clare's Hospital in East Seventy-first Street from a Bowery flophouse. The offers came from men and women who had read that, though he

had once played with the Pittsburgh Symphony Orchestra, he had been without a violin for more than 30 years.

The first instrument to reach the hospital was a gift from the Lighthouse, the institution for the sightless. It was delivered by a blind man. A nun took it to the octogenarian. He played it a while, tenderly and softly, then gave it back. He said: 'This is a fine old violin. Tell the owner to take good care of it.' The white-clad nun said: 'It is your violin, Mr. Stroetz. It is a gift.' The old man bent his head over it. He wept.

Those were among the last words Berger ever wrote. Two weeks after they were published, 'Mike' Berger suffered a stroke and, a few days later, died in University Hospital at the age of 60. A lengthy obituary ran the next day, and the man who had resolutely kept himself out of stories for more than 30 years finally became the subject of one. The following year, in the preface to a collection of Berger's 'About New York' columns, the *New York Times*' famed drama critic Brooks Atkinson wrote this, surely an epitaph that every reporter should aspire to:

> In the process of losing himself for the sake of his topic, he found himself more triumphantly than he knew.

Index

Photograph acknowledgements

Meyer Berger, circa Jan 1950, by Roy Stevens (Time Life Pictures/Getty Images); **Nellie Bly**, circa 1890, by H.J. Meyers (Library of Congress Prints and Photographs Division); **Edna Buchanan**, circa 1995, by Jim Virga; **James Cameron**, July 1965 (Getty Images); **Richard Harding Davis**, circa 1901 (Burr MacIntosh Studio/Library of Congress Prints and Photographs Division); **Floyd Gibbons**, circa Jan 1920 (Getty Images); **Ann Leslie**, Associated Newspapers Ltd; **A.J. Liebling**, circa January 1963 (Bettmann/Corbis); **J.A. MacGahan**, photo submitted by The MacGahan American-Bulgarian Foundations of New Lexington; **Hugh McIlvanney**, Sunday Times Pictures; **Ernie Pyle**, circa January 1945, by Bob Landry (Time Life Pictures/Getty Images); **William Howard Russell**, 1855 (Getty Images); **George Seldes**, aged 98, copyright 1989, Rick Goldsmith. All photographs reproduced by kind permission of the copyright holders.